The New Spatial Planning

Providing a critical examination of how devolution has influenced the ways that practices of planning have evolved, this book looks at how planning has sought to become more strategic, more spatial and better integrated with other policy sectors. It challenges traditional views of what planning is about and how best to study it. The book highlights the new spaces of planning – the devolved nations of the UK and a variety of new sub-national spaces.

Arguing that the reality of spatial planning is that it is producing better quality paper plans whilst still delivering poor quality physical development on the ground, this book takes a provocative tone questioning whether spatial planning is having the kinds of impacts its advocates would wish. Original research undertaken across Ireland and the devolved nations and regions of the UK is the base of the book, which emphasises the divergence of planning practices that devolution has allowed to unfold. Separate chapters present cases of spatial planning experience in Ireland, Northern Ireland, Scotland, Wales, and two English regions – the Thames Gateway and the Leeds City Region.

New insights into spatial planning, regeneration and territorial politics are clearly presented here, resulting in an invaluable source book on the first decade or so of planning experience post-devolution for researchers and students interested in urban and regional studies, geography and planning.

Graham Haughton is Professor of Human Geography at the University of Hull. His research is in the areas of spatial planning, sustainable urban development, local and regional economic development, and urban and regional regeneration.

Phil Allmendinger is Professor of Land Economy at the University of Cambridge. His research is in the area of planning and development.

David Counsell is Lecturer in Planning and Sustainable Development at University College Cork. His research is in spatial planning, sustainable development and planning and environmental planning.

Geoff Vigar is D̶i̶r̶e̶c̶t̶o̶r̶ ̶o̶f̶ ̶t̶h̶e̶ ̶G̶l̶o̶b̶a̶l̶ ̶U̶r̶b̶a̶n̶ ̶R̶e̶s̶... Newcastle. His r̶e̶... spatial planning p̶...

The New Spatial Planning

Territorial management with soft spaces
and fuzzy boundaries

Graham Haughton, Phil Allmendinger,
David Counsell and Geoff Vigar

Routledge
Taylor & Francis Group

LONDON AND NEW YORK

First published 2010
by Routledge
2 Park Square, Milton Park, Abingdon, Oxon OX14 4RN

Simultaneously published in the USA and Canada
by Routledge
270 Madison Avenue, New York, NY 10016, USA

Reprinted 2010

Routledge is an imprint of the Taylor & Francis Group, an informa business

© 2010 Graham Haughton, Phil Allmendinger, David Counsell and Geoff Vigar

Typeset in Akzidenz Grotesk by
Keystroke, Tettenhall, Wolverhampton
Printed and bound in Great Britain by
CPI Antony Rowe, Chippenham, Wiltshire

British Library Cataloguing in Publication Data
A catalogue record for this book is available from the British Library

Library of Congress Cataloging-in-Publication Data
The new spatial planning : territorial management with soft spaces and
fuzzy boundaries / Graham Haughton ... [et al.].
p. cm.
Includes bibliographical references and index.
1. Regional planning–Great Britain. 2. Land use–Great Britain–Planning.
3. Social planning–Great Britain. 4. Decentralization in government–Great Britain.
5. Regionalism–Great Britain. I. Haughton, Graham.
HT395.G7N46 2010
307.1'2–dc22
2009022361

ISBN10: 0-415-48335-2 (hbk)
ISBN10: 0-415-48336-0 (pbk)
ISBN10: 0-203-86442-5 (ebk)

ISBN13: 978-0-415-48335-3 (hbk)
ISBN13: 978-0-415-48336-0 (pbk)
ISBN13: 978-0-203-86442-5 (ebk)

Contents

Figures

Tables

Preface and acknowledgements

Several years ago now two of us attended a seminar at the offices of the main government department responsible for planning and local government. One of the speakers there was a senior civil servant who talked about the need for devolution to deliver if it was to continue to attract political support. From his perspective, devolution allowed the opportunity 'to let a thousand flowers bloom' in the post-devolutionary sun. If it worked well, then the hope was that successful experiments in one place could be learnt from and used to help create better policies elsewhere too. If it did not work, the opportunity might not come again for several generations and the likelihood of further devolution would be undermined.

This, it seemed to us, created an important research challenge. We had already been working on an idea to look at the integration agenda and spatial planning; we felt we had a reasonable theoretical context in place. What we gained from this seminar was a sense that a wide-ranging comparative piece of empirical research on the various devolved systems of planning then being unleashed would now be extremely timely.

Another central feature of our approach is that we wanted to decentre the analysis away from focusing largely on the role of professional planners and instead trying to think about the networked and relational forms of place-making now emerging within the state apparatus. By the state we mean here not 'government' but instead the broadly constituted institutional ensemble through which strategic directions and structural contradictions are struggled over as diverse actors seek to establish a stable regime for growth. In this understanding the state is not the source of strategic direction of itself but rather the site of contestations through which new understandings emerge (see Chapter 2). Planning provides just one small piece of this institutional context, albeit one which has a particular role in determining the spatial dimensions of future growth.

Our understanding of spatial planning evolved over time, but from the start we were clear that we wanted to understand how spatial planning operated as a networked activity which involved a rethinking of both bounded space and also the boundaries of various professions that might be implicated in broadly constituted processes of place making. Spatial planning it seemed to us would inevitably involve trained, professionally recognised planners, but we wanted to allow for the fact that it might not necessarily revolve solely or even largely around them. This approach proved helpful in developing our conceptual and methodological approach – and indeed the results justify our approach. There is considerable porosity in the workings of the new spatial planning, where many 'non-planners' are taking a lead in spatial planning activities, while many 'planners' are bringing their skills to the development process from outside the regulatory system of planning. One of the key findings of this book is in fact that innovation in spatial planning is often driven by those not trained as planners and involves a wide range of people thinking creatively about spatial and corporate development. In Wales, for instance, the Wales Spatial Plan is an integrative corporate spatial strategy deliberately developed separately from, though linked to, the bodies responsible for statutory local planning activities. Though we find signs of innovation emerging as part of the experiments with spatial planning, the book also reveals how little evidence there is of fundamental differences taking place in the shaping of new development, which is disappointing given the considerable hope invested in spatial planning. It is early days of course for the changes to work through to development on the ground – but if we are to accept this as an excuse, then we must be careful too about over-claiming both the potential and the reality of the changes brought about by 'spatial planning'.

This book then is about the diverse bodies influencing the way in which future development is conceived and managed by those trying to create long-term strategic frameworks for shaping future spatial development. It charts some considerable successes in terms of strategic intent and governance processes, but it also highlights the limited progress in influencing development on the ground.

To be clear then, this book is not simply about the planning system and its attempts to reinvent itself through 'spatial planning'. Rather it is a book about the processes of creating new state spatialities through what we broadly term spatial planning. This is not the only way in which new state spatialities emerge, but it is an important one. Though devolution was our starting point, one of our key findings has been the importance of what we term 'soft spaces', involving the multiplicity of newly created subnational spatial identities around which new understandings of spatial development possibilities are being created. These are not necessarily benign in intent or outcome, as the book clearly reveals, since by creating new areas which do not align with existing democratic institutions it becomes possible to subvert democratic processes of legitimation and sanction for any strategies that ensue. But equally, by operating outside the formal regulatory 'hard spaces' of planning that align to electoral boundaries, sometimes a level of creativity is unleashed and new possibilities for consensus building emerge in ways that do not necessarily exist through the formal planning system.

Formally speaking this book represents the main output of a two and a half years' Economic and Social Research Council (ESRC) project looking at spatial planning during the past ten to fifteen years. In practice, the process of putting a successful bid together, and more recently writing this book, means that we have been working on this research for five years. During this period we have enjoyed a huge amount of support from a wide variety of people. Particularly we would like to acknowledge the ESRC for its generous funding of the work reported on here, under grant RES-000-23-0756. We would also like to thank those who supported us in our application, especially those who provided us with critical comments on our initial drafts of the proposal, including officers of the Office of the Deputy Prime Minister (ODPM) and the Scottish Royal Town Planning Institute (RTPI).

Once approved, the project continued to benefit from advice provided by a steering group of policy-makers from stakeholder groups and from various arms of government, who were collectively and individually very generous in their time, advice and support during the project. We also established a network of academic experts who proved invaluable in providing us with context, contacts and advice, plus the stimulus to have confidence in our work and to be more provocative. We owe a lot then to Neil Harris, Chris Paris, Mark Tewdwr-Jones, Iain Docherty and Ger Mullally – thank you.

Many people helped us in producing this book. Work on the diagrams and maps was mainly carried out by John Garner at the University of Hull. Various people also read and commented on one or more draft chapters of this book and we are hugely grateful to all of those who took time to do this: Aidan While, Tony Baden, Iain Docherty, Trevor Hart, Tim Marshall, Chris Paris, Neil Harris, Ger Mullally, Niall Cusson and Andy Thornley. The usual disclaimers apply: the full and final responsibility for the contents of this book lies with us as authors. We are also grateful to those who have commented on aspects of this work when presented at various conferences and seminars, most notably the Regional Studies Association (RSA) conferences in London (2005), Lisbon (2007), Manchester (2007) and Leuven (2009), and at University College London (UCL) (ESRC workshop, 2005), Centre for Sustainable Urban and Regional Futures (SURF), Salford University (2009) and Manchester University planning department (2009).

Some of the material and ideas we have drawn on here have also been used to inform other things we have been writing, but we have tried to keep things separate, acknowledging direct borrowings wherever possible within the relevant chapters. In terms of direct permissions, English Partnerships kindly gave us permission to use the aerial photo of the Greenwich Peninsula. The photo on the cover of the paperback edition was taken by William Haughton, and the rest were all taken by Graham Haughton, David Counsell or Geoff Vigar. We were also given permission to use diagrams from Crown Copyright material, reproduced with the permission of HMSO and the Queen's Printer for Scotland (licence number CO2W002008). Further permissions were generously granted by the Scottish Government, Government of Ireland, Greater London Authority and Northern Ireland Assembly. If we have missed anyone from this list accidentally then we apologise and we will endeavour to ensure that due acknowledgement is provided in any later reprint.

Finally, many thanks must go to Georgina Johnson-Cook and the publishing team at Taylor & Francis for their support and especially for their patience with us as we kept missing deadlines. More than this their integrity in supporting our independence as authors has been exemplary – we could not have hoped for more. Thank you.

1

The new spatial planning

Territorial management and devolution

Introduction

Spatial planning is about better place-making. Like previous forms of planning, it involves the courageous act of looking into the future to imagine what kind of development we need to plan for now on behalf of society. In terms of the academic and policy rhetoric surrounding it, spatial planning is seen to be something that goes further than traditional planning in its aspirations to serve as a mechanism for collaborative visioning, for overseeing implementation of development by a diverse range of actors, and ensuring that all this is delivered in ways that meet the diverse and sometimes contradictory expectations of society. Such expectations include forms of development that are efficient and equitable, respect individuality and privacy, have positive environmental impacts, and produce a variety of high-quality environments, especially neighbourhoods for living and working in and diverse recreational spaces to be exercised, inspired, connected and rested in.

The emergence of spatial planning has been a recurrent theme in recent European and European Union (EU) policy and academic work on the governance of place (e.g. Commission of European Communities (CEC) 1999; Royal Town Planning Institute (RTPI) 2001; Planning Officers Society 2005; Nadin 2007). 'Spatial planning' though is an elusive concept and set of practices, defined as much by what it is not as it is by any clear or unified understanding of what spatial planning is. We should not be surprised by this: spatial planning is used variously within the literature as, first, a conceptual apparatus, second, a broad discourse about a particular moment in the history of planning thought and practice, which is presented as something of a paradigm shift within planning, and third, a still evolving set of understandings about what constitutes 'good planning' which is being codified and legitimised through academic usage and by professional and governmental bodies.

The academic literature on spatial planning has remained relatively narrowly framed, for the most part preoccupied with providing broad descriptive accounts of the term's meanings and origins alongside attempts to specify the constituent elements of spatial planning (e.g. Faludi 2000, 2002, 2004; Shaw and Sykes 2001, 2004; Nadin 2002, 2007). There have also been some notable academic attempts to evaluate the practices of spatial planning (e.g. Albrechts *et al.* 2003; Healey 2004a), which have frequently drawn rather negative conclusions about the achievements of spatial planning to date. However, such assessments are problematic, as Newman (2008) forcefully argues, because of their strong normative tendencies, seeking to judge spatial planning by derived principles and characteristics which are remote from the practices and aspirations of many planners. This is not to let spatial planners off the hook and say they should be judged only by their own preferred criteria, but rather to argue that spatial planning is a more diverse, fluid and malleable set of understandings and practices than it might first appear, such that reducing an evaluation of these to a singular set of desirable criteria is by its very nature going to produce negative conclusions. Indeed a central argument of this book is that the growing diversity of approaches within the broad heading of what is now broadly categorised as spatial planning is one of its key features. Fuelled by the twin processes of political devolution and the emergence of a whole range of subnational new planning spaces, it is now possible to argue that there is a range of spatial plannings emerging.

Alongside this widening of the scope and variety of spatial plannings, arguably there has been some diminution of the possibility of 'spatial planning' providing a radical alternative to mainstream planning, not least as most features of the previous approaches to planning have been in effect reinscribed as being part of an expansionary vision of 'spatial planning'. A key finding of this book is in fact that some of the most innovative 'spatial planning' practices are now being found outside the mainstream regulatory functions of planning. For instance, the Wales Spatial Plan is being taken forward by a group outside the main regulatory planning apparatus as a deliberate policy tactic, while initiatives such as the city regions of the Northern Way were invented outside the mainstream systems for plan-making and indeed arguably could not have been created within them. We return to these issues later. For now though, it is enough to emphasise that 'spatial planning' is a blend of the old and the new in planning, of the formal apparatus of 'regulatory approaches to planning' and a still emergent set of related spatialised forms of strategic practices which intersect in various ways with the statutory systems for strategic plan-making. This creates a distinct dissonance between the aspirations set out in official documents on spatial planning and the more prosaic realities of the detailed powers that are involved (Rydin 2004). Nonetheless, it is important not to underestimate the magnitude of the changes which the newly emergent 'spatial planning' represents, the wider set of practices it embraces, the more sophisticated understanding of territories that is emerging, and the diversity of approaches which the term 'spatial planning' now embraces.

Spatial planning is typically presented as an improved set of practices for bringing people together to think about future spatial development patterns and agree on actions to bring these about (Healey 2004b). In this context, spatial planning encourages reflexive and flexible approaches to emerge for dealing with societal complexity, not least in the face of changing technologies, uneven wealth and resource distribution within and across nations, and the environmental constraints of both local places and the planet itself. For professional planners engaged in spatial planning, much of their everyday work involves building understanding and consensus around how best to reconcile widely divergent views of what constitutes good design, sustainable development, 'the good society' and competitive economies. But looking outside this 'everyday work', spatial planning also speaks to a wider agenda for rethinking the role of the state and in the process generating more productive engagements between experts, decision-makers of all sorts, and the general public, involving experiments with new approaches to better governance (Healey 2007).

Grand aspirations then, reflecting in part a frustration with 'old styles' of development, whether market-led or state-led, that failed to meet the expectations and pressures for the present and the future (Planning Officers Society 2005). This is not to say that development in previous eras was inadequate or that 'planned' development is or has been superior. Whereas some older developments are highly valued (e.g. Georgian Bath or planned Letchworth) many others, including large areas of housing built in the 1950s and 1960s, were not. But added to this need to learn from the past there are new challenges such as climate change, societal diversity and demands for greater public involvement that also help create the context for the desire of planners themselves, government officials and others to develop a new role for and approach to planning. To understand the break with tradition that spatial planning represents, it is worth reflecting on the backlash against traditional planning, which became tainted by criticisms within the profession and beyond of the failures of comprehensive planning and comprehensive redevelopment during the 1960s in particular, that it was too technocratic, bureaucratic, top-down and insensitive to others. This was followed by the critique of the new right in the late 1970s and 1980s that planners had stifled enterprise with 'red tape' and engaged in counterproductive 'social engineering', most notably large public sector housing projects. In short, the popular mood shifted, with planning perceived to have become too powerful and needing to be reined in.

The result was a politically inspired rescripting of the parameters of planning, with a shift away from producing detailed long-term visions, towards supporting development rather than constraining it, and a narrowing of focus to land use issues. In time, this development-supportive planning and focus upon physical development as a panacea for social and economic problems in inner cities also came under critical scrutiny, subject to criticisms of short-termism, the privileging of private profit over public good, and concerns that unfettered free markets were leading to 'lowest common denominator' developments. Such views coincided with a growing environmental awareness and political activity since the late 1980s. The backlash against 'non-planning' combined with a new positive role for planning in helping create sustainable development (however that was interpreted) created an opportunity for all those involved in shaping the planning profession and the planning system, to develop a new, 'spatial' approach. It is not our intention here to provide a history of the emergence of spatial planning ideas, a process which is still in motion, but it is perhaps worth a mention here of some of the key shaping influences, such as the debates surrounding the publication of the European Commission's European Spatial Development Perspective (see below), the lobbying work of professional bodies for planners such as the RTPI and Planning Officers Society, the changes in guidance issued by the main government planning ministries, and, of increasing importance in both the UK and Ireland, the finance ministries and other government departments, not least as part of an emergent trend towards greater analytical attention to the impacts of subnational government expenditure.

In this context those promoting a new approach broadly conceived of as 'spatial planning' should not be seen as engaging in a project to restore planning to its former glories. Instead, to gain widespread acceptance among government officials, developers, lobby groups and others, the emerging approach to 'spatial planning' has been presented as something very different to what had gone before, in effect countering possible charges from opponents that spatial planning was simply more 'red tape' or a return to 'social engineering'. In this context the emergent official justification for a new approach to planning has sought to build legitimacy through addressing some of the problems of previous approaches while setting out how a revised form of planning could help address environmental concerns in general and climate change issues in particular within a context of economic globalisation (RTPI 2001; Department of Communities and Local Government (DCLG) 2007). The latter has involved growing economic connectivity between firms and the free flow of capital across borders. Nation states and regions have to compete to attract such capital, creating the necessity for capital-friendly regulatory frameworks of which planning controls are a part. In other words, planning's objectives were far-reaching but its scope for achieving them limited by constraints upon regulation.

Against this economic and environmental backdrop the 1980s and 1990s also witnessed a growth of the vocal and active citizen. People became more aware that planning involved consequences and its outcomes would create 'winners' and 'losers'. The upshot was that while involvement in national political processes and political party allegiance diminished, local political activity and single-issue politics grew. Planning found itself as a focus for this more active citizenry and embraced the notion of public involvement and participation. Not surprisingly in this context then, consensus building and participatory processes have formed part of the intellectual and professional underpinning of the emergent new orthodoxy of 'spatial planning', in an attempt to improve the legitimacy and credibility of the strategic processes themselves and also their outcomes, in the shape of spatial plans and deliverable policies.

This then is the context within which the emergence of spatial planning can be placed. The election of the Labour government in May 1997 provided further impetus to the emergence of spatial planning in the UK, not least given the new government's focus upon sectoral coordination. In Ireland too, policy coordination rapidly shot up the policy agenda during the 1990s. Since the mid-1990s 'spatial planning' has emerged as the new orthodoxy in UK and Irish planning, adopting elements of an approach common in continental Europe for some time. As should be already clear, the term 'spatial planning' is contested and what is meant by it changes and evolves over time, always subject to conflicting interpretations and aspirations. Nevertheless, at heart most variants stress four key dimensions. First, there is an emphasis on long-term strategic thinking and the creation of future visions in the form of agreed spatial strategies. Over time, spatial planning has become much more 'spatial' and 'connected' in nature, as it is used to broker agreements about longer-term spatial development patterns which help bring resolution to intractable local development conflicts about where particular forms of development should be welcomed or resisted.

Second, spatial planning is seen by government officials as one of several policy tools for bringing coherence to increasingly fragmented systems of governance (e.g. DCLG 2006, 2007). Spatial strategies in this view act as a mechanism for 'joined-up' policy-making, with planning seen as providing a credible forum in which other policy sectors can come to agree the spatial dimensions of future policy which will inform their own strategies. As such planning has been widened from its 'land use' orientation to take more explicit account of issues such as promoting economic development, environmental protection, and the provision of social infrastructure, such as policing, health-care, education and emergency services. This, it should be added, is very much a two-way process, as external stakeholders influence the content of spatial plans and as spatial plans are intended to shape other strategic docu-ments across government and indeed beyond. Linked to this, the more holistic approach implicit in spatial planning requires an opening up of the professional boundaries of planning.

Third, spatial planning is bound up in a belief that planning has a central role in moving society towards sustainable development (see e.g. Haughton *et al.* 2008). In Wales, for instance, sustainable development is a statutory duty for the Welsh Assembly, while in England legislation introduced in 2004 made the pursuit of sustainable development a statutory duty for planning, rooted in a definition of sustainable development which rhetorically presents social, eco-nomic and environmental goals as equally important and mutually compatible.

Finally, the new spatial planning emphasises inclusivity, reflected in an open-ing up of planning consultation mechanisms to wider groups in society, and in greater attention to addressing social inclusion issues within spatial strategies.

Spatial planning is best seen as an ongoing project which is not operating to a single template. Compared with earlier forms of spatial planning, the 'new spatial planning' which is now emerging is notable for:

- The growing diversity of practices, not least as a result of devolution, such that it would make more sense to speak of spatial plannings, a theme which runs through this book.

- Evolution from being presented as a largely transnational/European and national concept to a pervasive way of thinking that is now found at all levels of the planning system and which increasingly now informs what it is to be a planner, so that it is no longer an optional 'add-on'.
- In some places spatial planning has developed as an exercise in influencing integrated whole-of-government/governance processes to think more spatially, breaking out of the 'planning silo'.
- Its growing emphasis on 'delivery' in an era of public management where various managerial technologies, such as demands to meet short-term performance targets to speed up consideration of planning applications, run counter to processes of coordination and negotiation that might drive up the quality of built form. Thus, perversely, greater efforts to monitor and enforce planning processes run the danger of the whole system becoming more regulatory and less visionary, and inadvertently returning planning back to its roots, or sectoral silo, while also not tackling issues of environmental quality effectively.

In the next section we set out our approach to this book, focusing on how we constructed our comparative work on the evolution of spatial planning across the UK and Ireland. Following this we examine some of the rationales for devolution and a short introduction to the EU spatial planning approach, and finally a quick introduction to the devolved systems of governance that will be the focus of our individual case study chapters.

Analysing the new spatial planning in the UK and Ireland

The New Spatial Planning sets out to discover whether spatial planning and devolution are combining to create a different and more geographically variable approach to future development across the UK and Ireland. A related, central concern for this book is whether the emergent spatial planning paradigm is producing better plans for spatial development and whether new ways of turning these plans into reality are emerging. The underlying expectation was that both the nature of spatial planning and the wider devolution project within which it is situated would lead to a period of innovation and creativity.

At the heart of our intellectual inquiry is a critical interrogation of how spatial planning sits within wider systems of governance, given that within government there is a strong rhetorical commitment to embracing the new spatial planning as part of its wider apparatus for improving integration across different policy sectors. If spatial planning is to add the 'spatial' dimension to the wider corporate workings of government and its partners, informing, for instance, investment patterns in transport, health, economic development and education, is this changing the boundaries of planning itself? And if there is a remaking of planning evident, how is this playing out in different places – are some areas developing new practices more quickly than others, and if so, how, where, and why? Specifically, has devolution played a role in allowing greater experimentation and distinctiveness to occur in the strategies and delivery styles of the 'new spatial planning'? Rhetorically at least devolution was presented by its supporters as a way of allowing subnational partners to define the issues they faced and develop solutions sensitised to specific local conditions. We were interested in this context to see whether devolution had seen a top-down, centralised, hierarchical planning system abandoned in favour of a more networked, multilevel approach to planning, and if so whether this lead to innovative approaches to planning emerging across the British Isles. Tying all this together, our interest is to see whether spatial planning is making a difference, and if so where and how progress is most evident.

It is part of the distinctive nature of this book that it is empirically grounded in detailed interview work, from national governments to the governments of the new territorial administrations, regions, subregions, and local areas, right down to the neighbourhood level (in total 147 people were interviewed or took part in three roundtable events; see Appendix for more on methods). Drawing inspiration from theoretical work on relational geographies and associational networks, from the outset we felt that comparative research on planning in different areas could best be undertaken not at specific scales, such as 'regions' or 'localities', but rather across scales. To take this forward we adopted the analytical and methodological device of 'governance lines', working from EU/national scales, through to the local level. This approach allowed us to examine emergent national and subnational planning systems across the scales of planning, from the European, through the national (UK and Ireland in this case), the new nations (Scotland, Northern Ireland and Wales), through to regions, subregions, city regions, local governments and right down to the neighbourhood. In the event we chose six governance lines representing different devolution approaches, for Greater London, Ireland, Northern Ireland, regional England, Scotland and Wales. These each form the basis for the individual empirical chapters in this book.

The governance line approach is distinctive, for while many researchers talk of multi-scalar analysis, few studies have developed genuinely multi-scalar methodologies, typically honing down to either just one or two scales when it comes to linking analysis with empirical detail. In addition, from the outset we felt that if spatial planning was truly a process for improved policy integration, then it should be making impacts well beyond planning. We were interested in this context to find out the extent to which spatial planning involved working with a wider range of policy actors and institutional systems, and whether 'external' policy actors felt they needed to be embracing the new spatial planning. To meet this challenge we developed an approach that allowed us to look at spatial planning from the inside-out, while also looking at it from the outside-in. This has very much influenced how we set out about our research as we chose to interview not only the 'usual suspects' of much planning research, the planners themselves and their most vocal stakeholder groups, but also people outside this fairly established policy community. Guided by the notion that spatial planning seeks to be more integrative and holistic, we tried to identify people who ought in theory at least to be involved with spatial planning, even if in practice planning remained something of a foreign country to them. For instance, we wanted to talk to people involved in planning for new health, sports, culture, water and education infrastructure.

In setting about this task we undertook two main phases of interviews, with the first stage involving interviews with 45 key players in national debates in the UK, Ireland, Scotland, Northern Ireland, Wales and Greater London (see the Appendix for further details).[1] The intention in this phase was to develop a broad appreciation of how the various new systems for spatial planning after devolution were evolving, in the process helping us to identify examples of innovative approaches that might be followed up in our second round of interviews.

In stage two we undertook further detailed interviews for each of our selected governance lines (see Appendix). As part of this we had to draw on our stage one work to make choices about case study regions, subregions and localities, looking to identify areas taking innovative approaches. There was an important timing issue here, given that both the Wales and Scottish spatial plans were not published until 2004. While widespread consultation processes meant that much of their content was already in the public domain by then, the process of turning the strategies into practices was in truth still quite embryonic when we started our interviews in 2005 and 2006. Pragmatically, we selected areas where progress appeared to be already on the way and interesting new practices were evident. It is fair to say that our choices were not based on 'typical' case studies, but on those where strong spatial planning story lines had already emerged within their respective planning policy communities and which appeared to have the potential to influence future national policy.

The main empirical sections of this book are structured around our six governance lines, one for each territorial system, so it is worth providing here a quick overview of the rationale behind our choices. The decision to cover the UK was motivated by the rapid progress towards devolution made since the election of New Labour in 1997. Ireland was added to our case studies very soon after we started, once we realised how closely entwined the experiences of planning were becoming across the island of Ireland, and also how important Ireland was as part of the wider spatial planning policy community across the British Isles. At the case study level, we chose the Thames Gateway to explore how devolution was working in Greater London largely because it was such a substantial regeneration project, but also because it involved work across three English regions, providing us with a useful example of boundary issues within spatial planning. The Leeds City Region in Yorkshire and the Humber was chosen as an example of spatial planning in an English region, in part because it reflected an emergent policy debate around city regions. Cork and the growth area around Midleton were chosen in Ireland after our national interviews revealed a consensus that spatial planning in the area was leading the field nationally and already shaping national policy. In Northern Ireland, we chose to look at Derry as it had recently been proposed as part of an innovative cross-national 'gateway', linked to Letterkenny in the Republic of Ireland. The central belt in Scotland has a long tradition of strategic planning to build from and we wanted to see how this was influencing work in the new arrangements for city region scale planning in both Glasgow and Edinburgh. Finally, in Wales, we chose to focus on the challenges being addressed through cross-border planning work involving the north east of Wales and the Chester subregion in North West England.

With considerable access to senior policy figures nationally and in the newly devolved administrations, backed up by detailed interviews in the six case studies and analysis of background documentation (see Appendix), we have been able to piece together an intriguing picture of the sometimes radical departures, and sometimes hesitant subsequent progress in forging new ways of managing territorial development. We found strategic spatial planning – but not always in the places we expected to find it, nor was it being conducted necessarily by the usual people.

Devolution, spatial planning and territorial management

From a UK and Irish perspective the new spatial planning is firmly embedded within the new territorial management practices of devolution, since it provides one of the core policy responsibilities of all the newly created territorial administrations. The project of devolution is bound up in a series of experiments for reworking the scales and sectoral boundaries of the state, as new approaches are sought for stimulating economic growth. As Jones *et al.* (2005) point out, at the present juncture this in effect means that devolution is part of a series of experiments in neoliberal forms of economic governance. Neoliberalism in this context is best seen as an evolving and reflexive market-led approach to economic management, where a core concern with re-regulation in favour of market forces is accompanied by considerable diversity between territories in how the resultant processes of experimentation evolve. While broadly speaking it is true that neoliberal approaches lead to a subordination of social and environmental policy to economic policy (Jessop 2000), this should not be read as a crude universality. Sustainable development, social justice and climate change, for instance, are all powerful policy narratives that shape how economic policy must be presented and indeed constructed. Neoliberalism inevitably looks different in different countries, over time responding to its own contradictions and crises through mutating and seeking legitimacy through selective and purposive engagement with discourses such as sustainable development.

Reforms to both economic governance and spatial planning in this context can be seen as part of a profound reorganisation of the capacity of the nation state under neoliberalism, with devolved governance systems premised in part on a widespread belief that they will devise and deliver better policies. Likewise, the rescripting of the role of government has seen central governments seek to move away from the direct delivery of many former state functions in favour of achieving policy goals through other methods, from privatisation and contracting out to working in broadly constituted governance partnerships. We discuss issues of government, governance and metagovernance further in Chapter 2; here our focus is more narrowly on devolution debates.

Devolving greater responsibility for policy-making and implementation inevitably comes with a series of potential benefits and risks for those involved, and it is fair to say that the 'new regionalism' has sparked a lively critical debate (see e.g. Storper 1997; Cooke and Morgan 1998; Lovering 1999; MacLeod 2001). Articles on the international experience of devolution helpfully set out some of the possible advantages and disadvantages (Rodríguez-Pose and Bwire 2004; Rodríguez-Pose and Gill 2004, 2005; Jones *et al.* 2005). In summary, devolution might produce benefits through improved tailoring of policies to meet local priorities and needs, through promoting innovation by reducing central government interference, and through inter-territorial competition. Devolution can also stimulate greater accountability and engagement between government and citizens. In addition, there are important cultural and political drivers and rewards for devolution, particularly where strong cultural and historical issues are driving forward the momentum for political devolution, as in Scotland. Regional devolution then has the potential to improve economic performance, revive civil society and improve the effectiveness of state interventions.

In the face of such apparent benefits, it is important not to neglect the potential downsides, not least that devolved governments may bring about inequalities between territories, since richer regions will be better placed to resource innovative policies and reduce tax burdens. As more responsibilities are shifted down to devolved government systems, without adequate systems for inter-regional equalisation, the poorest regions are increasingly left to fend for themselves from a lower taxation base. There are potential inefficiencies too, for instance, by introducing counterproductive competition between localities over inward investment. Devolution can also add to institutional costs and therefore tax burdens. It can also be seen as a way for central governments to pass on responsibilities for problems without the necessary resources for addressing them. There may be a political price too if devolution brings resentments about the breakup of existing territorial identities, something which permeates UK debates, and also resentments about unfair representation in government (the so-called 'West Lothian Question' in UK politics asks why Members of the Scottish Parliament (MSPs) should be able to vote on English affairs, when English Members of Parliament (MPs) can no longer vote on issues devolved to the Scottish Parliament). Devolution then is neither the golden egg it is sometimes portrayed as by its proponents, nor is it a clear political act of munificence on the part of central government. As with any rescaling of government and governance, there is the potential for a radical reworking of the distribution of winners and losers in both societal and spatial terms, which may be progressive or it may be regressive. Taking this further, devolution's success or lack of it will be judged against diverse and often subjective criteria: if it is felt to be working, further devolution of powers might be expected; if it isn't then the pace and direction of change may be altogether different.

Given this broad context, it is helpful to situate the rise of political interest in regions in terms of the broader processes of the contemporary restructuring of the state, in terms of both 'rescaling' and the reworking of institutional and sectoral boundaries (see Chapter 2). This has many dimensions. At supranational level nations join together to create new trade rules or environmental conventions which in effect 'lend' powers upwards from the nation state to other regulatory institutions, from the European Union to the World Trade Organisation and the United Nations. This *upward* shift in powers has been accompanied by a tendency towards devolving powers *downwards*; indeed one of the European Union's clearest principles involves subsidiarity, that is powers should be devolved to the lowest level of government at which they can be effectively carried out. Since the late 1980s the European Union has promoted selective forms of devolution, particularly to 'regions', broadly defined as subnational entities which exist above the level of locality and below the level of the nation state. As we have already intimated, a key driving force in this has been debates about the 'economic dividend' expected of regionalism.

In addition to this *vertical* reworking of powers upwards and downwards, state powers are being reworked *horizontally*, linked rhetorically at least with a shift from 'government' to 'governance'. There is now a well-established international literature on the theme of an apparent shift from rigid, inward-looking, hierarchical systems of 'top-down' govern*ment*, to more porous, better networked forms of govern*ance* (Jessop 2000; Goodwin *et al.* 2005). In the new systems of governance, governments have sought to privatise, contract out, or otherwise deliver policy, sometimes creating new institutions which bring in new partners, for instance, business-led or community-led area regeneration agencies. In these new contracting or 'partnership' arrangements, government still plays a role as regulator and even as funder, but rhetorically at least the state is opening itself up to alternative forms of policy delivery, and in the process new ways of thinking and new policy communities are being introduced.

What we are seeing then is a whole range of interwoven ways of reworking the powers of the state, vertically and horizontally, a process which has led to considerable academic debate about the nature and extent of the so-called resulting 'hollowing-out' of the nation state and its subsequent 'filling in', not least with new regional institutional arrangements (Goodwin *et al.* 2005, 2006). What appears to be going on is not a simple redistribution of powers to other scales of government and governance, but a change to the ways in which the governments seek to pursue their aims, retaining for themselves a powerful role in setting the rules of the game, shaping how the new institutions work and are governed. As such we are seeing an enormous amount of experimentation with new institutional forms, much of whose legitimacy and funding is 'lent' to them by central government, which also sets up the regulatory frameworks within which they must operate and the goals which they must aspire to. In effect this is a form of metagovernance, which we might also think of as either the steering of governance or the governance of governance

(Jessop 2003, 2008; see Chapter 2 for further discussion). From this perspective, governments retain their power through the rules by which new governance institutions must conform, perform, be audited, evaluated and when deemed necessary replaced.

The result has been a period of huge institutional experimentation as new institutional forms and policy delivery mechanisms are introduced, a 'filling-in' process as Goodwin *et al.* (2005) refer to it. But this is a highly controlled set of experiments, which for all the policy emphasis on 'learning' and devolution retains a strong centralising tendency. Far from being a simple 'roll out' of new policy initiatives from the centre, new initiatives are invariably shaped by a diverse mix of local path dependencies and contemporary contestations involving diverse social forces working through state structures at all scales. The remaking of planning is a prime example of these issues. It is continuously being made and remade not by simple central diktat: instead diverse social forces struggle to shape the institutional forms of the state (and the planning apparatus) at all levels, as they seek to pursue their strategic ambitions. Some will seek to use planning to introduce greater regulatory control, others to reduce planning's regulatory 'burden'. Devolution in theory ought to allow greater diversity to emerge in the resultant accommodations, as power is reworked as new forms of state spatiality are introduced and peopled with new systems, institutions, laws, customs and expectations.

We will return to these debates in more detail in Chapter 2, but for now they provide an important introductory context for understanding why political and administrative devolution has been such an important yet disputed part of the policy process in recent years. There have been many high expectations for devolution, but underlying them all are the tensions of how much scope the new institutions will really have to create a distinctive subnational politics and distinctive policy approaches. For this book, the emphasis is on spatial planning not simply as an expression of devolution, but part of the wider restructuring of the state where devolution fulfils the important political and administrative function of encouraging diversity and distinctiveness in territorial management in the broader sense. Out of such experiments should come improved forms of territorial governance, which can then be shared and replicated to the benefit of all. Seen from this perspective, spatial planning after devolution should be a process of breaking out from previous styles of planning and unleashing the potential for new approaches to break through at subnational levels.

Asymmetrical progress towards devolution in Ireland and the UK

This book focuses on the emergence of new spatial planning practices across both Ireland and the UK, covering the recently devolved administrations in Northern Ireland, Scotland, Wales and Greater London, plus the move towards more limited regional devolution in England and Ireland. The expectation was that this breadth of coverage would allow a comparative analysis of emergent styles of spatial planning post-devolution.

To provide a quick introductory context, the UK comprises England and the devolved countries of Northern Ireland, Scotland and Wales, with a population of 60.3 million people and an economy (defined by Gross Value Added [GVA]) of over £1,000 billion. Both population and economic activity are unevenly distributed with a heavy weighting towards the south east of England, with London at its core. The devolved nations of Scotland, Wales and Northern Ireland share just 16 per cent of the UK's population and 14 per cent of GVA (Table 1.1).

The Republic of Ireland has a population of 4.2 million, which means its population is smaller than Scotland's but its economy is substantially larger. Government in Ireland has tended to be heavily centralised, and while local cultural identities are strong, there is not a strong tradition of regional policy. This is something which has to be put in the context of Ireland's relatively small population and its strong two-tier county and local government system. This said, under pressure from the European Commission, regional governance has started to emerge, as the Irish government has sought to maximise access to European structural funds (see Chapter 3).

Interest in devolution in the UK has been growing apace since the early 1990s (Table 1.2); this trend was substantially strengthened with the election of a national Labour government in 1997, leading very quickly to the creation of a Scottish Parliament, Welsh Assembly Government, Northern Ireland Assembly and Greater London Assembly. While political devolution has been limited in the regions outside London, there have been important reforms in regional governance, reforms which have been important for spatial planning.

Table 1.1 Comparative data on population and economy

Nation/region	Population (2006) (millions)	GVA (2005) (£ billion)
UK	60.3	1061.3
Scotland	5.1	86.3
Wales	3.0	40.9
Northern Ireland	1.7	24.5
England	50.5	909.6
North East	2.6	35.9
North West	6.8	106.1
Yorkshire and Humber	5.1	75.2
East Midlands	4.3	70.8
West Midlands	5.4	84.8
East of England	5.5	104.9
London	7.5	181.0
South East	8.2	166.3
South West	5.1	84.6
Ireland	4.2	150.1

Source: Central Statistical Office (2007).

Table 1.2 Selected milestones in devolution and the decentralisation of planning, UK and Ireland, 1989–2006

Date	Scotland	Wales	Northern Ireland	London	English regions	Republic of Ireland
1989					RPG introduced	
1994					Government Offices of the Regions established	Regional Assemblies (NUTS III)
1995		Separate Welsh policy guidance				
1998	Scotland Act	Government of Wales Act	Good Friday Agreement		RDAs/RESs New-style RPG/ Regional bodies	
1999	Elections to Scottish Parliament	Elections to Welsh Assembly		GLA Act Election to GLA		Regional Assemblies (NUTS II) National Development Plan
2000		A Winning Wales	Elections to Northern Ireland Assembly			Planning Act
2001	Review of strategic planning	Consultation of a national planning framework	Regional Development Strategy	Consultation on intent to prepare London Plan		
2002			Devolution suspended	Draft London Plan		National Spatial Strategy published
2003		Planning Green Paper		Public examination	Planning Green Paper	
2004	National Planning Framework published	England and Wales 'Planning' Act Wales Spatial Plan published in final form		Final version of the London Plan	England and Wales 'Planning' Act Statutory RSSs	Regional planning guidelines published

Table 1.2 continued

Date	Scotland	Wales	Northern Ireland	London	English regions	Republic of Ireland
2005	Planning White Paper			Subregional strategies	Failed referendum in the North East	
2006	Planning Act	Interim Sub-area statements	Resumption of devolution			

Later chapters reveal in more depth some of the events which led up to the different devolutionary settlements in different places, but this brief introduction highlights the major asymmetries in how devolution has unfolded across the UK and Ireland. In effect different accommodations have been arrived at in different places, reflecting in large part the very different histories and trajectories of subnational political coherence, voice and expectations (Goodwin *et al.* 2005; Jones *et al.* 2005; Keating 2005). It is important to emphasise then that devolution has unfolded as a multi-speed process, involving very different types of devolutionary settlement, with different levels of devolutionary powers and responsibilities arrived at (Tables 1.2 and 1.3). As a consequence of this there is now a considerable variation in approaches to territorial management emerging across the UK. These range from the Scottish Parliament which has primary legislative powers, to the English regions which have relatively limited responsibilities, including economic development, spatial planning and aspects of housing and transportation. Wales and Northern Ireland lie at different points in between these two extremes (Table 1.3). It is important to note that this is not a static picture, with changes emerging over time: for example, there is provision in the Government of Wales Act 2006 for the Welsh Assembly to gain further legislative competencies, while the new Scottish government elected in 2007 is keen to pursue further devolution.

Progress towards devolution since 1997 has been rapid, opening up 'uncharted territory for policy-makers around the UK to think reflexively and negotiate either to produce policy differentiation or policy convergence' (Jones *et al.* 2005: 400; see also Keating 2005), and with this differing approaches to seeking further devolved powers. Already we can see this leading to a diversity of territorial management styles across the UK and Ireland, which all reflect a marked shift away from previous systems of territorial management that were too highly centralised and hierarchical.

One of the criticisms of earlier forms of territorial management was that they did little to break down the 'silo mentality' between different policy sectors, while public spending patterns lacked a coherent strategic spatial framework, particularly for infrastructure. By contrast, the new territorial management emerging across the British Isles is characterised by:

Table 1.3 Summary of devolved and retained powers and responsibilities

UK government	Scottish Parliament	Northern Ireland Assembly	Welsh Assembly	Greater London Authority	English regions
Includes: defence, economic and monitory policy, designation of assisted areas, energy (with exceptions), rail regulation, air regulation	Primary legislation: health, education, culture, water, waste, economic development, environment, housing, local government, planning and transport, etc.	Primary legislation: health, education, culture, water, waste, economic development, environment, housing, local government, planning and transport, etc.	Secondary legislation: health, education, culture, economic development, environment, housing, local government, planning and transport, etc.	No legislative capacity, strategic economic development, planning, transport, environment, culture, plus fire and emergency services, police (part)	No legislative capacity, strategic economic development (RDAs), strategic housing, planning and transport (RAs)

- New systems of subnational governance, ranging from political devolution to improved systems for representation and accountability.
- Growing spatial sensitivity and transparency in national budget spending rounds, evident in both the UK and Ireland.
- Considerable work producing a variety of sectoral and integrative territorial strategies, each requiring engagement with a wide range of 'stakeholders' from the public, private, quasi-public and voluntary and community sectors.
- A central role for spatial strategies, providing a spatial framework for other sectoral strategies, not least with the aim of improving coordination of land use policies with infrastructure provision.
- Greater attention to promoting integration across policy sectors, through various consultative and strategic framework devices.
- An emphasis on joining up government initiatives vertically across the layers of governance, up towards the European level, downwards to the neighbourhood scale.
- An emphasis on improved policy learning, not only within government but also across the newly devolved territorial administrations and beyond, notably with other EU regions.

The reworking of planning then is part of a broader reworking of the politics of territorial management, involving struggles about territorial integrity, the forging of territorial coherence at a national level, and providing an opportunity for rethinking subregional or subnational territorial identities. While spatial planning after devolution could result in increased distinctiveness between and within the new territories, planning's governance arrangements and regulatory responsibilities mean that it also provides a potential vehicle for the subordination of devolved territorial management practices to wider state ambitions.

Planning then potentially contains the regulatory iron fist beneath the velvet glove of the governance and partnership structures of the new administrations. It is not of course the only such force – financial powers and EU directives, for instance, can both limit the discretion available to the new devolved administrations or impose particular directions, as we will see later in this chapter.

Integration, devolution and the modernisation of government

Modernisation of government has been a constant refrain for both the UK and Irish governments since the early 1990s, a process which found itself given further momentum with devolution, where, for instance, the Welsh Assembly Government has made efforts to create a distinctive 'citizen-centred' approach to government services a central part of its work (see Chapter 6). Central to this process has been a belief that with the increased fragmentation of governance systems likely to increase as devolution proceeded apace, there was going to be more emphasis needed on policy integration, between policy sectors and across policy scales.

We focus on the UK experience here, turning more to Ireland in Chapter 3. In the UK, devolved decision-making linked to better joining up by the centre was a central theme for the incoming New Labour government in 1997, alongside concepts of partnership, public/private initiatives, and stakeholder engagement, all of which were emblematic elements of Tony Blair's 'Third Way' political philosophy (Mawson and Hall 2000; Rhodes 2000; Ling 2002). Joined-up government has remained a pivotal aspect of New Labour policy (Ling 2002). The government's public sector modernisation proposals expressly set out to address a range of so-called 'wicked issues' which cross over departmental responsibilities (Cabinet Office 1999; Performance and Innovation Unit (PIU) 2000), many of which impinge on spatial planning:

> Many of the biggest challenges facing Government do not fit easily into traditional Whitehall structures. Tackling drug addiction, modernising the criminal justice system, encouraging sustainable development, or turning around run-down areas all require a wide range of departments and agencies to work together. And we need better coordination and more teamwork right across government if, for example, we are to meet the skills and educational challenges of the new century or achieve our aim of eliminating child poverty within twenty years.
>
> (PIU 2000: Prime Minister's Foreword)

Joining-up initiatives have been driven forward by the centre, through the Cabinet Office and Treasury, with central policy units playing a role (Rhodes 2000). A rash of policy documents on the policy integration theme was published in the period 1999–2000, triggered by the White Paper *Modernising Government* (Cabinet Office 1999). The Treasury has been at the heart of government modernisation and has introduced a raft of innovations designed to assist in the strategic planning of public expenditure. Perhaps the most innovative of these is the Comprehensive Spending Review, which shifted the emphasis away from annual negotiation towards multiannual budgets, with a greater prioritisation of expenditure in the education, health, transport and housing sectors emerging (Cullingworth and Nadin 2006).

Devolution has produced some interesting tensions in how coordination of policy can occur across the newly devolved territories, not least due to the substantial asymmetries in their devolved powers and responsibilities. This is particularly evident in the case of English regions, where there has been some limited devolution, but no equivalent to the powers granted to Greater London and other parts of the country. There is some confusion in that post-devolution some UK departments of state function essentially as English departments, but there is no separate 'national' English government (Jones *et al.* 2005; Keating 2005). The result is that 'England remains an enigma within the territorial politics of the devolved UK . . . England is sandwiched between the government's various UK wide policies and the activities of various regional scale institutions' (Jones *et al.* 2005: 429).

One Department of State that definitely does have a UK-wide remit is the Treasury, responsible for economic and monetary policy and setting expenditure limits for the devolved administrations. However, these expenditure ceilings are set according to a long-agreed formula – the Barnett Formula (Heald and McLeod 2005). Within the limits that the formula establishes, the devolved administrations can spend according to their own political preferences without reference to expenditure in England (Heald and McLeod 2005). Keen to exercise their new powers, the devolved administrations have indeed departed from English policy, for example, by abolishing student fees in Scotland and prescription charges in Wales.

The implications of the integration imperative for spatial planning are intriguing, not least given that spatial planning is itself seen by its advocates as a tool for integrative policy-making. Within the UK there is not a clear statement of 'national' government policy any more, given that spatial planning is a devolved responsibility to varying degrees in Scotland, Wales and Northern Ireland. Nonetheless, announcements by the planning department in Whitehall necessarily resonate around the devolved administrations and undoubtedly have an influence there. While the three new national administrations have all produced national spatial plans, there is no equivalent for England nor for the UK as a whole, indeed the government has been strongly resistant to any calls for such national plans. If these are the confusions, it is perhaps important to add here that the new national spatial strategies have all in their various ways sought to make links to work in adjacent jurisdictions, a theme we return to in our empirical chapters, illustrating something of the potential for spatial planning to be a more integrative device perhaps than pre-existing planning systems.

While competency for spatial planning is devolved to all three of the new 'national' administrations other matters which interface with planning – aspects of railways, airports and energy, for example – are 'reserved' by the

UK government (Keating 2005; see Table 1.3). These represent 'grey areas' in the devolution agenda. For example, the Scottish government is keen to bring wind energy on stream but is reliant on the UK government to upgrade the transmission network to allow the energy generated to be moved. Similarly, railways in Scotland, for example, are split between regulation (UK),[2] infrastructure (UK) and franchising (devolved) (Keating 2005).

Adding complexity, there are sectoral strategies at the UK scale which have clear implications for spatial planning. The *UK Government Sustainable Development Strategy* (Department for Environment, Food and Rural Affairs (DEFRA) 2005) is clearly crucial in view of the key role given to planning in pursuing sustainable development. Part of the new approach is that the UK Sustainable Development Strategy is then supplemented by sustainable development strategies produced separately by the administrations in Scotland, Wales and Northern Ireland. The result is a fairly loose UK framework, with the remainder of the sustainable development strategy document referring mainly to England and illustrating the current confusion associated with differentiating between the UK, England and the devolved administrations.

The European dimension to multilevel governance and devolution

In its pursuit of economic competitiveness, social cohesion and sustainable development, there is a clear spatial dimension to the activities of the European Union which is reinforced by policies in the fields of regional policy, transport, environment and agriculture (Cullingworth and Nadin 2006, p. 83). European cohesion policy is particularly relevant to territorial management, not least as it is backed up by the allocation of Structural Funds for regional conversion, which account for one-third of the total EU budget. The way in which the EU controls the disbursement of this considerable pot of money has been a powerful shaper in the development of regional policy in many member states (see e.g. Mullally 2004). As part of the Structural Funds, the European Commission also allocates considerable sums to various Community Initiatives, some of which are closely allied to spatial planning, notably the INTERREG (transnational planning), LEADER (rural development) and URBAN (urban regeneration) programmes.

Spatial planning as such does not come within the legislative competency of the European Commission, unlike transport where it has pursued the development of Trans-European Transport Networks, and the environment field where it has produced a range of Directives, for example, on Strategic Environmental Assessment, Habitats and Water. This said, the European Commission does have a strong interest in promoting a Territorial Cohesion agenda, not least through its regional structural fund system. The European Commission's work on spatial planning has focused on developing informal actions which aim to encourage member states to cooperate plus a system for making the release of structural funds for regional development conditional upon evidence of appropriate regional governance systems. The cornerstone of cooperation on spatial planning is the European Spatial Development Perspective (ESDP), which was approved in May 1999. This document reflects the culmination of work conducted during the 1990s on spatial planning both as a policy arena and as an integrative tool within Europe, resulting in moves to promote a spatial development framework for the whole of the European territory (Shaw and Sykes 2001; Faludi 2002). The ESDP does not set out to provide a master plan for the development of Europe as a whole; rather it provides a conceptual framework and language for thinking strategically about how to influence spatial development patterns. Its adoption by member states means that there was an initial broad commitment from national governments to take forward the ESDP's work in producing their own national and regional planning policies.

At an abstract level then the ESDP provides a conceptual and linguistic apparatus (polycentricity, gateways, corridors, hubs) which is useful to planners seeking to provide a way of presenting their policies as widely beneficial, rather than simply benefiting core areas. At a more practical level, engaging with European-level ideas and frameworks is helpful in accessing European money, and as such we find ESDP language is particularly evident in areas keen to attract European investment for transport infrastructure, Structural Funds and other initiatives.

The community initiative INTERREG requires that the projects it funds should be consistent with the aims of the ESDP and contribute to transnational planning strategies or frameworks (Cullingworth and Nadir 2006). The transnational dimension is vital to prove that there is a European role, otherwise under subsidiarity rules the Commission should not get involved. INTERREG has now produced five transnational strategies or 'visions', three affecting the UK, resulting in all British countries/regions with the exception of south east England being in at least two transnational regions and the Islands and Highlands in Scotland being in all three (Faludi 2004; see Figure 1.1).

These visions were intended to establish a bridge between the ESDP and national and regional strategies. However, it is important to emphasise that the transnational regional visions are produced as advisory documents which were not subject to approval by ministers and therefore do not have any formal status: 'All the spatial visions are in essence products of a small group of experts and the expression of the consensus reached by the groups' (Zonneveld 2003: 10). This lack of formal status has raised questions about who is responsible for the content of the spatial visions in the absence of any political legitimization (Zonneveld 2003). Another criticism levelled at the INTERREG spatial visions is that they make little attempt to provide a desired spatial structure for the INTERREG regions.

The status of these transnational strategies, and indeed the ESDP itself, is something of an issue in the absence of European jurisdiction for international spatial planning (Nadin 2002). The ESDP has been criticised for its lack of specificity, excluding maps in favour of pictograms and providing very generalised and generic policy principles and concepts (Zonneveld 2003; Faludi 2004). Likewise in their present generalised form, none of the spatial visions

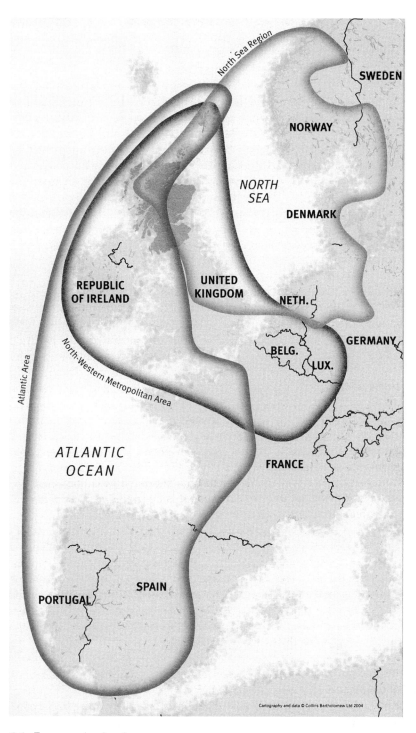

1.1 European 'regions'

provide a particularly adequate basis for implementing EU spatial policies at the national and subnational levels. Their roles are purely advisory, and inevitably in consequence their influence on spatial policy in member states varies. For example, in the British Isles, the first two 'national' spatial plans, the Northern Ireland Regional Development Strategy (RDS) and the Irish National Spatial Strategy (NSS), are both acknowledged to have paid regard to European thinking, evident in their use of European concepts such as regional gateways and hubs (Mullally 2004; Murray 2004; Walsh and Murray 2006). It is worth noting here that the various Community Initiatives have been powerful drivers of international policy learning within the EU. While there is only limited evidence of policy convergence in planning at the level of the enlarged EU (Adams 2008), within the UK and Ireland the research for this book reveals that some of the devolved administrations have developed strong linkages among themselves and also made selective use of EU networks to make connections into new policy communities outside the UK (see Chapters 5 and 9 in particular).

Conclusion

This chapter sets out an argument that as debates about spatial planning have matured and as the term has been used as a discursive technique for justifying particular approaches to planning practice, this has created the possibility for diverse understandings and practices to evolve. In other words, as spatial planning has matured as a debate and set of practices, so it has also become less of a unified set of understandings about a particular understanding of spatial planning and increasingly a wide-ranging set of practices. This is not simply about path dependency and local contingency however; it is the inevitable consequence of struggles over power at (and between) both national and subnational scales.

This book picks up from the fact that since the mid-1990s devolution has provided the opportunity for greater subnational experimentation in how to plan spatially and strategically, and, with this, struggles over how planning should be revitalised and indeed partially reinvented. Our approach involves the study of the reworking of policy across scales of governance. We see this process as one which works through and across the various informal and formal spaces of governance, not as a simplistic trading of places as one scale becomes more influential than another. In addition, since spatial planning is said to involve a lifting of the 'silo mentality' blinkers of policy-makers involved in making spatial strategies, we look in detail at the reworking of the boundaries of planning, particularly at how well planners are coping with the challenge of working more closely with those in other sectors, such as those responsible for providing transport, social (e.g. parks, health, education), environmental and economic infrastructure.

In Chapter 2 we take a more theoretically informed look at these debates, introducing new ideas about the ways in which fuzzy boundaries and soft spaces are emblematic of if not pivotal to recent work in this area. In the six chapters that follow we look in turn at the national and local experiences of spatial planning in Ireland, Northern Ireland, Scotland, Wales, regional England and London. Our concluding chapter then brings together these disparate experiences to return to the broad questions set out earlier in this chapter about whether the new spatial planning is indeed producing innovative and creative new approaches, and where signs of this are most in evidence.

To conclude this chapter, the implicit critique within debates about emergent approaches to spatial planning is that old styles of planning failed in various ways. Certainly it seems as if planners, politicians, the public and developers are all looking for a breakaway from an apparently moribund, conflict-ridden, slow, unimaginative, costly and inefficient approach to planning, which has led to new developments being unimaginative, stale, and sometimes downright ugly, not to speak of being inequitable and inefficient. There is a lot riding on the new spatial planning to produce not just better plans, but also better-quality places.

2

Rethinking planning

State restructuring, devolution and spatial strategies

Introduction

Chapter 1 traced the complex, evolving and uneven nature of spatial strategy-making across the UK and Ireland, highlighting the ways in which spatial planning is both an important influence in shaping future development patterns and an evolving practice heavily influenced by wider shifts in the nature of how nation states are governed. This chapter steps back and seeks to make sense of these changes by placing them in an historical context and engaging with a range of ideas and theories on state restructuring and the rescaling of governance and spatial strategy making. The broad points covered in this overview are:

- The scales and practices of planning are dynamic and contested. Any approach is a compromise between irreconcilable characteristics found in any planning system. This leads us to argue that there is no 'ideal' end-point planning system which manages to reconcile, for example, speed of decision-making with comprehensiveness of decisions. Nor is there at any one moment a planning system that will meet the aspirations of all.
- As a consequence a variety of approaches to and scales of planning have existed through time. Such approaches are temporary and reflect the outcomes of historical and contemporary socio-political struggles, in which path-dependencies also play a shaping role.
- Any approach, including reworking the scales and the scope of planning, will always favour certain interests over others.
- The boundaries and strategies of policy sectors such as transport and the environment are equally subject to socio-political struggles.
- The formal scales and processes of planning are being increasingly accompanied by the emergence of informal or soft spaces and fuzzy boundaries. Such new state spaces are fluid and one role of spatial planning is increasingly to provide 'glue' to the new, multiple spaces of governance, alongside other devices for policy integration.

- Taking these in total, we want to argue that planning has changed from a largely bipolar (local-central) scalar fix, towards being a more truly multi-scaled, networked activity. In this view a variety of policy scales coexist, and the shifting of powers, responsibilities and expectations between formal and informal scales is a constant process. More than this, planning and planners must now be embedded within, and achieve their policy goals through, a variety of planning and non-planning networks consisting of diverse stakeholders.
- This 'relational planning' provides new challenges for, and requires new skills and knowledge from, planners.

The upshot of this is that we should increasingly expect the practices of planning to vary over time and across space. But far from an unproblematic roll out from a particular ideological turn, the nature of these changes and local variations is always contingent to the specificities of place, where the pursuit of strategic political projects through new institutions and strategies is shaped by complex socio-political and geo-historical processes. The diversity of new planning styles represents a quickening of long-term trends: what characterises planning now is the significance and speed of change as well as the diversity of arrangements. We might also add that such diversity is now not simply an unintended consequence of planning, it is actually encouraged and even facilitated by central government.

Spatial planning, sustainable development and integration

The notion of spatial planning as practised in the UK and Ireland emanates from various sources, including domestic reactions against previous 'land use' planning approaches and perhaps most visibly through engagement with thought and practice at the European level. Particularly important were the debates leading up to and following on from the European Spatial Development Perspective (ESDP), with its emphasis on European notions of territorial competitiveness, social justice and sustainable development. The importance of this European inflection is particularly evident with sustainable development. This concept is inextricably linked with spatial planning in both the UK and Ireland, informing the ways in which planning systems are expected to find future development patterns that balance social, economic and environmental issues rather than privilege one 'pillar' of sustainability over the others. This 'balanced' or integrated approach is taken seriously in spatial planning, where it is a statutory duty in the case of the UK, and frequently sets it apart from the visions of future development held by those pursuing other strategic projects through the state, in effect setting planning on a collision course potentially with these other forces (Haughton and Counsell 2004; Haughton *et al.* 2008). That it does not quite work out like that may well reflect planning's other twin mandates in recent times: to be a powerful tool for policy integration and to provide a participative and deliberative approach to preparing strategic plans. It may also reflect that planning's subordinate role in the wider process of policy-making, where economic growth aspirations remain powerful drivers within the dominant discourses of neoliberalism (Counsell and Haughton 2003; Gunder 2006).

In both the UK and Ireland, spatial planning is rhetorically cast by government officials in particular as a way of knitting together diverse types of interested actors at and across various scales in an effort to create liveable or sustainable communities (as they are known in England); that is, areas that function well economically, socially and environmentally. In achieving this, spatial planning is implicated in widely varying policy agendas, from addressing economic competitiveness and creating local jobs, to tackling issues as diverse as global climate change and local obesity problems. Sustainable communities are as much defined by what they are not as by what they are – they are intended to be an antidote to poorly designed previous developments that underprovided in terms of local employment, community infrastructure, and recreational and public spaces, creating areas disparagingly thought of as dormitory suburbs, car centred rather than people centred, and having distorted demographic profiles in terms of age, race or class. The people expected to ensure that liveable communities emerge include planners, naturally, and also land owners, developers, utility providers, community organisations, and those responsible for transport, educational, healthcare, leisure and other infrastructure. Planners then may aspire to create sustainable or liveable communities, but they recognise that the means to achieving their goals lie elsewhere, within an increasingly fragmented system of governance for public services, a continuously reworked boundary between private and public provision of collective infrastructure, and the need to engage more with both communities and the private sector, which has its own sets of shareholders, stakeholders and regulators.

Spatial planning in this sense is a process for bringing people together to achieve aspirational goals at site level, at area level, and also contributing to wider regional and national aspirations for particular types of growth to emerge in pursuit of wider national policy goals. A central challenge for government officials in seeking to embed a spatial planning approach has been to achieve delivery of negotiated strategies at various scales through a process of consultation and collaboration with stakeholders and the public. This has produced increasingly 'thick' or 'congested' governance systems, designed to deal with complexity, distributed powers and networked resources (see Sullivan and Skelcher 2002). In principle these represent attempts to harness network power, rather than a hierarchical privileging of planning knowledge and governmental control, often involving work with private sector capacities to pursue governmental priorities. However, planning is always a site of political struggle and the notion of spatial planning is no exception to this. Spatial planning privileges some groups and interests over others and is a contested notion, particularly from those who see a far more limited and reduced role for planning and planners. As we discuss later, it is possible already to see a backlash against spatial planning, particularly in relation to housing and major infrastructure delivery.

There is already a considerable literature on how planners have sought to use an integrated approach to sustainable development, where its social, economic and environmental pillars are to be treated as equally important and policies devised which do not play one 'pillar' off against another (Haughton and Counsell 2004; Counsell and Haughton 2006a). For some this approach has simply been a Trojan horse, allowing economic growth arguments to pervade and dominate planning decisions (Gunder 2006), while for others it has provided planners with an intellectual apparatus for justifying a 'sustainable' approach to planning, which has at its heart an attempt to preserve the land resource through urban compaction policies based on densification, mixed use development, redevelopment on brownfield sites, improved urban design and place-making qualities. This latter approach has the advantage for government planners of helping them get around some intractable debates surrounding public sensitivities of the loss of rural land to new development, while allowing governments to provide the sites for new developments required to support economic growth. It is, to say the least, a problematic compromise, which some would say leads to town cramming and poor-quality urban developments in order to 'save' what is often rather unexceptional rural land from new development, in effect residualising alternative visions of sustainable spatial development, such as new settlements and creating a more green urban form with more gardens and public green infrastructure.

As Chapter 1 highlighted, one of the key distinguishing features of the new spatial planning is its aspiration to provide a tool for the integration of a wide range of policy domains, providing a focus for working through the spatial impacts of multiple government strategies, not just spatial strategies. In England this is made explicit in Planning Policy Statement 1 (PPS1: ODPM 2005b), which sees spatial planning in an integrative light as providing a spatial expression for other sectoral plans and strategies:

> Spatial Planning goes beyond traditional land use planning to bring together and integrate policies for the development and use of land with other policies and programmes which influence the nature of places and how they function. That will include policies which can impact on land use, for example by influencing the demands on, or needs for, development, but which are not capable of being delivered solely or mainly through the granting or refusal of planning permission and which may be implemented by other means.
>
> (ODPM 2005b: 12–13)

This approach contrasts significantly with the more regulatory land use planning approach characteristic of the 1980s and 1990s (see Table 2.1). Some characterised planning practice during the 1980s as 'project' led (Allmendinger and Thomas 1998), where planning was frequently cast as a regulatory function that reacted to proposals on a case-by-case basis, judging them on their merits. Spatial planning, on the other hand, has been characterised as:

Table 2.1 Differences between land use and spatial planning

Land use/regulatory	Spatial
Legal framework	
Scope prescribed by statute and case law	Scope significantly broader, though still prescribed
Boundaries are familiar	Boundaries to be established
Institutional	
Plan could be prepared in isolation from other agencies	Requires a collaborative approach with a range of agencies
Compatible with silo Council organisation	Predicated on Council having an integrated approach to strategy and delivery
Plan owned by the Council	Council leads preparation on behalf of Local Strategic Partnership and a range of agencies owned by a wider community
Planners could be peripheral to the Council, but still prepare the plan	Expects planners to be engaged in corporate strategy and policy-making
Content	
Vision not mandatory	Shared vision required
Objectives constrained to land use	Scope for diverse and more fundamental objectives
Site-specific and defined areas for operation of policies	Can contain non-site-based policies
Requirement for general conformity with higher level planning strategy	General conformity with Regional/London spatial strategy continues, but now also the requirement to have regard to the community strategy
Process	
Process generally of only legal concern	Process ongoing and important in itself
Consultation with communities focused on proposals	Early and ongoing engagement with communities, focused on needs, concerns and problems
Consultation with agencies on proposals	Requires consensus with agencies on strategy, integration and delivery
Monitoring a limited suite of data	Monitoring performance on delivery of objectives across the board

Table 2.1 continued

Land use/regulatory	Spatial
Implementation	
Delivery mainly through development control by the local authority	Delivery through a range of channels and a range of agencies
Focus on allocations and what gets built – outputs	Focus on delivery of objectives and all the elements which go together to achieve them – outcomes

Source: Planning Officers Society (www.planningofficers.org.uk/page.cp/pageid/100).

- **Broad-ranging**, concerning the assessment of the spatial dimensions of various activities and sectors, and interactions between them;
- **Visionary**, by opening up planning to a range of participants, and by relating processes of planning policy-making to notions of place;
- **Integrating**, through bringing together spatial issues relating to the development and use of land, and the users of planning;
- **Deliverable**, applying strategy to programmes for action, through proactive processes,
- involving coordination and choreography between different overlapping sectors and resources; and
- **Participative**, where planning is a facilitator and dependent on new forms of partnership and engagement with a range of bodies, stakeholders, businesses and communities.

(UCL and Deloitte 2007: 11, para 1.8; see also RTPI 2001)

A useful comparison between regulatory and spatial planning in the context of local government has been prepared by the Planning Officers Society (Table 2.1).

The integration agenda provides an integral part of our analysis. Arguably, planning in the 1970s sought sectoral policy integration around regional spatial and economic planning and the corporate agendas of local authorities. However, it was really with the emergence of the spatial planning agenda within government and professional bodies that a wider conception of the need for integration has emerged as part of the planning profession's reinvention of its role, raising a wider question about why planning found itself rediscovered or re-legitimised at the end of the 1990s, after nearly two decades on the margins, lacking policy salience and professional credibility.

There are a number of reasons. The first concerns shifts towards spatial planning as being an internal reaction within local government as it responded to pressures for improved internal efficiency, including better integrated decision-making. Bolton and Leach (2002) highlight three influences within this category. First, there were the increasing financial constraints within local government that led to a recognition of the need to ensure resources were used more effectively within local authority management. Second, they also noted the impact of a changing management ethos, which recognised the need to rethink local authority services in the light of client/contractor splits and partnership working in an era of fragmented governance. The shift towards greater contracting out of local government services (or privatisation as it was also known) often fragmented policy from implementation as it was usually the latter that was outsourced to the private sector. Finally, added to this was the commitment by all the major political parties to new management agendas and approaches focused on holistic service delivery rather than professionally oriented service units. Planning fitted into this changing zeitgeist with its expertise in strategy and policy formulation and its statutory, spatial basis. It may not always have been in the vanguard of change, but the planning profession in both Ireland and the UK was quick to recognise that it had much to gain from working with the grain of the emergent trend within government for producing coordinated long-term strategies.

The second reason privileges external, macro-economic and governmental trends and their consequences for local government. In other words, spatial planning is part of a much wider process of local government modernisation (Allmendinger *et al.* 2005). In relation to shifts towards integrated social and economic development, for example, Valler and Betteley (2001) note a number of broad influences. One is the reaction to the ineffectiveness of New Right market-led approaches to planning, urban regeneration and local economic development. Such approaches fragmented policy, establishing ad-hoc bodies and arrangements that focused on particular places and were underpinned by the notion of 'trickle down' or the social 'ripple effects' of physical, property-led regeneration. They also argue that spatial planning's role in policy coordination may reflect broader processes of restructuring driven by the economic liberalisation agenda globally and nationally, where privatisation, deregulation, competition and choice agendas all contribute to a more fragmented landscape of subnational governance.

Finally, fitting in with our understanding of the changing nature of planning, spatial planning can be seen as a reaction against regulatory planning that had dominated the 1980s. The 'project-led' approach that saw planning as a regulatory function had become increasingly criticised. Growing environmental concerns at the end of the 1980s linked to early awareness of climate change combined with reactions against numerous new settlement proposals in the south of England forced a policy 'u-turn' in the shift back towards planning as a spatially and sectorally integrative function. In many ways then, the integrative aspects of planning, its emphasis on sustainable development and inclusion, all chimed well with the expectations of the public that while major development might be necessary it should not be bulldozed through by government bureaucrats. Spatial planning in this sense provided an ideology for rethinking how the planning system could reclaim legitimacy through acting as a forum for debating how best to achieve better-quality development through partnership with a range of actors, rather than as a separate sphere of expertise which, in effect, told people how the government was going to work with the private sector to develop new housing and other forms of development. More than this, the explicit mandate for the planning system to pursue an integrated approach to sustainable development provided a twofold disciplinary task of ensuring that planners did not unwittingly take on the mantle of 'environment-first' policy approaches, while those wishing to navigate successfully through the planning apparatus had to recognise that a naive interpretation of sustainable development as economic growth and jobs at virtually any cost was no longer necessarily going to win out in planning debates.

That is the 'positive spin' on how spatial planning appeared to gain legitimacy and credibility within wider governmental circles. But in some parts of government spatial planning appears to be seen as adding to governance clutter, allowing those opposed to development to thwart it through seemingly endless consultation and involvement (see Chapters 7 and 8). The result is a series of government initiatives to 'rationalise' and 'streamline' planning, while also holding on to some of its core values, not least its role as a deliberative forum. In England, for instance, in 2007 the Planning White Paper also proposed to move away from a 'one size fits all' Local Development Framework adoption process in order to speed up the painfully slow process (DCLG 2007). Other mechanisms are also being put in place to encourage greater integration. The first is the strengthening of the role of Local Strategic Partnerships and Sustainable Community Strategies through Local and Multi-area Agreements. The second is to begin to engage with the emerging sub-regional agenda and give some coherence and formality to the soft and fuzzy spaces that planning is now beginning to grapple with.

Policy integration comes in various guises, with spatial planning just one expression. It can be about: integration across different types of policy domain, such as planning, economic development and transport; integration between different types of actors, state, voluntary, community and business agencies; or it may be about pursuing an integrated approach to the social, economic and environmental dimensions of 'sustainable development' (see Haughton and Counsell 2004). The broad point is that integrated approaches, including spatial planning, are far from neutral policy devices (Vigar *et al.* 2000) and far from unproblematic. As with other policy changes, the push towards greater policy integration, including a stronger role for spatial planning, will typically encounter diverse forms of resistance:

> Purposive attempts at change are hard to achieve. New institutions in local governance are likely to be resisted (or 'hijacked') by those who benefit from existing arrangements or see new rules as hostile to their interests. They are likely to be adapted in ways that suit locally-specific institutional environments. Organizations and groups have an immense capacity to co-opt, absorb or deflect new initiatives.
>
> (Lowndes 2003: 280)

As Bolton and Leach (2002) and Hardy *et al.* (1992) point out, there is a good deal of evidence of resistance to policy integration from professional and departmental interests within local government; reference to 'warring baronies' and 'independent fiefdoms' were commonplace in studies of local government policy integration during the 1980s. Professionals, who can feel that their status is being challenged, may provide barriers to greater integrative working. However, other studies have suggested that such departmentalism and professional antipathy have been breaking down, particularly during the 1990s (Leach *et al.* 1994). Organisation cultures may also prove to be an impediment to greater integrative working – both internally and externally – particularly where strong management hierarchies exist (Stewart *et al.* 2000). Progress on such new initiatives can often be because of the resources that follow rather than any real commitment (Valler and Betteley 2001: 2410). This, as we will see in later chapters, is a real concern for those working on spatial plans as they seek to move from designing long-term spatial visions to seeing them through to implementation. It is rarely clear cut as to whether resources follow plans, plans follow resources, or whether there is simply a 'muddling through'.

Spatial versus regulatory planning

Key to understanding the changing arrangements for, and scales of, planning is an appreciation of the basic tensions inherent within it. The history of planning in the UK and Ireland has always been characterised by a shifting settlement between a range of conflicting tensions and views, as well as experiments with reworking or re-regulating the role of planners via both 'hard' and 'soft' spaces. Most significant over the period of 'modern planning' (roughly from the middle of the twentieth century) is the tension between, on the one hand, a regulatory view of planning and, on the other, a more comprehensive (spatial) approach (Allmendinger and Haughton 2007: 1484). A regulatory view sees planning as intervening in land and property markets to control what economists refer to as negative externalities (e.g. noise, pollution, overcrowding). It is focused on facilitating and delivering development. There is a recognised need for some form of intervention in land and property markets by even the most ardent proponents of free markets. However, this does not necessarily involve state intervention (see e.g. Pennington 2000). A range of tools and mechanisms such as private covenants would, some argue, achieve the same ends as regulatory planning without the attendant downsides of state control. More comprehensive and more spatialised approaches give planning a much more positive and interventionist role in securing wider objectives and integrating a range of policy sectors at different spatial scales. In this view spatial planning is about the nature and pattern of future development processes, allied increasingly to a concern to oversee delivery of the plan's aims through diverse implementation bodies, and to monitor progress. To some extent then, the shift from regulatory to spatial planning parallels the shift from 'government' to 'governance' systems and, as we will argue later, the emergence of metagovernance.

It is in this context that policy integration and delivery coordination appear increasingly frequently in the planning literature (e.g. Glasson and Marshall

2007), involving both 'vertical' (across scales) and 'horizontal' (between policy sectors) integration, where no single scale or policy sector assumes primacy, and in theory all work together towards agreeing and achieving common goals. Spatial planning in this sense is about bringing together actors and institutions to agree a process for imagining better-quality physical environments and persuasive powers to engage others in moving towards achieving these agreed aspirations. It is not about a group of experts deciding among themselves what needs to be done in the interests of some abstract thing called 'society' or 'the economy' and then using regulatory systems to require others to comply with this vision. It is much more about working with others to create a vision of what might be that inspires others enough to join in and support its achievement.

This is what those pushing a spatial planning agenda in government and the planning profession appear to aspire towards – the system is not yet there yet, and perhaps never will be. If nothing else, the history of planning tells us that at various times and in different places the planning system has swung between regulatory and spatial approaches (and myriad positions in between). But the tension here is always that both systems ultimately place high value on conformity and predictability in the development process, in a world where conformity and predictability are neither achievable nor necessarily seen as desirable. As such regulatory and spatial planning remain in perpetual creative tension with each other in how to achieve the unachievable. There is a further tension here in that there are elements of the spatial in the 'regulatory' approach, and spatial planning necessarily relies on its incorporation of aspects of a regulatory approach. The rhetorical presentation of differences between spatial planning and previous 'regulatory' approaches sometimes seems to be as much about political legitimacy and the moral high ground as about changing the practices of planning. Both approaches are presented as aspiring to higher-quality physical development which is better planned and coordinated. The difference is that each is associated with particular preferred methods for achieving their goals, involving a delicate balancing of addressing people's desire for the protection of individual freedoms with the achievement of collective aspirations and needs. Indeed this tension is one of the main reasons (the other one being ideological) why planning seems to be perpetually 'reformed'.

Trying to ground this rather abstract account of planning's perennial tensions, Table 2.2 provides a highly simplified overview of the changing nature of planning since the early 1930s. England is used to illustrate these changes, simply because it would be too complex to include in one table the many subtle and not so subtle differences with the experience in Ireland, Scotland, Wales and Northern Ireland. The main theme that Table 2.2 brings out is the shifting emphases in both the *scales* and *styles* of planning throughout this period, highlighting the recent refocusing upon spatial and regulatory planning.

There are four relevant points that emerge from these experiences or changing phases of planning. The first is that there is nothing inevitable or

Table 2.2 Selected key changes to the scales and styles of English planning, 1932–2005

Phase	Scales of planning	Styles of planning
1932–1947	Detailed national guidance and model policies. Detailed zoning plans at the local level	Prescriptive zoning. No separate planning permission required
1947–1968	National level takes on a more guidance and supervisory role. Two-tier development plans comprising a county map (broad allocations) and more detailed town maps (detailed land uses and densities)	Discretionary rather than prescriptive zoning approach. Separate planning permission required
1968–1979	Oversight and prescription of centre strengthened through introduction and approval of county structure plans. Local plans to be in conformity with structure plans	Discretionary approach with separate plan and permission
1979–1990	Increased central role through dictating content and scope of plans. National planning guidance extended. Downgrading of the significance of structure and local plans in detailed planning controls. Plans no longer required to be prepared. Reintroduction of prescriptive zoning in Enterprise Zones and Simplified Planning Zones	'Project-led' planning era with combination of discretionary decision-making based upon 'case-by-case' basis and areas where no separate permission required
1990–1998	Significance of central government guidance maintained through the introduction of the 'plan-led' system. Devolution of central government departments to English regions and responsible for regional planning guidance. Structure and local plans again required	'Plan-led' approach under S.54 of the Planning Act 1990 aims to give greater certainty and clarity to decision-making. Performance targets introduced
1998–2000	Further devolution to Scottish Parliament, Welsh Assembly and English regions. Elected London Mayor. Creation of Regional Development Agencies and Regional Chambers/ Assemblies to prepare regional planning guidance	Sustainable development logics integrated into process and decision-making. Planning's role in tackling climate change rises up the agenda

2001–2004	Launch of Sustainable Communities Plan and later the Northern Way and city region agenda. These non-statutory documents appear to drive much of the 'filling in' of subnational planning structures. Planning and Compulsory Purchase Act 2004 introduced Regional Spatial Strategies (RSSs) as statutory documents. Sustainable Community Strategies introduced as policy and spatial coordinating mechanisms at local level	Planning Delivery Grant introduced, rewarding speed of process in development control and emphasised process over outcome. Plan-led approach re-emphasised (s. 38 of the 2004 Act). Treasury introduces PSAs, driving change in planning practices again to reward speed
2005–	Proposed strengthening of delivery role of regional planning through combining RSSs and RESs and giving responsibility of preparation to RDAs. National-level guidance intended to be scaled back	Targets shifted from process to delivery with Housing and Planning Delivery Grant. Regulatory aspects of planning strengthened through provisions in Planning White and Housing Green Papers

Source: adapted from Allmendinger and Haughton (2007).

pre-given about any approach to planning. Planning has changed in its scale and scope with (almost predictable) regularity. Second, while we are currently in a phase (2005 onwards) characterised by spatial planning, there are already clear signs of another phase transition back to a more regulatory emphasis. The reaction against elements of spatial planning is becoming increasingly vocal (e.g. Confederation of British Industry (CBI) 2005; Barker 2006), including a slow though discernible refocus of planning back to concerns with core aspects of delivery and development (DCLG 2007). This is proposed through the standardisation of developer contributions, the introduction of a fast-tracked process for major infrastructure projects and a new emphasis upon the link between plans and infrastructure provision. In addition, local authorities in England will be incentivised through the Housing and Planning Delivery Grant to speed up plan making. Any phase, therefore, does not represent the 'end of history': phase transitions between different planning approaches are usually precipitated by backlashes against what are perceived to be the drawbacks of the current approach. Thus, the dominance of regulatory planning in the UK during the 1980s led to criticisms that it lacked any sense of the 'big picture'. In particular, the growing concern over environmental issues towards the end of the decade necessitated a more spatial approach.

But spatial planning also has its drawbacks: it tends to take more time and come up against a range of complex issues of integration between policy sectors and across spatial scales. In periods when there are particular demands to accelerate the rates of building new residential properties (as in the first decade of the twenty-first century), spatial planning can be portrayed as serving to thwart development rather than ensure that better-quality, more integrated and sustainable development ensues. At the time of writing in both the UK and Ireland, there is a strong emphasis from central governments on housing delivery, with UK ministers beginning to voice frustrations with planning in general and development control in particular.[1] (It is worth noting, however, that housebuilding dropped significantly towards the end of 2008 not because of the planning system but because of the global credit crunch.) There is also concern in some quarters that planning remains slow and cumbersome and imposes high costs upon developments, with little evaluation of the benefits.

Figures 2.1 and 2.2 provide a schematic representation of the shifting nature of planning between its different forms (e.g. spatial versus regulatory) and the different phases outlined earlier in Table 2.2. In Figure 2.1 different approaches to planning are represented as compromises between opposing characteristics, seen as a spectrum of possibilities rather than necessarily mutually exclusive. On the horizontal axis certainty and flexibility are cast as opposites. The British and Irish planning systems both privilege flexibility and administrative discretion, allied to a strong emphasis on property rights. In contrast, civil law systems such as those found in continental Europe emphasise greater administrative certainty.[2] In reality, all systems are flexible to a degree though the difference is whether such flexibility is formal or informal (Booth 2003). Thus there exists a tension in planning between certainty of outcome and flexibility of process: the greater the certainty of the process and

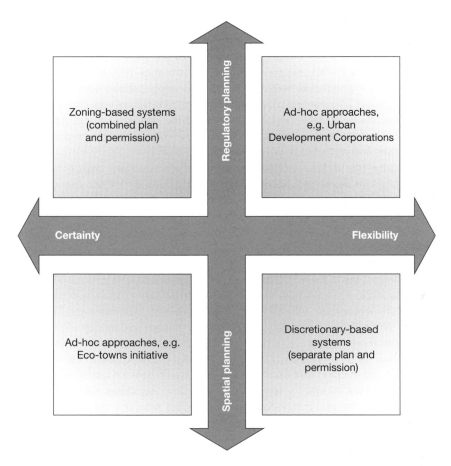

2.1 A typology of planning approaches

Note: these axes are intended to show a spectrum of possibilities, not mutually exclusive bipolar opposites.

criteria upon which decisions are taken the less flexibility or discretion there is for the decision-taker, and vice versa. The vertical axis highlights contrasts between regulatory and spatial planning approaches. Any system will also involve a compromise between, on the one hand, speed of decision-making and, on the other, comprehensiveness of decisions. In other words, the quicker the decision the less information or inputs into the process, including public involvement, are likely, and vice versa.

Having set out this basic framework, we then attempt to map on to it various ideal-typical approaches to planning. In Figure 2.1 zoning-based systems that combine plan and permission are characterised by high degrees of certainty and a regulatory focus and can be placed in the top-left quadrant. In such systems no separate planning permission is required providing the proposal conforms with the zoning criteria. The British systems with their current emphasis upon spatial planning and flexibility are to be found in the lower right.[3] Here, separate planning permission is normally required and development plans are more indicative than prescriptive. Decisions do not have to be taken in accordance with the plan (though they normally are). In the other two quadrants bespoke and ad-hoc approaches such as Urban Development Corporations can be plotted; these in effect can be portrayed as limited experiments in breaking away from the dominant paradigm, or as ways of dealing with special cases, where the standard planning practices of the day are not expected to work.

In reality, this is an inevitable simplification of what are unique systems of control: zoning-based approaches will unavoidably reflect the characteristics of each territory, and indeed with greater political devolution we would expect to see greater variation in practices occurring. Further, it is difficult to ascribe 'one' approach to the UK and Ireland given the separation of plan from permission: it could be argued that England, for instance, has a spatial development plan approach and a regulatory development control system. Nevertheless, the division of planning systems into 'families' is a common and useful heuristic against which to compare the inevitable messiness of practice, particularly the unique nature of the British approach (Newman and Thornley 1996). What Figure 2.1 usefully highlights is the political nature of planning approach: there is a range of different approaches to planning vying for the attention of those charged with shaping national planning practices.

Having established that planning systems vary in type we can now turn our attention to time. Inherent in largely unitary, centralised states such as the UK and Ireland is the ability to reform law and policy relatively quickly. As mentioned above, planning has been no exception to this. Regular changes to the planning system can and have been made and these can be plotted against the typology (Figure 2.2). The periods of planning style and scale in Table 2.2 form the basis of the approach. Six phases are identified with associated exceptions where appropriate. For example, the broad approach of the period 1932–1947 was more akin to the continental European style of planning, though this changed significantly under the post-1947 approach which introduced a more discretionary and spatial regime. Since then there have been a variety of different settlements, though there have also been special arrangements that depart from the overall approach. For example, while the post-1947 approach was discretionary, special arrangements for the building of new towns were made that have been used again recently, though with modifications, for the development of areas under the Sustainable Communities Plan of 2003 in Thurrock Thames Gateway, East London (including a number of local authorities and also covering the Olympic Games sites) and West Northamptonshire. A similar model also underpins the current Milton Keynes Partnership Committee.

Such bespoke solutions have also been used in other eras. Between 1979 and 1990, for example, the planning system shifted incrementally towards a more market-oriented approach, with two further ad-hoc arrangements represented where the governments of the time would probably have liked

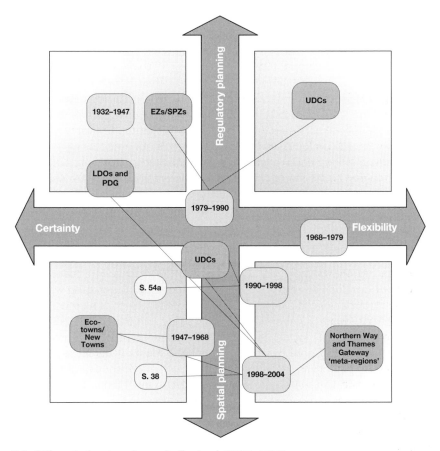

2.2 Different planning phases in England, 1932–2004

Note: these axes are intended to show a spectrum of possibilities, not mutually exclusive bipolar opposites.

the whole system to move (Allmendinger and Thomas 1998). Enterprise Zones and simplified planning zones represented a much more zoning-based approach to land use regulation while the Urban Development Corporations (UDCs) under the early Thatcher administrations also represented a very development-oriented regime. However, both are located within a wider discretionary system and though the governments of the day made much of their symbolic and political importance, they remained largely outliers within the planning system, acting as independent experiments in a more flexible, business-friendly approach to planning.[4] In the case of UDCs, they were created in three phases and a degree of learning from experience characterised their evolution as a result, so while the emphasis remained on speed of process and certainty for business, they also became much more focused on issues such as achieving greater community engagement and higher design standards as time went on.

Similar outliers to the standard planning system have been introduced in Ireland, where the government can designate areas of strategic importance for expedited social and economic development, most recently with Integrated Area Plans, introduced in 1998, and Strategic Development Zones, introduced in 2000. These occupy similar roles to their British counterparts in terms of being within the planning system, but allowing a degree of flexibility to deviate from 'standard practice'. Indeed many national governments introduce such special schemes – the point here is that the English experience which we have been focusing on in this section is not exceptional.

Returning to the English experience, a fragmented approach has also been taken in recent times, though in a slightly different way. There are essentially two ways in which the orientation of planning can be changed. The first is to change the system (i.e. the legal and policy context). The second is to manage the process. In practice, governments have sought reform through both approaches. The system of development planning has largely though not exclusively been recently reformed through legislative change, in the UK primarily the Planning and Compulsory Purchase Act 2004. This introduced a new system of development plans and aimed to speed up plan making while also moving towards 'spatial planning', including greater emphasis on community engagement, strategic coordination and policy integration (DCLG 2007). Development control (or development management as the government now likes to call it in England) has been reformed in recent times largely through management processes, including the setting of performance targets and the introduction of financial incentives to authorities to meet them. The regulatory and management approaches are both involved then in strengthening the link between the two halves of English planning through the 'plan-led' approach. Legislation first introduced in 1991 and then updated in 2004 requires that any determination of an application '*must be made in accordance with the plan unless material considerations indicate otherwise*' (S. 38(6) of the Planning and Compulsory Purchase Act 2004). This could be interpreted as a move towards a more zoning-based approach in creating greater certainty.

In terms of locating this approach in Figure 2.2 the two 'plan-led' approaches (identified as S. 54a and S. 38 in the diagram) seek (in theory) to increase certainty in planning in general and development control in particular. In addition, Local Development Orders (LDOs) will introduce a zoning-based approach while the increased use of performance targets and performance-related incentives in the form of the Planning Delivery Grant (PDG) also have the effect of increasing certainty and emphasising the regulatory nature of development control.

The positioning of different phases of planning in Figure 2.2 is not by any means clear cut: the separation of plan from permission and different 'styles' of planning in different localities mean that ascribing a position is illustrative of the changing aggregate characteristics of planning through time. For instance, Regional Spatial Strategies (RSSs) comprise elements of regulatory and spatial planning, combining certainty (over housing number allocations, for instance) and flexibility. The point here is not to ascribe or map a definite place that represents the different approaches towards planning but to highlight the changing nature of the settlement between competing tensions through time.

Third, and related to the above point, it needs to be stressed that phases are not binary. During a phase dominated by spatial planning, regulatory planning still exists. The UK and Irish approaches to planning separate plan from permission, i.e. land allocated in a development plan still has to obtain separate planning permission. In continental European countries plan and permission are combined. However, in both the UK and Ireland the dominance of a particular approach to planning always sits alongside the less dominant approach. Since the mid-1990s or so, for example, regulatory planning has had a 'Cinderella' role compared to the focus on spatial planning, though it has still existed and been an important element of any local planning regime. Finally, there is a range of planning styles possible within any given phase. Though slightly overstretched, Brindley *et al.* (1989, 1996) highlighted how different places have discretion to pursue different styles of planning within national contexts or phases. Interestingly, while the first edition of this influential book identified six planning styles, in the introduction to the second edition they note that within a matter of a few years they had largely collapsed into one dominant approach. The important point here is that the scope for autonomous local planning is tightly prescribed and open to challenge if it conflicts with national priorities. Though their observations were based on local scales of planning the same principles arguably would apply to other scales.

While much of the preceding discussion has focused on the English experience, from 1999 onwards it is more appropriate to talk of UK plannings and, for the purposes of this book, Irish planning. Devolution has played an important role in breaking up the largely centralised and hierarchical nature of UK planning, though it has been far less of an influence in Ireland, where devolution is still at an early stage. The key issue in Ireland has been the decision to create a national spatial strategy in 2002, and running alongside this a system of regional planning guidelines and informal systems for metropolitan planning. The Irish experience adds a new dimension to the previous discussion though because of the importance there of the link between the new systems of spatial planning and investment planning. So while the NSS is a statutory plan, it has only a limited role in terms of, for instance regulatory targets. It is more strategic and broadbrush than, say, English RSSs. But it has perhaps a stronger 'regulatory' force than this implies because of the introduction of mandatory requirements that all departments of government give an explicit account of how they will support NSS objectives in bidding for their investment budget, and moreover each department must provide annual reports on progress against NSS objectives. This is an entirely different type of control to the legalistic forms we have been discussing in the English case.

Introducing Northern Ireland, Scotland and Wales into the discussion adds further complexity. In Northern Ireland the main 'national' spatial strategy is the Regional Development Strategy (2001). As Chapter 4 reveals, this combines aspects of both spatial and regulatory planning, but it struggles to enforce or even oversee either aspect given the fragmented governance system for planning introduced post-devolution. There is an interesting parallel here with the experience of the regional economic planning councils in the UK in the 1960s and 1970s, which ranged in ambition from long-term spatial visions to providing wider-ranging corporate frameworks for decision-making, attempting to provide a spatial dimension for coordinated government policy-making and investment in the regions (Glasson and Marshall 2007). In Scotland, the National Planning Framework (2004) was initially a non-statutory document, though this is in the process of being changed. In Wales, the Wales Spatial Plan is a statutory document of the Welsh Assembly government, but it is not a statutory part of the Welsh planning system. So, as in Northern Ireland, local plans are expected to have regard to the national spatial plan, but they are not required to conform to it. The Welsh approach is also notable for its deliberate decision not to allocate new housing figures among constituent local author-ities, leaving this to a mixture of local discretion combined with a central steer and joint working between local and national planners. In other words, if the English experience revealed the extent of fragmented trajectories in planning over time through an 80-year time horizon, when we start to think of divergent practices since devolution in the late 1990s and the innovations introduced by the national government in Ireland, we begin to see the scope for diversity in planning systems across the British Isles. More than this, there is con-siderable policy learning going on across the new territorial administrations, as they seek to rethink how to plan for their territorial development in ways that mark a distinctive break with the past.

We discuss in further detail in later chapters of this book how different regions of the UK and Ireland are developing their own distinctive approaches to planning in general and regional planning in particular. However, what we can already begin to see from the present discussion is that there is a wide range of complex formal and informal influences between the emergent planning systems and their own phases. The outcome of such centripetal and centrifugal forces towards conformity or difference cannot be 'read off' (Allmendinger 2001a, 2001b), though at this stage it is worth highlighting that the gradual and periodic phase changes in Table 2.2 may now be replaced by more punctuated and/or quantum forms of change in other parts of the UK: following a change of political leadership, Scotland or Wales could decide to move towards a more radically different approach to planning, for example. Further, the tension between regulatory and spatial planning approaches may itself be replaced, particularly if parts of the UK follow a more continental system of planning or a more radical approach as found in other parts of the world. It was always the case that planning history did not follow a linear logic, and as we have sought to emphasise throughout these first two chapters, 'spatial planning' is not some logical end-point evolving out of previous approaches. Instead we try to emphasise here some of the perennial tensions within planning that re-emerge in different guises during each new phase of experimentation. What is particularly interesting about the current period of experimentation, which we might broadly think of as 'spatial planning', is that the devolution agenda and the proliferation of new planning spaces that has accompanied this (see below) have increased the possibilities for divergent subnational planning approaches to emerge even within the context of what superficially might appear to be a strong orthodoxy.

Rescaling, regions and spatial planning

Another dimension that is critical to any understanding of spatial planning is the changing scales of both regulatory and spatial planning. Planning in the UK is multi-scalar; that is, policy and plan making are made by different bodies at different spatial scales. Table 2.2 highlighted aspects of this dimension, which Figure 2.3 elaborates on through a schematic representation of the changing nature of scale in English planning, with increasing governance congestion standing out in the contemporary period. The three different-sized ovals provide an approximation of the significance of each scalar element, while the arrows highlight a deliberate shift in scale (e.g. legislative change). What stands out in Figure 2.3 is the incessant reworking of scale within planning.

One question that this diagram throws up is what are the underlying systemic forces that drive these changes? (The same question could be asked of the different approaches in Table 2.2.) It is important to stress that the scales at which planning operates and the changes to them are part of a process driven by socio-political struggles, with the state providing a site in which these forces play out. Rather than seeing the state as fixed or an embodiment of regulation, it is instead best seen as 'a terrain upon which different political forces attempt to impart a specific direction to the individual or collective activities of its different branches' (Jessop 1990: 268). As such the state (and, we would add, planning) reflect a continuous struggle by various bodies, institutions and interests for privilege and advantage:

> The geography of state spatiality must be viewed as . . . an outcome of continually evolving political strategies . . . The spaces of state power are not simply 'filled', as if they were pre-given territorial containers. Instead state spatiality is actively produced and transformed through regulatory projects and socio-political struggles articulated in diverse institutional sites and at a range of geographical scales.
>
> (Brenner 2004: 76)

It would be wrong to assume that the state imposes its own will or is always subordinate to dominant economic interests. Instead, some interests are more influential than others at any geo-historical conjuncture:

> Particular forms of economic and political system privilege some strategies over others, access by some forces of others, some interests over others, some spatial scales of action over others, some time horizons over others, some coalition possibilities over others.

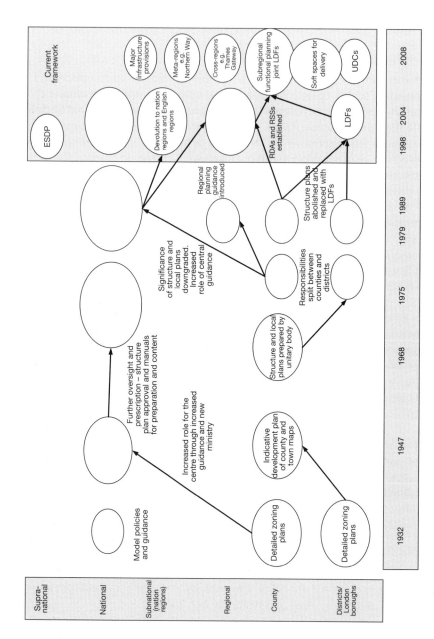

2.3 Scalar flux and increasing governance 'congestion' in English planning

Structural constraints always operate selectively: they are not absolute and unconditional but always temporally, spatially, agency, and strategy specific. This has implications both for general struggles over the economic and extra-economic regularization of capitalist economies and specific struggles involved in securing the hegemony of a specific accumulation strategy.

(Jessop 1997: 63)

Of course the corollary of this is that at any particular spatio-temporal conjunction some interests are less influential than others and their aims are more difficult to achieve. The point is that such 'spatio-temporal fixes', as Jessop (1997) terms them, are dynamic and contested. For example, environmental concerns have grown more influential in recent years, one consequence being that the role and influence of the Environment Agency in planning matters has been strengthened. Thinking about the dominant scales of governance and planning at any particular moment is important as they can shift not only the points of access to the planning system, but also the ways in which planning struggles are played out. Good examples of this include the abolition of the former metropolitan counties and the shift of powers to unitary local authorities in 1986, and the decision to reduce the role of county councils in the planning system in 2004 (see Chapter 7 for further discussion of this). In this context, the rescaling of planning represents a perennial search for some combination of governance structures stretching from neighbourhood to national, and even EU scales, which align with wider goals such as pursuing national economic growth, social justice, or sustainable development. Planning in this sense is a site of socio-political struggle, where its regulatory and institutional structures are contested and reworked in ways that are revealing of wider societal and ideological debates about the role of the state in relation to markets and civil society.

The notion of governance is usually portrayed as a shift away from rigid, hierarchical systems of state-centred government, where power is largely exerted from the top down mainly through regulatory forms of enforcement. By contrast governance is seen as a more networked form of arrangement, which brings a broad constellation of actors into the policy-making and delivery arena. Governance is typically presented as a more porous form of decision-making, where agreements are brokered through multiple actors, and where network power is more important than coercive power. Jessop (2002) defines governance as a system of reflexive self-organisation, where actors combine in complex systems of reciprocal interdependence, engaging in dialogue and sharing resources in pursuit of mutually beneficial work. Given this, who participates in the different governance structures is important in understanding what types of understanding and agreements arise out of particular constellations of governance actors – add in new actors, or subtract some, and new understandings are likely to emerge. This is why the changing nature of governance systems matters, whether these are changed through rescaling or opening up to new sectoral influences, or some combination. In practical terms, at the subnational level in particular, we are now seeing a proliferation of governance bodies which bring together stakeholders from various organisations in government and beyond, selectively empowered to undertake work that might once have been largely viewed as the work of 'government'. We have already mentioned examples of these new governance approaches, the UDCs, for instance, plus various forms of regeneration partnerships. In consequence, as one leading commentator puts it: 'We have entered a post-elected local government era and are moving to a new era of local governance populated by a more diverse and varied set of institutions and processes' (Stoker 2004: 9).

Running parallel to the shift from government to governance is the shift from government to what Jessop (2003) refers to as metagovernance in the shadow of hierarchy. Metagovernance is the process of steering or shaping the diverse systems of governance which have emerged in recent years, embracing the ways in which rules of the game are set and interpreted by those involved, linking these governance bodies to each other and to wider strategic imperatives. It provides a way of ensuring that systems of governance operate in complementary and mutually reinforcing ways (Jessop 2003). Rather than see this as simply a further example of dispersed, network power, 'in the shadow of hierarchy' suggests that metagovernance practices will be part introduced through reflexive self-organisation and part shaped by dominant interests. Metagovernance then is not simply the imposition of governmental priorities through the shaping of the rules of the game, though this is a factor. It is best seen however as a more complex process for creating shared understandings of acceptable behaviours, enforced through diverse mechanisms, not least the shared involvement in creating strategic documents required by the policy integration agenda, and agreement on the instruments for ensuring conformity, such as sustainability appraisal, performance targets and integrated policy appraisal. Interlocking the processes for preparing economic development and sustainable development strategies, for instance, helps determine the parameters of discretion within individual sectors and brokers' shared understandings around broad principles and direction of travel. Metagovernance is also multilevel, working at and across different scales. For instance, Jessop (2008) sees the European Spatial Development Perspective as something which is at one level seeking to consolidate a European approach to territorial integration, with its emphasis on infrastructural networks, for instance, Trans-European transport routes. In the process it creates a new scalar division of labour that asserts a dominant European-level understanding of spatial planning concepts and practices, while simultaneously constituting national and regional actors as 'nodal' rather than dominant scales (cf. Collinge 1999).

Jessop (2003) also refers to the need for requisite variety in looking at governance and metagovernance, ideas which have a particular resonance for planning. His argument is that like markets, governance and metagovernance are always prone to failure and must learn to anticipate and deal with this. Requisite variety in this sense concerns the need to cope with systemic turbulence through a wide repertoire of responses, allowing flexibility in dealing with rapid change. Dealing with complexity might usefully involve building multiple, interlocking governance structures, which may at times result in governance congestion or over-governance (Sullivan and Skelcher 2002). On the positive side, however, what this governance complexity also does is provide alternatives for one mode of governance failing, so that not all institutional memory is lost. Jessop's work also highlights the need for reflexive capacity within governance systems to make choices over which type of 'acceptable failure' their decisions might lead to. It is important for cohesion and therefore the chances of achieving 'acceptable failure' that all maintain publicly their support for the agreed strategy (Jessop amusingly refers to this as 'requisite irony'). This is important in practical terms when it comes to negotiations for advanced infrastructure in large-scale new developments. If planning cannot provide certainty then it is not in the interest of infrastructure providers to provide excess capacity in advance of demands.

Devolution, which is at the heart of this book, in this context provides new challenges for metagovernance, which in turn create opportunities for existing policy communities to be reworked and new ones to emerge (Keating 2005). Most notably here, the process of developing strategies and plans at newly empowered scales of governance allows new policy communities to emerge, as stakeholders seek to shape not only the strategy itself but also subsequent policies for implementation. It makes sense then to think of devolution not simply as a given number of separate territorial entities each evolving their own systems within behavioural parameters imposed from above, but instead as an interconnected set of networks, working to build stronger territorial and extra-territorial alliances, with which they can then reshape the rules of devolution. This complex process of engagement through interlocking, porous networks is very much part of metagovernance, where power is multidirectional, multifaceted and always being remade through formal and informal systems of rules and understandings.[5]

When governance systems are opened up, or where new policy domains emerge, things tend to be relatively fluid with new networks and policy communities being formed, as in the case of developing national spatial strategies in newly devolved territories. This creates the opportunity for existing policy communities to adapt to the new circumstances, or for new policy communities to form. As part of this process, constituent actors are opened up to new ways of thinking and required to acknowledge the values and understandings of different bodies of professional expertise and scientific knowledge. The polity from which new scalar (e.g. regional) and sectoral (e.g. sustainable development, spatial planning) strategies emerge is thus made up of diverse communities which are variously interlocking and shifting in composition and placed within the broader multi-scalar polity. In these ways planners are exposed to new ways of thinking about the problems they face, while when they engage with other communities of practice they bring with them their more 'spatialised' forms of knowledge and understanding. This study reveals how this process of remaking policy communities has been occurring not simply at the level of the newly devolved territorial administrations, such as Scotland, but also at a range of other scales, as new institutional geographies are brought into being within or alongside existing planning spaces. We return to this theme later in this chapter when we discuss the issues of 'soft spaces' in planning.

The right-hand side of Figure 2.3 represents the dynamic and fragmented nature of rescaling in planning. However, this is not the whole story: since devolution there has been a further dimension to rescaling as variant forms of devolution have emerged. It was always anticipated that one of the benefits of devolution would be the policy innovation that it sparked, unleashing differing levels and types of divergence from national policy, not least given the path dependencies arising out of previous devolutionary initiatives (Keating 2005) and the asymmetrical nature of contemporary devolution (Cooke and Clifton 2005). Cooke and Clifton (2005) claim that it is already possible to identify variant forms of devolution emerging across the UK. They summarise these as Northern Ireland demonstrating 'constrained governance' allied to an economic 'coordinated market policy approach', whereas Wales is characterised as 'precautionary governance' linked to 'state-centric' policy and Scotland as having visionary governance and a liberal market policy approach. Each of these interpretations is open to challenge given the rapidly evolving nature of the devolution project and the fact that approaches to spatial planning may reveal different policy approaches. Nonetheless, this analysis is helpful in opening up the issues of how devolution styles might have a bearing on the relationship between rescaling, spatial planning and what we term the scope of policy.

New territorial management: the question of scope and spatial planning

We do not want to engage too deeply here with recent debates on scale, relational geographies and territorial politics, simply to acknowledge them briefly because they do infuse much recent literature in this area (for a useful overview see the special issue of *Regional Studies* 'Whither Regional Studies?': Pike 2007). At the risk of oversimplification, the recent resurgence of interest in regional-scale governance has sparked an increasingly lively debate about the politics of 'rescaling', relational geographies which emphasise the importance of stretched networks of relationships that transcend hierarchical and rigid notions of scale and bounded regions, and the social and cultural construction of regions. In recent times there have been helpful efforts to reconcile these different perspectives (Morgan 2007; Jessop *et al.* 2008). Morgan's work is particularly helpful in this respect in trying to avoid unhelpful oppositional readings of territorial politics and relational perspectives. Relational, non-territorial approaches in this reading argue that in an era of globalisation society is comprised of transnational flows and networks which render traditional readings of place politics centred on spatially bound units and institutions unhelpful. With its emphasis on flow, porosity and connectivity (Allen *et al.* 1998; Amin 2004; Allen and Cochrane 2007), a relational approach brings into question not simply the usefulness of regions as an analytical unit, but also the nature of territorial politics. Morgan (2007) argues that those pursuing a relational approach are in danger of overstating their case, providing crude caricatures based on a binary reading of relational and territorial readings of place, which portray territorial politics as 'antediluvian, parochial, or even reactionary' (Morgan 2007: 1248). Backing up his argument he points to the potentially progressive, non-insular policy approaches that devolved administrations have undertaken, for instance, in engaging with global networks on development, notably in Africa. More than this, bounded spaces matter if for no other reason than that politicians are held to account through territorially defined elections, at various scales of government. Likewise devolution, for all its limitations, matters because it does bring about new spaces for debate and in the case of elected devolved governments, new forums for democratic deliberation and engagement.

For Morgan, accepting the value of relational thinking, with its emphasis on connectivity and porosity, does not logically mean that territorial politics are no longer relevant. In this context, he calls for a more nuanced reading of spaces as 'bounded *and* porous, territorial *and* relational' (Morgan 2007: 1247). A more culturally inflected reading of regions (e.g. Allen *et al.* 1998; Paasi 2001) helps in this respect, with its insistence that analysis should not focus simply on regions as pre-given, bounded entities, but instead as fluid and contested processes, in which various understandings of regional cultural identity are struggled over and played out. Thinking of regions in motion, where regional identities are socially and politically constructed rather than predetermined, helps make sense of many of the practices we look at in this book, where planning is implicated in the thinking through of new understandings of regional identity at the levels of both newly devolved territories and the spaces within them, not least in terms of what we will later refer to as 'soft spaces'.

For our purposes, debates over the rescaling of planning highlight the value of developing a more relational understanding of how policy development and implementation takes place. In other words the networks of policy communities aligned around a particular strategy or issue stretch across different scales and policy sectors. Consequently, in addition to an understanding of the shifting nature of planning, the changing nature of governance and state rescaling we also need to look at how other policy sectors have been affected by and, in turn, have affected planning. The expansion of governance reflects a response to greater societal complexity, which has resulted in governance systems becoming more functionally differentiated, an increased fuzziness of institutional boundaries, and the multiplication and rescaling of spatial horizons, and a need for reflexive knowledge and understanding to cope with this complexity (Jessop 2003). Following on from Jessop's argument we could argue that the boundaries of various sectors, including planning, are continuously struggled over as part of the rescaling process: for instance, the objectives and processes of planning are a focus of struggle to privilege, say, environmental over economic interests. In local economic development and urban regeneration too there is a continuing ideological struggle over just how to deal with community-based alternatives and social justice issues. In other words the politics of scale inevitably intersect with struggles over sectoral policy parameters, as the boundaries of activities such as economic development and planning become variously more interwoven, more porous, fuzzy and more malleable. The upshot is that planners must learn to work with professional, sectoral and geographical fuzziness, such that much of their work at a strategic level involves orchestrating how best to work with others across sectors and scales.

The rescaling of planning and other policy sectors outlined can be seen as part of what might be thought of as 'scalar complexity' or 'scalar flux' (Brenner 2000; Jones 2001) (see also Figure 2.3). Scalar complexity highlights the fact that empowering new or different scales of governance or policy intervention requires finding ways to negotiate governance complexity through improved efforts to coordinate, regulate or integrate multi-scalar processes, structures and institutions (Jones 2001). Taking this argument further, Brenner (2000) argues that institutional turbulence is the emergent 'norm', with governance powers, resources and legitimacy being reworked selectively and more or less continuously across scales and, we would argue, across policy sectors and policy actors (Allmendinger and Haughton 2007). It is possible to see a link here to Jessop's 'requisite variety' rule, so that governance complexity is an outcome not only of dealing with societal complexity, but also of dealing with governance complexity itself. In other words, as governance systems become more diverse and complex they need to self-regulate more effectively, with new systems of governance or metagovernance sought to bring coherence to the system overall. This is not achieved through one overarching metagovernance approach, but through introducing multiple ways for interlocking diverse governance systems. Planning in this sense is both a form of governance and metagovernance, as it provides a vehicle for achieving greater spatial coherence among different strategic, sectoral governance systems. In turn, through its intersection with other strategic work, planning itself becomes subject to their shaping influence.

Spatial strategies and 'soft spaces' in the reworking of the politics of scale and scope

Given this background we can begin to rethink the way in which spatial planning is being performed at various scales. So at one level we can see the way in which the ESDP functions as a form of metagovernance, seeking to build agreement around the new practices of spatial planning, codifying these within a particular set of 'identifiers' or principles for spatial planning and a new vocabulary, of connectivity, polycentricity and settlement patterns reinscribed as gateways, hubs and corridors. It is in this context that we can begin to make greater sense of Jessop's (2008) interpretation of the ESDP as a means of asserting a form of intellectual and scalar dominance, which is intended to be carried through by planners at different scales, notably the national and regional.

Recent devolution has seen the emergence of new territorial entities that are using the concepts and tools of spatial planning as part of interpreting and writing about their territorial identities. This needs to be seen in terms of an imperative to develop in parallel both a clearer 'national' message of spatial futures, and an opportunity to rethink and reinvent new internal territorial geographies, be these known as regions, areas or subregions. Ideas such as gateways can be used to rethink spatial priorities of the new nations or regions, with the consultative processes of planning used to both test and legitimise these new understandings. We see this quite clearly in the work of the spatial strategies produced in Wales in particular, and to a lesser extent in Northern Ireland, Ireland and Scotland. English regional planning remains stuck with the boundaries of 'standard regions', which seem to change only slowly and sporadically (for the emergence of an Eastern England region, see Haughton and Counsell 2004), but they can and do reimagine their internal geographies, with new subregions and most recently an emphasis on city region scale. We can see the rescaling of English planning then in terms of the recent creation of statutory regional spatial strategies, which since 2004 have been invited to intervene in providing subregional strategies. There has been considerable work on promoting city region thinking in economic development in particular, not least as the limits of rescaling at the 'regional' level became apparent with the failed referendum for political devolution in the North East region in 2004 (see Chapter 7). This has in turn permeated through to planning, where thinking for the city region level is undergoing something of a renaissance.

In the devolution literature there is often discussion of the prospects for, and likely impact of, 'double devolution' taking place, a process whereby devolution to, say, a new territorial government or regional scale might then see power and resources further cascaded down to local government level and then to neighbourhoods (Mulgan and Bury 2006; Morgan 2007). Although there is undoubtedly a stronger interest in promoting local government by both the UK and Irish national governments, and also in Northern Ireland, elsewhere there is little evidence of the double devolution dividend taking place. Instead, the experience of planning suggests that insofar as there is a double devolution taking place it is not simply reallocating roles and responsibilities to the formal apparatus of local government and local planning, but instead to new spaces of governance, an issue which we turn to next.

One of the main driving forces behind new state spaces concerns process as well as output. As we discussed earlier, one of the downsides of the spatial approach to planning is the time taken to coordinate and integrate plans and strategies and involve various stakeholders in the process. For national planning officials a key outcome of their reforms is that spatial planning should be more effective in achieving its outcomes, whether this is viewed as time taken to process planning applications, or turning strategic visions into actual development. This can be achieved by overall system reform, and also by changing the ways in which the system deals with specific development problems. One advantage of the flexibility and discretion in the UK and Irish planning systems that we outlined earlier is that the formal scales of plan making and rigid processes can be supplemented, complemented or subverted when they are accompanied by alternatives.

We term such alternatives 'soft spaces' (see Haughton and Allmendinger 2008; Allmendinger and Haughton 2009). Examples might include some of the recent work in planning for subregions that cross regional boundaries, plus the whole host of regeneration initiatives that are not coterminous with the boundaries of local government or standard regions, for instance, the UDCs, Enterprise Zones, and more recently the government's Sustainable Communities plan 'growth areas' such as the Thames Gateway and housing market renewal pathfinder areas (ODPM 2003c). The chapters that follow highlight that much of the real work of 'strategic planning' is taking place outside the formal and/or statutory mechanisms of planning. Formal planning mechanisms with their legal responsibilities are primarily rooted in statutory local and (to a lesser extent) regional plans. These are the 'hard spaces' of governmental activity, involving statutory responsibilities, linked to legal obligations including democratic engagement and consultation all of which take time, and come with a particular set of public and professional expectations around their choreography. Such statutory processes and outputs are formal arenas for interest mediation. They can be slow, rigid, bureaucratic, expensive and exclusive, by virtue of the costs, specialist language and legalistic format associated with participation. There is also a mismatch between the spatial scales at which such planning is undertaken and the more amorphous, fluid and functional requirements of development and sectoral integration.

The emergence of 'soft spaces' in addition to the 'hard spaces' of formal planning as a distinctive feature of the new spatial planning has previously led us to four conclusions (Haughton and Allmendinger 2008):

1 Soft spaces represent a deliberate attempt to insert new opportunities for creative thinking, particularly in areas where public engagement and cross-sectoral consultation has seen entrenched oppositional forces either slowing down or freezing out most forms of new development.
2 The 'hard' and 'soft' spaces of governance are mutually constitutive, such that one cannot work without the other. The aim is not to replace 'hard' institutional spaces with new 'softer' ones, rather to create complementary and potentially competing opportunities for development activities to focus around, whether at some kind of 'sub' regional or 'sub' local government scale.
3 The soft spaces of governance are becoming more numerous and more important as part of the institutional landscape of spatial planning and area regeneration.
4 Soft spaces often seem to be defined in ways that are deliberately fluid and fuzzy in the sense that they can be amended and shaped easily to reflect different interests and challenges.

As highlighted in Figure 2.3, new state spaces including fuzzy and soft spaces amount to a further round of rescaling. Such spaces are informal though condoned by government. How can such spaces be governed and how do they link to systems of metagovernance? Our view is that they are part of the glue that binds more formal scales of planning and governance together, with spatial planning providing a means for exploring the spatial dimension of how the building blocks of government and governance systems come together. Seen from this perspective spatial planning at local and regional levels is tasked with providing the spatial and sectoral 'glue' of coordination and governance. Whether it is up to the job is very much the focus of this book.

Conclusions: spatial planning as the continuous remaking of planning and the spaces of planning

This chapter points to new ways of conceptualising the current phase of planning history, in particular the importance of understanding the fuzziness of professional and sectoral boundaries, and the multiple scales of planning, which we see not as a reworking of the hierarchical scales of planning, but as a reinvention of the scales of planning and how they work together. Thinking about the interplay of the hard and soft spaces of planning helps us to make connections to the way that planning actually works rather than the way the statute books suggest the planning systems should work. The same way of rethinking what it is to 'practise' planning is helpful. The emergent practices of spatial planning challenge planners to be more 'relational' in their thinking, building a capacity to work more creatively and closely with those with complementary expertise and viewpoints (Healey 2007). This agenda is not wholly new but it does imply an increased emphasis on working with other policy sectors.

It is in this sense central to spatial planning that it places sustainable development and social inclusion issues as part of its core rationale. But this does not give planners the right or the role to go out and 'enforce' a particular interpretation of these issues on others that they work with as they seek to develop spatial strategies. Nor does it mean they should stand back and merely 'facilitate' in some form of deliberative or communicative role. Rather, spatial planning requires an awareness of the value that comes from more networked form of interaction with other professions and different parts of the general public, bringing in viewpoints that challenge not simply the dominant paradigms of planners themselves, but of those they work with. In this sense the role of spatial planners is not about introducing or creating or sifting or disseminating planning knowledge. It is about interpreting multiple understandings of complexity and seeking to use these to inform their spatial planning work and how they work with other parts of the governance system, accepting that if they do indeed work in a system with requisite variety and requisite irony, some good may come of their endeavours.

There are some important tensions that run through the spatial planning that we have already begun to highlight, and we summarise them here as they are themes that recur throughout this book. These tensions include the following:

- The search for improved integration as a way of reducing confusion and overlap, yet integration can also result in lowest common denominator compromises, or the distorted insertion or prioritisation of particular approaches masked as integration.
- The aspiration for certainty and predictability, which can run against the desire for flexibility and recognition of the reality of societal complexity and flux.
- The relative ease of gaining consensus around non-statutory plans may disguise difficulties in getting stakeholders to subsequently accept responsibility for implementing them.
- The search to embrace multiple perspectives and the desire for agreement around a unified strategy can lead to tokenistic 'mentions' of diversity but little in the way of tangible policy in order to present a public face of unity.
- There is a tension too for planners in managing their relationship with other strategy-makers, between using spatial strategies to achieve sectoral outcomes and working on sectoral strategies to introduce greater spatial awareness.
- If it is to be successful, spatial planning by its very nature has to be carried out not just by professional planners but as a corporate and collective activity. This creates tensions around ownership, and when is a spatial plan really a corporate plan not a document 'owned' by the planning system.
- Non-statutory processes in local authorities and elsewhere can generally deliver their parts of the spatial planning agenda more quickly and flexibly than the statutory development plan process, creating a risk of systemic imbalance as matters progress at uneven rates within the 'spatial planning' system.
- Finally, further devolution and a rebalancing of governance in favour of the local level is needed if spatial planning is to deliver local and regional distinctiveness. The retreat that this would require from central control remains unlikely given for as long as central government feels that housing market activity requires more rather than less central direction.

One final point to emerge from this chapter is the high level of hyperactivity in policy, legislative and institutional change since the mid-1990s or so. This multidimensionality provides us with difficulties in mapping, never mind understanding and analysing, contemporary planning. However, it is worth bearing in mind that planning as an activity including its scope and practice is not fixed. Paraphrasing Jessop, it is a terrain upon which different political forces attempt to impart a specific direction to the individual or collective activities of its different branches.

3

Irish spatial planning and the Cork experience

From grabbing growth to managing it

Ireland's rapid economic turnaround since the late 1980s has been widely regarded as an international success story, characterised by a startling transition from economic stagnation and net population decline to an unprecedented period of growth. This period of economic growth ended as Ireland entered recsssion in 2008. With an annual average rate of economic growth of 20 per cent between the years 1995 and 2000, the Irish economy grew at a rate which was three times greater than the European average (Lynas 2004; Matthews and Alden 2006). Frequently referred to as the Celtic Tiger, this rapid economic growth was fuelled by substantial foreign investment and high-quality jobs in the information technology and pharmaceutical sectors, bringing with it a reversal of populations trends, as some Irish migrants returned home, out-migration reduced and immigrants from elsewhere were attracted in (Matthews and Alden 2006). There is considerable debate on the key ingredients of this success, but favourable rates of corporation tax, historical connections to the United States, good educational levels, the English language, plus eligibility for substantial EU investment as an Objective 1 region during the 1990s all appear in most accounts.

Less frequently mentioned is that the planning regime was also a factor, with investors rarely finding it difficult to overcome any opposition to plans for new sites. Growing affluence also led to a major housing boom, reflected in escalating house prices and a rush to build new housing. After years of economic stagnation, the planning system struggled to cope with the scale of new development and to anticipate the cumulative impacts that this might create. In short, the system did not have the necessary experience and structures in place to cope with rapid growth, with canny developers quick to exploit any weaknesses in the system as they sought to find new land to develop (McDonald and Nix 2005). More than this, however, the mood of the public and consequently the political consensus favoured development over those calling for planning constraints. The result was too much scattered, poorly designed development with inadequate infrastructure in place. There has also been growing unease about the uneven nature of growth and spatial balance across the nation, particularly as Dublin boomed while many areas fared less well. More than this, Dublin in particular quickly came to be regarded by many as a victim of its own success, as congestion increased, while ribbon development and poorly designed new housing littered the surrounding countryside, widely known as 'bungalow blight'. Transport infrastructure in particular struggled to keep up with the pace of new development, while sprawl into rural areas led to growing concern about sewerage and pollution (McDonald and Nix 2005). The combination of housing sprawl, locally inappropriate development, congestion and groundwater pollution came to be associated in the media and political debate more generally with allegations of incompetent or (near) corrupt local planning practices, where developers seemed to have the upper hand over planners, while the probity of some local politicians came under suspicion (McDonald and Nix 2005).

The need for better growth management and coordinated infrastructure investment inevitably started to emerge as a major issue for the country's politicians by the late 1990s, with a growing consensus that the country needed to maintain the good aspects of its recent growth while doing more to improve standards of development if people were to enjoy an improved quality of life. The European Commission has played a supporting role in promoting change, not least by attaching a series of conditions to its provision of funds which forced the Irish government to take seriously issues such as environmental impact assessment. It is only fair to say here that the European Commission was simultaneously forcing the UK government to address some of its shortcomings through its Structure Fund procedures, not least in terms of greater engagement with local communities (Haughton *et al.* 1999).

It is worth briefly setting out a bit more the context of Ireland within the British Isles. Ireland emerged from British colonial rule during the early 1920s, with governmental powers defined in the constitution in 1937. The Irish Free State became the Republic of Ireland in 1949. Successive Irish governments struggled hard to modernise the economy, hindered by a legacy of poor economic and physical infrastructure plus continuing high levels of out-migration. Things started to change rapidly in the late 1980s, assisted by a deliberate government policy to reduce corporation taxes in a bid to attract foreign investment. The country currently has a population of 4.2 million and a GVA of £150.1 billion (see Table 1.1). To put this in perspective, Ireland's GVA is currently nearly twice that for Scotland and generated from a smaller population base. Both population and economic activity are concentrated in the Greater Dublin Area, which has a population of some 1.7 million (Central Statistical Office 2007) and nearly half of the national GVA (48 per cent) (Department of Environment, Heritage and Local Government (DoEHLG) 2002). Ireland's western and northern edges have long suffered economically from their peripheral rurality, while the border with Northern Ireland exhibits more than the usual border problems, given the unique problems associated with the history of religious division and conflict on the island (see Chapter 4).

More recently Ireland has begun to suffer the hangover after the party, as growth has slowed down and the housing market bubble punctured (Matthews and Alden 2006).

This chapter looks at the Irish experience of reforming its governance and planning structures, initially to attract investment and economic growth and more recently to manage the impacts of growth more strategically in ways that deliver better spatial, social and environmental outcomes than during the early years of the boom. We look at the case of Cork as an example of an area that has been innovative in its pursuit of a spatial planning approach, notably the 2001 Cork Area Strategic Plan, known as CASP.

Remaking governance and the creation of an Irish regional system

Since the mid-1990s the Irish government has engaged in a steady programme of modernisation of its systems of governance, including reforms to the planning system. The Irish government also has a strong commitment to promoting 'all-island' approaches to policy, including energy, tourism, transport and more recently spatial planning, a theme which we return to in Chapter 4. A 'Delivering Better Government' initiative was begun in 1994, some five years earlier than the equivalent reforms appeared in Whitehall, led by the Department of the Taoiseach (Prime Minister) and the Department of Finance. The need for better integrated government was emphasised as part of this process, with the rationale set out clearly in the second report to a coordinating committee of ministers:

> There are many vital national issues which can no longer be resolved from within the functional remit and skill base of a single Department or Agency. Indeed, many of the most pressing issues which must be addressed require the expertise and commitment of a variety of Departments and Agencies in order to achieve successful outcome . . . These new approaches challenge traditional Departmental and functional boundaries.
>
> (Department of the Taoiseach 1996: 17)

One of the responses to these challenges was to establish a number of Cabinet subcommittees, chaired by ministers, to coordinate key aspects of government policy, including one on Housing, Infrastructure and Public– Private Partnerships which coordinates and monitors work on the National Spatial Strategy (NSS) (Murray 2004).

The Irish Sustainable Development Strategy (1997) provided a further important marking point on the journey towards improving policy integration, reflecting the growing international consensus around an integrative definition of sustainable development where social, economic and environmental issues are expected to have equal prominence (Haughton *et al.* 2008). As an example of how this works as an integrative device, City and County Development Boards (see below) are expected to policy proof their strategies against the sustainable development strategy, along with the anti-poverty strategy and equality and gender issues (Ellis *et al.* 2004)

Perhaps the most important corporate policy driver in the Irish government is the National Development Plan (NDP), which establishes spending priorities, currently over a six-year period. The NDP process provides the framework for allocating both Irish Government and European Structural Funds, and indeed it came into being as a result of the 1988 reforms which saw the whole of Ireland designated as an Objective 1 region. In terms of its regional consultation processes the first NDP (1989–1993) was largely a cosmetic exercise to draw down European funds, but further reform was prompted by the European Commission's insistence on a stronger regional engagement in the next round of Structural Fund programming (NDP 1994–1999). The Irish government responded pragmatically by designating eight regions at NUTS III scale in 1994, largely charged with public services coordination (Mullally 2004).[1] With improved economic circumstances meaning that the country as a whole no longer met the Objective 1 threshold, the Irish government decided subsequently to designate two larger regions at NUTS II scale in 1999, allowing Objective 1 funding to be retained in one region while the other attracted 'transitional' status (Mullally 2004; Matthews and Alden 2006).[2] The NUTS II regions have Assemblies of nominated elected members from local authorities, while NUTS III regions have Regional Authorities, again with nominated elected members from local authorities. Both are charged with overseeing the regional implementation of the NDP and EU structural fund programmes.

These represent major changes for the Irish governance system. Historically government in Ireland has been highly centralised without any tradition of a regional scale, in part reflecting the country's relatively small population size, leading to a continuing debate about whether there is any need for an Irish 'regional' approach (Mullally 2004). There had been a brief dalliance with regional planning in Ireland during the 1960s, notably with the publication of the Buchanan Report in 1968, which in the spirit of planning thinking at the time proposed a set of regional growth centres. This approach was to all intents and purposes ignored, as political pressures dictated that such growth as there was be diffused more widely to include smaller towns and rural areas (Murray 2004; Scott 2006).

It took the lure of European funding to bring about what appears to be a more enduring set of regional structures. In this context it is worth emphasising here that Ireland's Objective 1 status has resulted in substantial European funds entering the country, bolstering the national GDP by several percentage points at its peak, and also subsidising massive infrastructure expansion. For the Irish government, with its weak, indeed near non-existent, regional governance systems, accessing this funding required the rapid invention of regional scale structures. These were largely bureaucratic creations, not reflecting any sense of historical regional cultural identities, more a pragmatic desire to attract European structural funds, with the new regional structures subsequently being back-filled with policy mandates (Mullally 2004). This was an issue picked up on in some of our interviews with planners:

So there isn't a strong regional identity . . . people don't have the
sense of being in such and such a region. . . . It's purely pragmatic
. . . and opportunistic . . . A region can be anything it wants to be in
this country.

(Interview IR17, academic (former local planner) 2006)

In essence the new regional structures have provided a platform upon which
a gradual programme of regional devolution has been built, with the new
regional authorities increasingly important within the governance system of
Ireland not least in providing a regional voice to negotiations around government investment (Boyle 2000). Though a top-down administrative tool of
convenience initially, seen as an evolving system of regional governance their
importance should not be underestimated.

The National Development Plan for 2000–2006, published in 1999, took a
major step in linking government investment to a clearer agenda for spatial
development across the country, with proposals included for five regional 'gateways', including Cork, plus a clear commitment that the government would go
on to prepare a National Spatial Strategy (NSS), subsequently published in
2002. The most recent National Development Plan (2007–2013) takes this link
forward, including, for instance, a detailed commentary on the NSS and
regional development issues in individual gateway areas. Significantly, it also
established that the Irish government was prepared to invest directly in
improving cross-border infrastructure development with Northern Ireland in
ways that had hitherto not been politically feasible. Perhaps most importantly it
introduced a formal requirement that all government departments must justify
their spending against the objectives of the National Spatial Strategy. The NDP
process then is much stronger and politically more mature than its counterpart
in England, the Regional Funding Allocation (see Chapter 7), with stronger
political support and a clearer cross-governmental commitment to thinking
about the spatial impacts of spending.

Irish local government is long established and has a strong role in the
governmental hierarchy, although its functions are limited in some areas, for
instance, with little involvement in education, healthcare and policing. There is
a two-tier system of county and district councils, with single-tier city councils
in the main metropolitan areas. Substantial reforms of local government have
included the Better Local Government initiative, which was notable for ensuring that sustainable development concerns became mainstreamed into local
authority practice (Ellis *et al.* 2004). The Local Government Act 2001 paved
the way for improved planning practices in a series of measures designed to
modernise local government, improving its democratic credentials, with new
structures introduced to strengthen the role of elected members and improve
community participation in local government. Strategic Policy Committees
(SPCs) and County and City Development Boards (CDBs) were introduced
in 2000, and given a statutory basis in the Local Government Act 2001. Both
are intended to improve local democratic processes and policy integration,
with CDBs particularly important in bringing together various community

bodies with local government and other governmental agencies to provide an overview of strategic matters, including strategic planning documents (Kelly *et al.* 2004).

The Irish planning system in brief

Until recently the Irish planning system was strongly local in character, but this has changed markedly in the past decade as Ireland has developed a hierarchical system of spatial planning consisting of the National Spatial Strategy (Department of Environment, Heritage and Local Government 2002), regional planning guidelines (RPGs), city and county development plans and local area plans. This system came about through a recognition of some of the failings of the previous system, one of which was that local planning authorities found it very easy to ignore the wider context in which they worked, something which was less of an issue in a period of slow growth but became a major concern once development accelerated:

> Our problem with planning in Ireland was that planning was very localised . . . the local authority had all the planning powers. . . . Our problem was we had the development plan at local level . . . we had things like the national investment plan at national level, but we had no link between the two.
>
> (Interview IR4, civil servant, 2005)

The introduction of the NSS and RPG system represented a deliberate attempt to provide this link. We deal with the NSS in greater detail in the next section, focusing on the regional and local levels of planning here. In 2002 the National Spatial Strategy introduced a requirement that the NUTS III regions each produce a regional planning guidelines document. The intention was that this new tier of planning would roll out the NSS approach to regional level, and in turn cascade it down to development plan level (Matthews and Alden 2006). By 2004 RPGs had been produced for all the Irish regions.

Development plans are the responsibility of county and city councils with local councils involved in preparing local area plans. A new system of development planning was introduced in 2000 with a six-yearly cycle, which means that all Irish development plans have now been able to take on board policies set out in the National Spatial Strategy of 2002. Local Area Plans provide a more detailed framework, with scope to produce Special Local Area Plans (SLAPs) where appropriate, for instance, where large-scale development is anticipated. Introduced under the Planning Act 2000, subsequently the Planning and Development (Amendment) Act 2002 required that these be consistent with the objectives of the development plan.

The result is that on paper the Irish planning system has a model hierarchy of plans, but one which has yet to fully live up to its potential in practice (Scott *et al.* 2006). One of the tensions is that there is a strongly embedded culture of wariness about central government overriding local government, so to date there has been very little tradition of central government planners sending local plans back for fundamental reconsideration. Partly reflecting such concerns, there is some weak phrasing in the words setting out how the different tiers of planning should take account of each other:

> There is a strong ethic of competition between counties. That [com-petition] has frustrated efforts to get a higher level of vision . . . the difficulty here is that the legislation around regional authorities is weak . . . and compliance is in the form of voluntary compliance. It's very weak language.
>
> (Interview IR1, academic, 2005)

Officials responsible for planning nationally readily admit the system is still bedding in and expect to continue to refine it, including clarifying statutory responsibilities:

> I think there is a growing realisation that . . . how in effect the hier-archical cascade between NSS, RPG and development plans is delivered needs to be strengthened in legislation . . . so that the mem-bers . . . in arriving at a decision on a development plan clearly know that they are working within a legislative framework.
>
> (Interview NI14, civil servant, 2006)

As noted earlier, local authorities are required to cooperate with a range of other service providers through County and City Development Boards, preparing integrated strategies for local service provision in a similar way to sustainable community strategies in England (see Chapter 7). Following a government review in 2005, all CDBs were asked to prepare a review of their activities, including proposals for better integration of public services at local level and setting out a limited number of key priorities (Cork County Development Board 2005). This seems to have been a welcome opportunity to refocus the work of the Development Boards, addressing some of the concerns of those who felt that the integrated strategies did not appear particularly closely integrated with spatial plans, as one Cork planner told us:

> They don't have a direct role . . . it's difficult to define what their powers are . . . There is a requirement that when we are preparing our development plan it must be in line with the strategy . . . They haven't really been fully incorporated into the system.
>
> (Interview IR12, planner, 2006)

In the context of recent urban growth in particular, the metropolitan planning system has been the site of some innovation, reflecting that the current hierarchy of statutory plans struggles in terms of linking cities to their new functional hinterlands. In Cork, for instance, the city council is a relatively tightly prescribed area, so much of the city's suburban area is the responsibility of the separate county council. To overcome this potential barrier to coherent spatial planning at the city regional level, Cork has been at the forefront of metropolitan scale planning, with the Land Use and Transportation Studies (LUTS) of 1978 and 1991, and the Cork Area Strategic Plan of 2001. Others have attempted to follow this path, but none have been as successful, largely because they have failed to build an effective political consensus and administrative apparatus.

Metropolitan planning such as CASP is one of several forms of soft space governance to be found in Ireland, with perhaps the most well known being the designated urban regeneration areas, such as the dockland areas in Dublin and Cork. These initiatives have a substantial pedigree. The Urban Renewal Act 1986 defined 'Designated Areas' in Dublin, Cork, Limerick, Waterford and Galway, intended to encourage private sector investment in both commercial and residential buildings (Drudy and Punch 2000: 231). In 1997 these were superseded in the case of Dublin with the creation of the Dublin Docklands Development Authority, which by the end of that year had produced a 15-year masterplan, a pioneer of a new integrated approach to urban regeneration, Integrated Area Plans (IAPs), which were introduced in 1998 and applied nationwide (Bartley and Kitchen 2007).

The emergence of the National Spatial Strategy as a force in national policy

Prepared over just two years and published in 2002, the NSS is the responsibility of the Department of the Environment, Heritage and Local Government, which has a relatively small NSS team within it. Various forces appear to have combined to prompt the development of a National Spatial Strategy for Ireland, including the political agenda for improved policy integration, the development of European Union regional policy and pressure from within the country to address the growing problems of congestion in Greater Dublin which required action at a greater than local scale (Walsh and Murray 2006). The result was pressure on the government from various sources, including the Sustainable Development Strategy and various academic and independent reports (Matthews and Alden 2006; Walsh and Murray 2006). As we have already seen, the NDP 2000–2006 provided an unequivocal commitment to produce the NSS, a logical consequence of the attention to balanced regional development across the country in successive NDPs.

The European Commission influence is a common refrain in most accounts of the emergence of the National Spatial Strategy, both in terms of the financial imperative of attracting Structural Funds and the way in which the NSS was strongly influenced conceptually and linguistically by the European Spatial Development Perspective. For instance, the NSS overtly adopts ESDP concepts and terminology such as 'balanced development', 'urban–rural balance', and working towards 'polycentric development' through the designation of a series of 'regional gateways' and 'hubs' (Murray 2004; Scott 2006). The set of circumstances that led to this approach were helpfully summarised for us by an academic close to the policy-making process:

> In terms of being able to win structural funds last time . . . it was impor-
> tant to come in with something novel . . . and so the ideas of gateways
> and new ways of linking urban and rural areas . . . ESDP ideas . . .
> they're in our National Development Plan . . . Our Department of
> Finance was in the business of maximising Structural Fund receipts
> and we realised early on that an aspatial approach was not going
> to work. We picked that up from feedback from people in the
> Commission who looked at the drafts of the NDP . . . and were very
> excited about these references to gateways and a regional policy that
> was grounded on achieving potential and moving away from redis-
> tribution. So there's political gamesmanship going on.
>
> (Interview IR1, academic, 2005)

The NSS designated eight national 'gateways' in addition to Dublin, which is seen as an international gateway. Four of these had already been identified in the NDP for 2000–2006, all of them already major urban centres with strong growth potential (Cork, Limerick/Shannon, Galway and Waterford). The four new centres were seen to be capable of achieving high growth provided substantial infrastructure investment occurred (Dundalk, Sligo, Letterkenny/ Derry and Athlone/Tullamore/Mulingar). It was envisaged that collectively the gateways would constitute a national network of strong centres that could act as a counterbalance to Dublin, without undermining the capital. In addition, eight national developmental 'hubs' were designated around the country to help bring growth to surrounding rural areas. These concepts were subsequently used to shape both regional planning guidelines (Figure 3.1) and local plans.

The hubs and gateways approach represents a limited attempt to break away from previous patterns of local patronage which worked against concentrating government resources in the main towns. In practice the sheer numbers of gateways and hubs was seen by some as watering down the official rhetoric of concentrating growth in areas of potential (McDonald and Nix 2005), while others complained that the approach neglected small towns and rural areas in the push for growth. These tensions probably help explain why just two years after the publication of the NSS the national government announced a major decentralisation of national civil service functions, involving dispersal mainly to smaller rural settlements rather than to the gateways and hubs designated under the NSS. Unsurprisingly this led to considerable media and political speculation that the NSS was not really the powerful unifying document it had previously been held up to be (McDonald and Nix 2005; Scott 2006). For the critics, the NSS approach was still essentially one of political appeasement of the various local lobby groups around the country, all keen to be seen as central rather than peripheral to the national growth project (McDonald and Nix 2005).

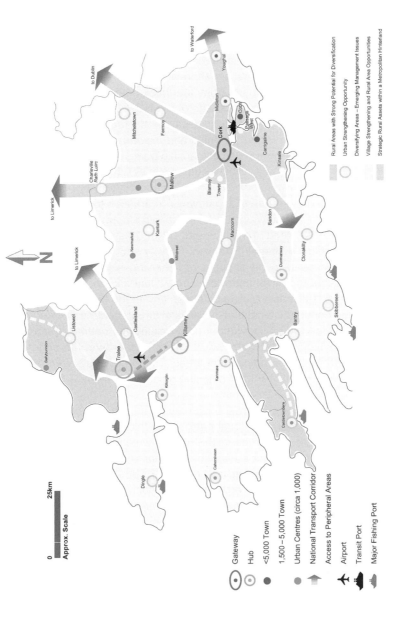

Approx. Scale

0   25km

○ Gateway

◎ Hub

● <5,000 Town

● 1,500 – 5,000 Town

○ Urban Centres (circa 1,000)

National Transport Corridor

Access to Peripheral Areas

✈ Airport

Transit Port

Major Fishing Port

Rural Areas with Strong Potential for Diversification

Urban Strengthening Opportunity

Diversifying Areas – Emerging Management Issues

Village Strengthening and Rural Area Opportunities

Strategic Rural Assets within a Metropolitan Hinterland

3.1 National Spatial Strategy: key diagram for the South West Region

Source: Department of Environment, Heritage and Local Government (2002).

The policy of balanced regional development was also heavily criticised in a study commissioned by the think-tank Urban Forum (Dublin Institute of Technology 2008), which promoted an alternative growth strategy based on concentrating development on an East coast in a corridor from Belfast to Waterford. This alternative approach would, it argued, make more economic sense and sustain the levels of growth needed to transfer funds to the less advantaged areas in the west. This is not dissimilar to the controversial argument put forward in England by the think-tank Policy Exchange in favour of concentrating growth in the South East at the expense of northern cities (Morris 2008). Not surprisingly the Urban Forum study attracted widespread media attention followed by statements of support for the NSS from the Irish Planning Institute and central government politicians (Siggins 2008).

One of the other key features of the NSS was a strategic desire to consolidate growth within existing urban areas and discourage rural sprawl. As the popular and political consensus was that growth itself was desirable and should be encouraged, the preferred solution was to attempt to keep as much physical expansion as possible within the designated growth areas through a major programme of infrastructure investment, especially transport. In particular the NSS acknowledges the problems caused by the gravitation of investment and population towards the greater Dublin area, pointing out that 'There are increasing contrasts between areas encountering congestion due to the concentration of economic activity, and areas experiencing under-utilisation, because of a lack of competitive and balancing locations for economic activity' (DoEHLG 2002: 14). The result was a massive expansion in transport investment in the capital, though this did not lead to a commensurate increase in the proportion of new development within the city area, leading to some concerns among national planners about the need to strengthen implementation processes.

Spatial planning, policy integration, consultation and sustainable development

One of the themes in both the NDP and the NSS is the need for improved sectoral policy integration, both vertically across the tiers of government and horizontally across policy sectors. While the hierarchy of plans begins to address the vertical integration theme within planning itself, it invariably hits against the fact that as a small country the tradition in many other government departments has been one of strong centralised control over spending, as those involved readily acknowledged:

> One of the difficulties in Ireland is that sectoral policy is very centralised . . . We have no local education boards for example . . . education is effectively run by the government department here. Health is the same . . . Transport tends to be quite centralised as well . . . and enterprise agencies generally operate on a national basis.

> So there is a difficulty there between the local development plans and
> the sectoral policies and their implementation.
>
> (Interview IR4, civil servant, 2005)

However, this compartmentalised approach has begun to break down over
recent years, with more progress towards cross-sectoral working and devolution of decision-making in some departments than in others. One of the key
drivers of this process has been the NSS and beyond this the decision to
introduce regional planning guidelines, with some departments choosing
to engage actively with these processes. Foremost among these is the
Department of Transport, which includes as the first of its five high-level goals:

> To ensure an integrated approach to the development and delivery of
> transport policy by providing a coherent policy framework . . . and by
> the integration of transport with other government policies, particularly
> sustainable development and spatial/land use policies.
>
> (Department of Transport 2005: 7)

Interdepartmental support for the NSS and spatial planning in general appears
fairly high if somewhat uneven, undoubtedly facilitated by the development of
a reporting structure direct to Cabinet. This involves a Cabinet subcommittee
of relevant ministers that receives regular reports on progress against the NSS
objectives. This committee reports to Cabinet and is supported by a parallel
steering committee of officials. The interdepartmental steering committee
draws its membership from a wide range of departments – Agriculture and
Rural Development; Enterprise, Trade and Employment; Tourism, Sport and
Recreation, Health and Children; Taoiseach; Finance; Marine and Natural
Resources; Arts and Heritage; Education and Science; Public Enterprise; and
Social, Community and Families. Underpinning this bureaucratic apparatus is
the introduction of a formal requirement under the NDP that government
departments are allocated a multiannual investment envelope, but in return
they must each provide an annual report on their progress that takes explicit
account of how their spending has supported NSS priorities.

   The result of this multi-stranded approach is a growing awareness of the
role of spatial planning on wider policy agendas:

> In fairness it is dawning . . . in wider government departments that
> there is an extremely strong link which should be there between what
> they are trying to advance in terms of the design and discharge of the
> capital envelope and what's happening at local level . . . So I think
> more widely through the government system there is anxiousness to
> watch this spatial planning area and if necessary to come in.
>
> (Interview NI14, civil servant, 2006)

Inevitably some departments have bought into this process more than others
– our interviews revealed a general concern that education and health had

been slow in changing their thinking, but that others such as Transport and Enterprise had been quick to get involved with the NSS and its related systems:

> To say there's an NSS now and a lot of departments are thinking spatially . . . I don't think that's happened . . . but I certainly do think that people consider the world in a different way.
>
> (Interview IR3, civil servant, 2005)

The production of the NSS was considered by those involved to have met some of spatial planning's emphasis on improved public engagement, with considerable efforts made to take the draft of the NSS around the country to regional workshops, with ministers attending many of them. For those involved there was a belief that this had led to a sophisticated debate around key issues at all levels, from the very local up to cabinet. As a result of this engagement process, when the NSS was published,

> There was some controversy . . . about individual towns that were left out of it, but by-and-large there was a fair bit of acceptance that the ground had been well-prepared. There were no great surprises in this and that was deliberate.
>
> (Interview IR4, civil servant, 2005)

Against this and similar positive assessments by insiders, Murray (2004: 240) describes the NSS as 'skeletal in design' and 'oriented to securing a government-led political vision of the future' compared to the community consensus approach to spatial planning in Northern Ireland. At the local level, there was a concern too that while advances had been made to improve consultation processes in recent years, they lacked genuine community engagement from the beginning of the process, tending to focus heavily on paper 'consultation' around already well-advanced plans. As one civil servant put it:

> In terms of the pyramid of participation . . . we are very much at the bottom in terms of what we are doing . . . whereas the top of that pyramid would have them working in there with us.
>
> (Interview NI14, civil servant, 2006)

However, there is growing evidence of community activism, rooted in part in reaction to poor local planning decisions, which is stimulating changed political attitudes at the local level, which in turn was sending signals to politicians and officials at national level:

> I think increasingly there is a sophistication building in . . . I think people are wise-ing up to how this process goes on . . . I suppose the pace of change and the extent of change is driving that, you know . . . Some communities are becoming quite vocal.
>
> (Interview NI14, civil servant, 2006)

One of the other main themes of spatial planning is sustainable development, which on paper is certainly something that runs through the hierarchy of plans in Ireland. Our interviewees tended to agree that in practice the economic pillar had been very much to the fore so far. This perhaps made sense in the early years of the boom, but increasingly officials are turning their attention to how to develop a stronger public awareness of sustainability issues and their relation to planning. At all levels of the planning system, officials are now seeking to move on to add sophistication to how they approach sustainable development, not least thinking through more carefully the implications of the massive road-building plans on future development and the dangers of promoting car dependency. For instance, in CASP there is a clear statement that previous planning had been based on accommodating motor transport to homes and businesses, promoting car dependency (Atkins 2001: 9). Nationally too, planners were looking to develop their thinking and practice in this area:

> We haven't really got to debating those kinds of issues . . . There's been a headlong rush just to deal what we're dealing with . . . there are houses that need to be built today . . . because people don't have homes . . . There's gridlock that needs to be addressed because that's a huge political issue. You have the three pillars of sustainable development and the economic is very much in the ascendancy here at the moment.
>
> (Interview IR2, civil servant, 2005)

In summary, the Irish experience of spatial planning is largely positive, if mixed. It has made reasonable progress in improving its systems for public and wider stakeholder engagement, and it has certainly produced strategies and institutional frameworks that seem to support balanced development. Least progress is perhaps evident in terms of adopting an integrated approach to sustainable development, with economic growth still very much a priority. The most remarkable progress though has been in policy integration. Irish practice illustrates a transparent two-way relationship between national investment planning and spatial planning, with the National Spatial Strategy providing the spatial policy framework for the National Development Plan. Even with these linkages though, there was concern among some of the people we interviewed that government decisions did not always take the National Spatial Strategy into account. Nevertheless the degree of coordination between the National Development Plan and National Spatial Strategy in Ireland is something which UK administrations should perhaps aspire to match.

CASP, Cork and 'go east'

Early on in our work we encountered central government officials praising the 2001 Cork Area Strategic Plan (CASP) as a successful approach to spatial planning, very much influencing our decision to use it as part of our Irish governance line. The hierarchy of plans for this governance line is the Irish

National Spatial Strategy (NSS) (Department of Environment, Heritage and Local Government 2002); regional planning guidelines for the South West (South West Regional Authority 2004); the Cork Area Strategic Plan (Atkins 2001); revised county and city development plans; and a network of local area plans, including a SLAP for Midleton, adopted jointly by the county and town councils. We use Midleton to illustrate the local end of our Irish governance line.

Cork is Ireland's second largest city, with a metropolitan population of 345,000 in 2000, served by two local planning authorities, Cork City Council, which is responsible for the inner area, and Cork County Council, which covers the outer area. Future growth is expected to be strong, with CASP initially envisaging a 28 per cent growth in population by 2020 (to 440,000), and a 35 per cent increase in jobs by 2020 (from 155,000 to 210,000). In the 2008 draft update for CASP, the population projections were increased by a further 65,000 and employment by 15,000 jobs. The metropolitan region has no formal statutory status, but the two authorities have had a strong history of cooperation over spatial planning between the city and county of Cork going back to 1978, when the first Land Use and Transportation Strategy (LUTS1) for greater Cork was prepared jointly by the two local authorities. This was updated in 1991 (LUTS2). Locally these were both well regarded at the time, credited particularly with a succession of improvements to the road infrastructure. However, the public transport aspects of the plans were relatively neglected such that by the time the CASP document was being prepared poor public transport infrastructure was widely acknowledged to be contributing to major congestion problems in parts of the city, notably the city centre. In addition, there had been a major growth in housebuilding in the more prosperous western and southern parts of the city region, leading to local concern about the negative consequences of this as infrastructure investment had not followed at the same pace. Finally, growth within the city was uneven, with some areas still lagging. In particular local planners were concerned that the Northside area of the city had been left behind, remaining beset by social problems, while parts of the city centre, more particularly the docklands, were seen as underdeveloped.

Unsurprisingly in this context, growth management was a central theme in the Cork Area Strategic Plan published in 2001 (Atkins 2001). CASP's main features include a clear spatial strategy, attempting to shift the focus of growth from the south and west to a new growth corridor linking the north and east, an emphasis on integrated land use and transport planning, within an overall approach that called for infrastructure-led development. For those at the centre of the process, though, it was the economic growth agenda that most clearly shaped the plan:

> So whereas the LUTS study was primarily a traffic study . . . CASP was more economically driven. What we're about is providing employment . . . that's the key driver of any region's success.
>
> (Interview IR19, planning consultant, 2006)

The plan itself was produced for a joint committee of the two councils and published a year in advance of the National Spatial Strategy. The process of developing the plan and consulting on it was led by a team of consultants, which is a common practice in Ireland and seen by many within the formal processes of planning as a useful way of ensuring parochial politics does not compromise strategic thinking. However, for some stakeholder groups this was seen as problematic, with claims that consultants had no subsequent responsibility for their work.

Despite such misgivings, very quickly CASP came to be recognised as an innovative document and its approach was embraced and confirmed by the National Spatial Strategy. Part of the reason for this was that as part of the plan preparation process government officials had been involved and some quickly bought into its key features, most notably a major investment to create new railway infrastructure running from the north and the east to the city centre. When it came to preparing regional planning guidelines in 2004, again much of the work had already been done by CASP, so the RPG for the South West also endorsed the CASP approach, as have subsequent development plans for the City and County. So though a non-statutory plan in itself, CASP has in effect become part of the statutory system through its absorption into other plans.

Perhaps the most notable feature of CASP was its clear intention of integrating spatial planning and infrastructure provision. This chimed well with a central government aspiration to invest heavily in infrastructure expansion, particularly where it fitted the NSS agenda for integrated policy-making and for balanced regional development through gateways and hubs. Central to the CASP approach was that 'infrastructure (including roads, public transport, water and sewerage) and community facilities are provided ahead or in tandem with housing and other uses in all new development areas' and the provision of 'an integrated transport system based upon "state of the art" public transport facilities and a well managed roads system' (Atkins 2001: 27).

This approach became important in justifying a radical attempt to alter the pattern of new development, involving an attempt to constrain further development in the overheating suburbs and villages to the south and west of the city through much tighter controls over new development. Most people readily acknowledge that the legacy of under-investment in public transport since the LUTS plan had meant that new developments were in essence car dependent. The proposed constraint policy seems to have been slow to take hold, however, with the proposed revisions to CASP published in 2008 noting that the overall population projections in CASP proved accurate for the period to 2006, but population in the city declined more than expected, while growth in rural areas and around the ring towns was faster than expected. In other words, the pattern of growth had not been radically altered at all during the first five years of CASP.

Running parallel to the call for constraint in the west, CASP outlined a vision for a new growth corridor linking the north of the city (Blarney/Mallow) to the east (Midleton). Central to this was reworking part of the existing intercity rail route to allow commuter rail, and reinstating an abandoned railway line to the east, initially to Midleton, but potentially in the future further to Youghal (Figure 3.2).

Rather than repeat some of the mistakes made in the previous ten years, CASP argued that reopening the railway line would allow higher density, high-quality development to be supported, with other infrastructure provided in an orderly manner, including water and sewerage connections. Crucial for the proposal's success would be whether the planning system could deliver higher density development around the planned railway stations. This was important as without a reasonable catchment of commuters the commercial viability of the new line would have been in doubt and national government would have been unwilling to invest in opening up the disused railway line.

In many ways CASP provided a useful way for national officials to prove their serious intent to develop the gateways, allowing them to demonstrate that substantial investment would only be released in support of good-quality, integrated plans. After a feasibility study had reported positively on the commercial viability of reinstating the railway lines, the Department of Transport quickly agreed the funding for the work to go ahead. The feasibility study suggested that regular commuter services to Midleton and Mallow/Blarney were both potentially viable provided the amount of development proposed in CASP took place and that parking restrictions were introduced into Cork city centre. In addition to new stations in expanding settlements, a new station on the Midleton line is to be provided linked to a park and ride facility (Figures 3.3 and 3.4). These improvements will be part funded by a special levy on developers; the Planning Act 2000 makes provision for such special contributions in addition to standard developer contributions, which will apply to residential, retail and office developments within one kilometre of the new rail stations (see www.corkcity.ie/ourservices/developmentplanning/development contributionscheme/supplementarydevelopmentcontributionsscheme/).

This approach is now frequently cited as an exemplar for integrated land use and transportation planning in Ireland. Indeed, one central government official told us how this model was being used to try to influence planners in other parts of the country, using the potential for transport investment as a lure:

> So that would be the way we are trying to have the Cork model rolled out. We've supported the buses . . . we've supported the rail link because of the development patterns that were proposed around it . . . and hoping that the others will follow suit.
> (Interview IR3, civil servant, 2005)

The local end of our governance line was Midleton, which along with the neighbouring area of Carrigtwohill, is now targeted for substantial new development, plus the new railway connection. The railway line is already complete and is expected to open in 2009. CASP had also embraced the idea of priority Green bus routes, with upgraded infrastructure for high-speed commuter

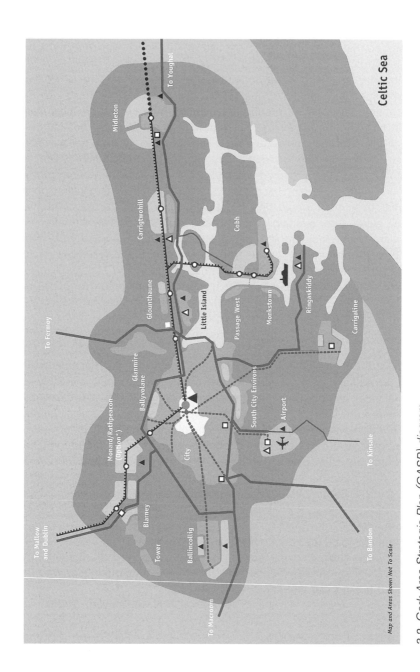

3.2 *Cork Area Strategic Plan (CASP) diagram*

Source: Atkins (2001).

buses, supported by national government funding, with Midleton being one of the beneficiaries.

Midleton is a small town in its own right, with a population of 10,315 in 2006. The original CASP document proposed increasing this to 21,010 by 2020, a target revised upwards to 23,429 in proposed revisions of CASP published in 2008, necessitated by increased government population projections. The growth is higher than this suggests, with the 'Carrigtwohill and Midleton hinterland' area also expected to grow from 9,685 in 2006 to 20,303 under the revised CASP targets. The intention then is to more than double the population in around 12 years. New development around the new railway

3.3 Derelict railway station site at Midleton, 2006: the Cork–Midleton line was reinstated in 2009

3.4 New-build, low-density sprawl close to the new Midleton rail station: this development makes nonsense of the promise to ensure high-density development in this area to support the railway line's reopening

station is already strongly present, but much of it is low density and appears to have got planning permission before the CASP recommendations on higher density around the railway corridor were worked through into formal plans, rather undermining the intentions for the area set out in CASP. A Special Local Area Plan for Midleton was adopted in 2005. The town's employment base is expected to remain largely service and tourism based, with the implication that much of the new population is expected to commute into Cork city centre. A northern relief road is planned for the town, along with improvements to local water and sewerage services.

Between plan and reality

> That document [CASP] has actually hoodwinked us . . . it's a way of keeping us quiet . . . It works beautifully . . . But when we go and say why aren't you doing this, they say it's just a guideline . . . it doesn't mean sod-all . . . just a waste of paper.
>
> (Interview IR26, environmental group, 2006)

There was widespread agreement that the hierarchy of plans for the city and county of Cork were all good as written documents. The local planning authorities in the Cork City region have worked closely to produce spatial plans which make much of an integrative approach, tying together policies across key policy sectors and across scales. This has undoubtedly been facilitated by the fact that there are just two principal authorities, and that the new regional authority very much took CASP to heart in producing its own regional planning guidelines. As we noted earlier, it is significant that national government officials had also actively engaged with the production of CASP. The result is that Cork provides a good model of how to technically plan for spatial development in a city region (Haughton and Counsell 2007). However, our interviews with stakeholders and policy-makers highlight mixed opinions on whether it works out as well in practice as it does on paper.

The regional planning guidelines were seen as largely uncontroversial in themselves, but there was a consensus that they were not really being used to broker difficult decisions on projects that had region-wide significance. Part of the reason for this is that they are guidelines rather than statutory plans. In so far as their authority comes from being part of the regional assembly there is an issue that these comprise nominated local councillors rather than directly elected representatives. Moreover, the particular history of the creation of regional authorities such as the one for South West Ireland meant that they were not rooted in a strong cultural sense of identity. In effect therefore regions and their regional assemblies were seen as creatures of central government, designed to push through NDP and NSS priorities; indeed, one of our academic interviewees went so far as to argue that 'Like most decentralisations in this country, it's highly centralised!' (Interview IR15, academic, 2006). Regional authorities then appear to be perceived by many as part of an essentially hierarchical system of government rather than a more networked system of governance. For some at least the result was a system still essentially based on mistrust:

> I'm fairly sure that government see regional authorities as subservient to them . . . Counties don't like regional authorities to any great extent . . . towns don't like counties to any great extent.
> (Interview IR14, local government officer, 2006)

As we noted earlier, the constraint policies for the south and west of the region proposed under CASP have yet to show much sign of working, which may partly reflect previously granted planning permissions. But for many of those we talked to the problem was simply that the relevant local authorities were not heeding the higher level plans, succumbing still to pressure from developers:

> They're now . . . with the blessing of the local authority . . . putting quite a lot of houses into those areas which we would say absolutely not . . .
> But they'll carry on regardless with housing . . . big new housing developments . . . it's happening all over . . . where there's no public transport . . .

> We're not in the position to enforce things on the local authorities
> . . . And the local authorities will decide . . . and to hell with those
> policies . . . We can rant and rave all we like . . . but we can't do an
> awful lot more than that.
>
> (Interview IR18, regional body, 2006)

Ballincolig, once a small village to the west of Cork, has recently undergone massive housing expansion, which for some people was emblematic of how under-serviced development in the area was having detrimental effects, not least for those living there. Belatedly a new town centre is now being developed on a former army barracks, with shops, offices and other facilities, seeking to turn it into something other than a car-centred, dormitory suburb of the city. Meantime, more housing continues to be built. All of this makes some sense in terms of using the windfall brownfield site to retro-engineer a more mixed use form of development, but it does show up the shortcomings of the previous approach and the difficulties of achieving the new constraint policy.

There was a similar strong policy for locating most new economic development and associated jobs in the city centre and the central industrial areas around the docks, to serve the planned population expansion in the north east corridor. The logic here was clear, that new transport investment would serve these areas, hopefully reducing the amount of commuter car journeys in the region. Cork Docklands in particular was envisaged as a major focal point for new employment generation, requiring substantial investment in land preparation and that competing out of town greenfield site development be constrained. Cork City Docks was designated as an Integrated Area Plan in 1998, and a masterplan was prepared in 2001 (Cork City Council 2005). The masterplan identified a capacity for 6,000 new residential units and 100,000 square metres of non-residential development. The proposals were incorporated into the Cork City Development Plan in 2004. While progress is underway in the Docklands, implementation has been patchy. The underlying problem is that the city council oversees the central area while the county council has responsibility for outlying areas. Naturally there is a tension which emerges here, as the county is called upon to engage in a certain amount of short-term self-sacrifice for the wider long-term regional good. Rather than engage in such noble self-sacrifice, however, county planners understandably argue that within the wider context of CASP's drive for economic growth it was unrealistic for them to turn away potential investors:

> These companies come down to Cork and say 'I'm not going to wait
> until the docklands is up . . . I want to come in now, where can I go'
> . . . and they see these green fields . . . They are going to places like
> the airport because . . . greenfield site . . . low development costs . . .
> and low rentals . . . whereas the city centre is more complicated to
> develop and the costs will be higher.
>
> (Interview IR8, local government officer, 2006)

The development of new employment parks around Cork airport to the south of the city symbolises this tension. Though nominally land was released to allow airport-dependent businesses to locate there, in practice it has been a successful general business park, not constrained to airport-related usages. This has been frustrating for those at the regional level who seek to enforce regional planning guidelines, apparently with limited success: 'the county keep on doing this . . . we've tried to put a full stop on the county . . . but the officials say you can't stop this' (Interview IR18, regional body, 2006). It is perhaps still early days, however, with those responsible for development in the Docklands area relatively sanguine that as their own efforts start to create a stronger local alternative, things would alter.

There is a strong dissonance evident between the official view of CASP's achievements and those of people who were less fully engaged with it. For those involved CASP represented a clear breakthrough, and while problems were acknowledged these were seen to be essentially ones of synchronisation:

> In the 1980s we used to prepare plans but there was no money to implement them. Now we can prepare plans with the confidence that they will be implemented . . . there's public money as well as private money to implement them. With the pace of development . . . particularly in the south of the county . . . it's still difficult to get everything synchronised . . . but the money's there.
>
> (Interview IR12, local planner, 2006)

While there was acknowledgement that there had been massive investment in roads, and some investment was starting to come through for public transport, more generally there was a feeling that the system was not quite delivering as it should. In our Midleton case study, for instance, we found evidence that despite being part of the CASP priority area for future development, when it came to implementation all was not going quite to plan:

> The plan is to develop the land between the railway and the dual carriageway . . . the idea being that people can use the train and reduce car usage . . . But a prime example of where it didn't work was a developer bought a plot of land on the far side of the dual carriageway away from all of this . . . and he's building huge numbers of houses now . . . and it's nothing to do with the local area plan.
>
> (Interview IR25, environmental group, 2006)

> Cork County Council granted planning permission for 600 units . . . that generates a fairly high level of traffic . . . the only way to go anywhere is to come in through the narrowest street into Midleton . . . right into the centre of the town . . . and it doesn't matter where they are going, that's the way they must come . . . pure and absolute chaos.
>
> (Interview IR14, local government officer, 2006)

Hidden behind some of the concerns we encountered about the realities of development was that not everything was transparent. The theme that developers seemed always to get their way, even when this ran against official planning policy, ran through many of our interviews and it was very much in evidence in our joint meeting with local environmental groups, where one participant summed up the general feeling of those present:

> Whatever way the system works developers seem to get their way. You think what's the point in drawing up this plan. That's the way it's always been . . . we're too politicised.
>
> (Interview IR23, environmental group, 2006)

One of the features of the new spatial planning that particularly interested us was that it potentially offered the opportunity to reconnect planning with a stronger social agenda, if only through the role of guiding the location of social infrastructure. In Ireland most social infrastructure investment still comes through heavily centralised government departments rather than local government, notably health, education and policing. Not surprisingly then when it came to local-level planning there was a widespread sense that in this respect spatial planning was not actually working as well as it could as an integrating policy device. In particular there were issues in zoning for social infrastructure within large-scale developments, something that Cork planners were aware of but struggling to work around.

In Midleton the national education department was working on plans to provide new schools, for instance, but one of the issues locally was getting developers to provide appropriate land, in a system where planners could require land to be provided but were reluctant or unable to specify where. The problem with this is that it means the most accessible sites for an area as a whole may not be designated. We asked what this looked like from the local council perspective:

> [You appear to be working closely with the Department of Education without going through the county council?]
>
> No, no . . . we're not dealing with that at all in fact . . . That's another issue I suppose of local government in Ireland . . . the number of functions is very limited compared to other countries . . . we don't have any direct input into education . . . nor policing for example.
>
> [How do you get over the message that we need twice as many police and so on?]
>
> What we do is write to the minister . . .
>
> [So you go direct to national government?]
>
> We do . . . yes
>
> [But not through the county?]
>
> No.
>
> (Interview IR14, local government officer, 2006)

This direct access to central government is something which has much to recommend it. It seems to be working in Midleton and surrounding areas because it is of such prominence within CASP's ambitions for managing future growth, the support for CASP nationally, and the 2005 Special Local Area Plan. Alternatively it seems to be a time-consuming process for all, and one where transparency is not always apparent, leading to some frustration among planners and local government officials about whether they were always getting the best possible outcomes for their areas.

Conclusion

What our new planning legislation did [2000] was to provide a statutory basis for a hierarchy of plans from the NSS . . . to regional planning guidelines for the eight regions . . . and following through into the local . . . And the idea was that each would be consistent with the other . . . and so decisions on national investment priorities would be taken on the basis of the NSS and would feed down into the local planning policies. Having said all that . . . that's the theory . . . whether it's being achieved? . . . It is starting to be achieved . . . but it's going to take us some time to get there in practice.

(Interview IR4, civil servant, 2005)

It is still perhaps premature to engage in a full assessment of the new Irish planning system. But already it is possible to see some major advances that have been made, not least the very fact of having a National Spatial Strategy. That the NSS is in turn strongly linked into the budgetary processes of the state through the National Development Plan is entirely laudable, bringing a clearer spatial and long-term direction to government investment. In broad terms assessing recent initiatives for spatial planning at the national level it is fair to say that there has been steady but patchy progress in terms of improving policy integration and consultation processes. Less clear cut is progress towards sustainable development, where the Irish model remains strongly focused on economic growth and looking beyond the rhetoric there is not much evidence that this approach is strongly tempered by social and environmental considerations. In terms of achieving balanced development across the national space, again the rhetoric is strong, the policies are clearly there on paper, but there is still some way to go before it can be said that Dublin's growth pains are behind it and that growth is genuinely being spread more evenly across the rest of the country.

In metropolitan Cork, CASP provides a spatial strategy which is widely supported by national, regional and local bodies. However, there remain real concerns that the strong paper plans and the evidence of better directed government investment in infrastructure are yet to fundamentally transform recent patterns of development. The result is that the existing pattern of unbalanced development across the Cork city region is likely to continue for some time yet, and with it problems of localised congestion, pollution and under-serviced development.

It is perhaps appropriate to end on a more positive note. Until the late 1980s or so, the Irish planning system was mainly struggling to come to terms with stagnation or even decline, particularly in population terms. Very quickly both the planning system and the wider public that it serves have had to get used to dealing with the consequences of rapid growth. In this context, there has been a growing sophistication about how growth needs to be handled and cumulative longer-term impacts anticipated. More than this, however, systems have been put in place that put most other countries to shame in attempting to synchronise infrastructure investment with the projected future development needs of local and regional areas, tied together with a national overview which favours balanced territorial development. If the system has not quite delivered to its full promise yet, that is not to say that major advances haven't already been made.

We end with a conclusion that contains two hypotheses which might be useful to bear in mind as we read through other chapters. First, the Irish experience suggests that spatial planning is most likely to bring in other government departments if it is strongly tied into systems for allocating departmental funding, allied to regular monitoring of spending patterns against the spatial plan. Second, even where this happens, little effective impact will occur at local level unless government departments find better ways of working at local level directly with local partnerships.

4

Spatial planning in Northern Ireland and the emergent North West region of Ireland

Introduction

Northern Ireland has some of the most distinctive planning issues of any covered in this book, not simply because of the political border issues but also because of the turbulent history of the province and the sectarian politics associated with this. With a population of 1.7 million in 2006, it is much smaller in population size than any other region of the UK. However, Northern Ireland's particular history means its political significance is far greater than its population alone might suggest. In this chapter we focus on how spatial planning has been embraced in the period since the 1998 Belfast Agreement (also known as the Good Friday agreement), which signalled a new era in Northern Ireland politics and in relations between the Republic of Ireland and the UK.[1] Two themes dominate the chapter, the first of which is the development of the 2001 Regional Development Strategy for Northern Ireland, widely regarded at the time as an early exemplar for spatial planning in the UK. One of its most widely noted successes was in public engagement, while its main problems have been in achieving implementation.

The second focus is on the Derry city region and emergent plans for cross-border spatial planning for the North West region, covering parts of both the Republic of Ireland and Northern Ireland. We chose to examine Derry and the North West region in part because it was relatively understudied in the planning literature (though see Paris and Robson 2001; Paris 2005, 2006; Murtagh and Kelly 2006) but mainly because of the fascinating cross-border issues emerging since 1998. Demilitarisation of the border as part of the post-1998 'Peace Process' unleashed a rapid growth in cross-border activity, commuting and housing development in particular, in the process creating new opportunities and some distinctive challenges for integrated policy-making and for spatial planning.

The early part of this chapter draws particularly on interviews with seven 'national' stakeholders in 2005, three of them academics. It is worth noting that in the particular circumstances of Northern Ireland, academics have played an important role as critics of and participants in aspects of the planning process, notably including the consultation processes for the Regional Development Strategy (see McEldowney *et al.* 2002).

Spatial planning in Northern Ireland

Just as there is no single spatial plan for mainland Britain, so there is not a single, all-island spatial plan for Ireland. While there are moves towards greater coordination on planning matters between Northern Ireland and the Republic, in practical terms there remain considerable differences in approach to spatial planning between the north, with its centralised and technocratic planning system (Neill and Gordon 2001; Ellis and Neill 2006), and the south, where there is a stronger local scale of planning activity. We have already introduced the national planning approach of the Republic of Ireland in Chapter 3, so here we will focus on Northern Ireland and make connections to processes in the Republic based on the assumption that the reader has already picked up the broad picture.

It is important to provide some background to the contested nature of territorial politics in Northern Ireland at this stage.[2] As Ellis and Neill (2006) succinctly put it, Northern Ireland was created by the Government of Ireland Act 1920 in a move that satisfied the aspirations of neither the unionists (for continuing union with the UK) nor the nationalists (favouring being part of an independent Ireland). In consequence much of the subsequent history of the province is rooted in strongly entrenched and opposing senses of cultural and territorial identity, in part defined through their opposition to each other. Territorial complexity and struggle manifests itself in many ways, including disputes over nomenclature, with differing bodies finding specific cultural meanings and symbolic resonance in the use of Northern Ireland, region, province, 'six counties' or Ulster, and in the naming of Derry/Londonderry.[3] There is a distinct cultural contrast too between a predominantly nationalist west (west of the River Bann) and unionist east, associated with continuing sensitivities about under-investment and higher levels of poverty in the west. At the micro level too, communities can be sharply divided, with enclave communities living in the midst of majority communities.

After 1921 the UK government devolved responsibility for administration and policing, in the process asserting political sovereignty over Northern Ireland, excluding the Irish Free State from participation in the affairs of the region, while itself adopting a stance of non-intervention in the region (Anderson and Dowd 1999a). This stance in effect gave considerable power to unionist governments to develop policies that clearly favoured certain groups over others, leading to long-standing concerns about the unfair impacts of partisan politics in building and allocating housing and in guiding infrastructure investment. In consequence there was, and still is, enormous sensitivity within Northern Ireland politics to spatial and social inequities. Concern with unionist policing, 'gerrymandered' electoral systems and housing allocation and location policies grew rapidly during the 1960s, in part responding to civil unrest elsewhere, including the United States, and in part to the welfarist logic of UK politics at the time, with its emphasis on universal and equitable access to education, housing, and health facilities (Anderson and Dowd 1999a). The result was growing internal and external pressure for change, accompanied by growing sectarian violence from the early 1970s.

Devolved government in Northern Ireland was suspended in 1972 as a result of growing civil unrest, sometimes referred to as the Troubles, replaced by Direct Rule from Westminster, with a minister for Northern Ireland and administration through the Northern Ireland Office. Under Direct Rule planning became highly centralised, with a single central government department providing both strategic plans and local development plans, with development plans typically covering several local government areas. The 26 local government units in Northern Ireland are small in size, limited in function and for the most part not trusted by the UK authorities. As such they had no formal say in deciding planning matters, only a consultative role. The resulting planning apparatus is generally portrayed as centralised, lacking sensitivity to place, yet over-sensitive to the political tensions of the province, as we found in some of our interviews:

> What is interesting about the Planning Service is that they have relied very heavily on a professionalised, bureaucratised system . . . it is very much a sanitised planning world. The capacity to think outside that regulatory planning framework is much reduced and part of that is due to the violence . . . the way the state was threatened . . . These big bureaucracies were pretty much centralised . . . they were just about regulation . . . nothing to do with segregation . . . Planning had become quite politicised under the old Stormont Unionist Administration . . . The NI Planning Order came in 1972 when Stormont was suspended . . . and since then planning has relied on technical values . . . on professional status.
>
> (Interview NI3, academic, 2005)

This view of a technocratic planning apparatus, remote from local communities and with a tendency to fudge decisions is widely held. However, most would also allow that this approach was rooted in some very difficult circumstances, as planners sought to deal fairly with planning matters in the context of a deepening sectarian divide which was creating a complex internal reterritorialisation along ethno-religious lines (Neill and Gordon 2001; Ellis and Neill 2006).

Though formal political contact between the governments of the UK and the Republic was maintained from 1920 onwards in various forms, the practice was at best patchy. Consequently while there is a long tradition of cross-border activity in Ireland, this was selective and historically at its most successful where the governments were not the key players. The borders with the Republic became increasingly militarised during the Troubles, making movement between the two countries more difficult for most people. At governmental level, political sensitivities tended to inhibit meaningful cooperation on border or other issues. This said, things did begin to change for the better when both countries joined the EU in the 1970s. From the 1980s onwards the European Commission has played a central role in promoting strong cross-border links, funding a variety of cross-border infrastructure projects in Ireland, stimulated by a general Commission concern to address negative border impacts in light of the Single European Market and cohesion policies (Anderson and O'Dowd 1999a; Paasi 1999; Perkmann 1999; Scott 1999; Yarwood 2006).

A major breakthrough came with the Belfast Agreement of April 1998, which established a basis for ending the political troubles. Under this agreement the UK government undertook to revise the Government of Ireland Act 1920 and the Irish government to drop the territorial claim to the north from its constitution. The Agreement also provided for devolved government through an elected Assembly, which in turn elected an Executive. It also established a number of formal north–south institutions, such as the British–Irish Council covering the British Isles, the British–Irish Intergovernmental Conference, and the North/South Ministerial Council. In total twelve north–south functional areas for cooperation were agreed, with six to be covered by new bodies, five by existing arrangements and a new private company for joint tourist marking (Anderson and O'Dowd 1999a).

The resulting assemblage of institutions, when combined with local government, a host of local partnerships, and elected representatives in Westminster and the European parliament, meant that the 1.7 million people of Northern Ireland became 'probably the most heavily governed in the world' (Anderson and O'Dowd 1999a: 692). More positively, some have argued that the new arrangements represent a concerted effort to turn the border into a bridge (McCall 2003), or as Anderson and Dowd (1999b: 595) put it, border regions are 'at once gateways and barriers to the outside world'. We return to this theme later in the chapter.

Internally, a central part of the devolution process involved the creation of an elected Northern Ireland Assembly, where power-sharing between political parties would form the basis of executive government. However, stable government, initially at least, proved difficult to maintain (Knox and Carmichael 2005) and the Assembly was suspended on a number of occasions, the longest between October 2002 and May 2007 during which period there was a return to direct rule through the Northern Ireland Office. Following the St Andrews' Agreement (2006), devolved government resumed in May 2007.

In the early days of the Northern Ireland Assembly and the power-sharing agreement, a total of eleven ministries were established in Northern Ireland, one for each member of the Northern Ireland Executive, consisting of the First Minister and ten ministers. Responsibility for planning matters was consequently divided between four different departments with their own ministers and civil servants. For planning, this saw the end of concentration of responsibilities in the Department of Environment (Northern Ireland), as different roles were spread across the new ministries The resulting pattern was of a still centralised administration, but with internally highly fragmented responsibilities. Responsibility for the province-wide Regional Development Strategy (RDS) rests with the Department of Regional Development (DRD), which also has responsibility for the Regional Transport Strategy. Development plans, on the other hand, are prepared by the Planning Service (Department of the Environment), while urban regeneration and housing are the responsibility of the Department of Social Development (DSD), and rural development rests with the Department of Agriculture and Rural Development.

The Regional Development Strategy: innovative spatial plan or irrelevance?

Northern Ireland has a history of planning at the national (referred to in Northern Ireland as 'regional') scale, continuing from the Belfast Regional Plan published in 1964, and including the Regional Physical Development Strategy for 1975–1995, which proposed a decentralised settlement policy as part of a proposed spatial rebalancing of development in the region. Between 2002 and the resumption of devolution in May 2007, all major services were administered by the UK government's Northern Ireland Office, in some cases through agencies such as the Planning Service and the Northern Ireland Housing Executive. The centralised town and country planning service in Northern Ireland was established in 1973 and, as the Planning Service, became an executive agency of the Northern Ireland Department of the Environment (DoE) in 1996. Under restored devolution, it remains responsible for preparing development plans and undertaking government planning functions including development control. Strategic planning, specifically the Regional Development Strategy, remains the responsibility of a separate department, which as we will see generates some tensions.

The Belfast Agreement of 1998 gave added impetus to strategic planning – the preparation of a regional development strategy was a specific requirement of the Agreement, giving it quasi-constitutional status (Ellis and Neill 2006). The British government pledged to prepare:

> a new regional development strategy for Northern Ireland for consideration in due course by the Assembly, tackling the problems of a divided society and social cohesion in urban, rural and border areas, protecting and enhancing the environment, producing new approaches to transport issues, strengthening the physical infrastructure of the region, developing the advantages and resources of rural areas and rejuvenating major urban centres.
>
> (Belfast Agreement, p. 19, cited in Ellis and Neill 2006: 129)

Earlier consultations in 1997 had focused on a proposed Belfast City Region plan, which created concerns that it represented a return to previous approaches, said to have had a 'Belfast bias' (McEldowney *et al.* 2002). Moving to a whole region approach was politically welcomed by most.

Recognising the need to tackle the problems of divided communities, the approach adopted for preparing the Regional Development Strategy was geared to achieving 'internal societal consensus' (Murray 2004: 240). It deliberately set out to provide an inclusive approach, incorporating an extensive process of public consultation and an examination in public (Neill and Gordon 2001), seeking to secure a broad consensus on the future planning framework for Northern Ireland both within the community at large and within government. A government-appointed Consultation Consortium carried out consultations with 477 voluntary and community groups, the large number reflecting the growth of civil society given the limits of local democratic accountability during the Troubles (Neill and Gordon 2001; McEldowney *et al.* 2002). The findings from these consultations were fed into the Draft Regional Strategic Framework for Northern Ireland, which was published in December 1998. The examination in public was held in December 1999, and the final plan was endorsed by the Assembly, prior to its suspension, and subsequently published in late 2001 (Murray 2004; Ellis and Neill 2006).

Held up as an innovative model spatial plan when it was produced and in the vanguard of thinking on European spatial planning (Royal Commission on Environmental Pollution 2002; Albrechts *et al.* 2003; Healey 2004b), the Regional Development Strategy adopted the conceptual language of the European Spatial Development Perspective (ESDP) (European Commission 1999; Healey 2004b). The spatial development strategy is described as pivotal, with a hub, corridor and gateway approach (see Figure 4.1)

> designed to promote balanced and integrated growth across the network of Cities, Main and Small Towns, and their rural hinterlands, to enhance equality of opportunity in all parts of the Region, and offer the locational choice to meet the variety of needs in a divided society.
> (Department of Regional Development (DRD) 2001: viii)

Concentration of development in the gateways and hubs is variously justified on the grounds of spatial equity, economic dynamism and sustainable development. Tackling issues of sprawl, urban decay and infrastructure pressures by focusing on existing urban areas, this approach also addressed development pressures on the countryside and the need to tackle concerns that dispersed rural housing was weakening smaller settlements. Indeed, adopting a relatively strong stance on sustainable development issues was a strong feature of the RDS, particularly as it predated by several years the release of a formal sustainable development strategy for the region (Haughton *et al.* 2008).

There is an interesting debate locally about the impact of the ESDP on the strategy. Murray (2004) is upbeat about how it provides a common technical conceptual language, of gateways and hubs, which was subsequently also adopted in the Republic of Ireland's spatial strategy, opening up the possibility for stronger integration between the two. Focusing on the strategy's development, Murtagh and Kelly (2006) argue that consultation played a much

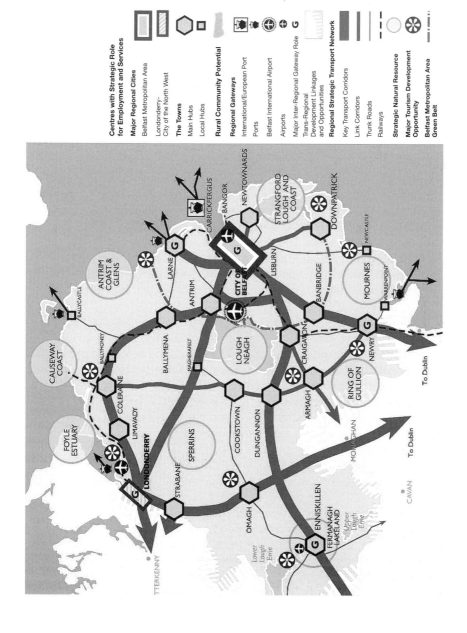

Centres with Strategic Role for Employment and Services

Major Regional Cities

Belfast Metropolitan Area

Londonderry-
City of the North West

The Towns

Main Hubs

Local Hubs

Rural Community Potential

Regional Gateways

International/European Port

Ports

Belfast International Airport

Airports

Major Inter-Regional Gateway Role

Trans-Regional
Development Linkages
and Opportunities

Regional Strategic Transport Network

Key Transport Corridors

Link Corridors

Trunk Roads

Railways

Strategic Natural Resource

**Major Tourism Development
Opportunity**

**Belfast Metropolitan Area
Green Belt**

*4.1 The Spatial
Development Strategy
for Northern Ireland*

Source: Department of
Regional Development
(2001).

greater role in bringing about changes to reflect the priorities of rural and non-metropolitan Belfast issues than anything coming out of engagement with ESDP thinking. Ellis and Neill (2006) go further, arguing that the RDS lacked a substantive debate on possible spatial futures, instead focusing on achieving consensus around the neutral concept of territorial equity and balanced development, not tackling hard issues such as the relative merits of concentration versus dispersal, or public transport-led development patterns. While there was a view among our interviewees that the ESDP had contributed to the conceptual and rhetorical basis for the strategy, and that greater consultation was one consequence of this, more generally there was a degree of scepticism, captured well by one of our academic interviewees:

> I think there is a certain cynicism outside DRD . . . and everywhere is something . . . a hub or a gateway . . . It was just too politically fudged . . . and codified as ESDP . . . polycentric development . . . Quite a political document in some senses . . . keeping everybody on board and everybody happy with it.
>
> (Interview NI8, academic, 2006)

So while EU thinking clearly played a role in providing acceptable wording, and to an extent policy directions for the RDS, there remains a concern that rather than flushing out debates about preferred futures for the spatial economy, it instead provided a means for accommodating and hiding from view underlying tensions. The advantage of this was in building consensus on a region-wide approach in a way which was, according to some of our interviewees, remarkably non-sectarian. But the disadvantage was that the opportunity was lost for considering any radical spatial reorganisation and more interventionist policy regime.

While early academic assessments of the RDS were largely positive (Healey 2004b) and the five-year review (Department of Regional Development 2008) revealed an official position that little needed changing in relation to the RDS, subsequent academic assessments have highlighted some major areas of concern, as did our interviews for this book.

Several issues stand out. The first concerns the consultation process involved in producing the RDS. It is important to emphasise the achievements of this process first – it was wide-ranging and did appear to help bring about changes between the initial and final draft of the strategy, specifically in terms of making it more spatially informed and more sensitive to cross-border issues. The balanced approach to spatial development, with its gateways, hubs and transport corridors, was widely seen as a useful corrective to the Belfast-dominated strategies of the past. In particular the RDS promotes Derry/Londonderry's development as a second regional 'gateway' (Belfast is the other gateway), giving development in the area a priority it had not hitherto enjoyed. Indeed, one of the frequent comments in our interviews was that the RDS enjoyed considerable support in the west of the region. While much of this was innovative and welcome when the document was published, five years later people had begun to question what if anything had been achieved. Some people felt that the designation of hubs had been an essentially empty gesture for ensuring political buy-in across the region, rather than a genuine effort to bring about a reorganisation of the spatial economy. In essence most decisions, including housebuilding numbers, appeared to be made still on grounds such as existing share of population or employment, rather than any major redistribution. A former civil servant heavily involved in the early stages told us how it worked:

> While my logic as a planner was that we should be tackling it on a city regional basis . . . that was not the main game here. And in the end the motivating factor overall was not to upset the balance . . . to allow economic development to be attracted to the east and west . . . to the same ratio as the projected population at the time. They then started to allocate the projected population to the twenty-six district councils . . . it was really as crude as that.
>
> (Interview NI2, former civil servant, 2005)

One of the regular criticisms we encountered was that by including housing numbers in the RDS, it got derailed from being a strategic spatial document to a politicised process for distributing new housing across areas and for introducing a UK government policy that 60 per cent of new housing should be on brownfield sites. Using sustainable development rhetoric to justify an urban consolidation approach, such policies ran into practical and political problems when it came to negotiating issues of territorial equity. In the context of Northern Ireland, the history of contested, uneven development of infrastructure raises issues about whether policies that in effect maintain the status quo are also perpetuating past discriminatory patterns:

> Because some groups in the region feel that west of the River Bann . . . the western part is largely non-Unionist . . . has been traditionally for decades under-developed. So if you were to look at future development simply on the basis of existing infrastructure, it is not an even playing field . . . And that is only going to perpetuate that pattern of uneven development. Now there are different views on this . . . that's from a nationalist point of view. Unionists would say that that regional pattern is simply in line with how many regions developed . . . that peripheral areas beyond the main urban corridors were very difficult to develop . . . so what has happened in the past is simply in line with the market. It was very difficult grappling with these different perspectives.
>
> (Interview NI5, academic, 2005)

In practice, the historical legacies and contemporary political pressures made it difficult to achieve consensus around anything that might upset the status quo too much. For two of our interviewees, there was a concern too that planners dominated the process, so that while it was ostensibly about creating a wide-ranging 'spatial planning' perspective, in practice it remained largely land use oriented and technocratic in nature. Breaking out from existing mind-sets was also a problem for some of those being consulted. As one of those involved pointed out, this was something they had struggled with, aspiring to ask what kind of future society people wanted and how this might translate into spatial terms:

> Now in practice, of course we found that when you go out, the closer to the ground you go, the more difficult it is to get people to think conceptually about those broader things. In a society that has been highly ghettoised . . . where people have been used to living in small spaces for security . . . horizons are narrowed accordingly. To get people at that level to talk about what is the vision for Northern Ireland we want to see in twenty years' time is very difficult.
>
> (Interview NI5, academic, 2005)

Reviewing the work of themselves and others on the consultation process for the RDS, McEldowney *et al.* (2002) reveal how for all its achievements in reaching out to communities largely isolated from planning decisions in the past, the consultation process was not quite as successful as they had hoped. Most notably business interests proved difficult to engage with through the open workshops, leading the authors to question whether the power structures had been realigned in any fundamental way. Under-represented groups had been brought into the process, with considerable gains in mutual learning and understanding, but still powerful lobby groups preferred the semi-legalistic framework of the Examination in Public (EiP). The frustration was palpable in the comments of some of those who participated, including one who told us:

> What had happened was that we had undertaken this amazingly comprehensive consultation . . . more than anything you would usually find in Britain at a regional level . . . and yet when you came to the EiP these people like developers, landowners, housebuilder associations and their very expensive legal advocates . . . were there around the table. They had not participated in any of the public discussions but they had simply brought their case to the end point . . . We were there representing the groups we had consulted and we felt that this was not the proper way to weight these different voices. We had done this comprehensive discussion with a whole range of people over a long period of time . . . but it seemed as if that was simply put on the table alongside somebody who was a legal representative for the housebuilders.
>
> (Interview NI4, academic, 2005)

Perhaps the most widespread criticism we encountered in our interviews was a concern that the strategy was a fine paper document, but that it had not been fully bought into by other departments, resulting in little progress when it came to implementation. More than this, nearly all our interviewees were scornful about progress towards a more coordinated approach to policy across government departments as a result of the RDS or devolution more generally. In the context of the fragmentation of responsibilities for different aspects of planning across government departments and resultant interdepartmental 'turf demarcations' (Neill and Gordon 2001: 41) difficulties quickly emerged in negotiating implementation of the Regional Development Strategy through the complex network of departmental and public agency responsibilities in Northern Ireland. At the heart of these problems lies the fact that responsibility for strategy preparation and monitoring of delivery is separate from decisions about investment and the agencies of delivery. Adding further complexity has been the political fragmentation involved, with Democratic Unionist Party (DUP) members initially refusing to participate in the new Executive, despite taking up their ministries. Our interviews revealed widespread concerns that in the key early phase of implementation of the plan, for political and related bureaucratic reasons departments remained distant from each other.

The interdepartmental rivalries and lack of cooperation were essentially part of the institutional landscape of Northern Ireland, something officially denied, but in practice acknowledged by all, whether within the system or outside, with one environmental lobby group summarising the general mood well:

> There is a very strong silo mentality here among civil servants both within departments and between departments . . . and the overarching strategies that have been developed such as the Biodiversity Strategy and the Sustainable Development Strategy . . . they inevitably end up being housed in a particular department and then become ghettoised as a result. There are major fault-lines between departments that really should be working closely together.
>
> (Interview NI17, environmental NGO, 2006)

Such downbeat assessments of the implementation difficulties for the RDS were more or less shared across our interviewees. Amidst petty political squabbles and administrative rivalries, the grand visions and good intentions of planners come down to earth with a solid bump.

More generally, the political aspirations for a cross-sectoral approach were seen to have been short-circuited by departmental and party politics, which meant that when it came to crucial investment decisions, for instance, on major hospital investments, the RDS was not considered as a factor. Economic development and infrastructure were frequently cited as areas in which policy coordination remained an illusion in general terms, and spatial policy appeared to be a marginal consideration. Even within the planning system itself, with its responsibilities fragmented across departments, there was felt to be little consistency between the RDS and the new generation of development plans being produced:

> Look at the content of those plans and see to what extent they come within the context of the RDS . . . and have embraced the rhetoric of it. What you find is that those area plans are relatively unchanged from what they were twenty-five years ago . . . they are land use plans with very limited agendas . . . it's where you put the houses basically and bits and pieces of infrastructure. I'll give you an example . . . Down Council complained about the lack of attention to economic development in their area . . . the rebuttal was 'it's beyond our remit'.
>
> (Interview NI4, academic, 2005)

The interesting fault-line which emerges here is that while the RDS was approved with no public dissent in the Assembly, one of the reasons for this is that it did not in fact have any legislative status. This was felt by some of our respondents to be symptomatic of the slippery politics of the early days of the Assembly, where people were willing to nod through policies for which they had no responsibility and little intention of backing subsequently if local politics dictated otherwise. At a more practical level, a common concern among our respondents was that disagreement between the main departments involved led to a major debate about whether development plans must follow the RDS or not, resulting in a compromise wording of being 'in general conformity', a weak phrasing in legal terms, stronger than 'have regard to' but weaker than 'consistent with'.

There was also the issue of reversion to Westminster rule rather than devolution for much of the initial period after the RDS was adopted. For instance, we were told that policies aiming to encourage more people to move from private to public transport had been discussed early on, but later came to nothing:

> Under the devolved assembly the minister was willing to commit to that . . . but the direct rule minister is unwilling to commit to any move to encourage people to get out of their cars and onto a public transport system . . . That's where we're falling down . . . ministers of the UK take the easy option . . . they won't take the tough decisions. So there is a large degree of disappointment whereas a locally devolved assembly might well have gone further to support some of these things that would have supported the RDS.
>
> (Interview NI6, former civil servant, 2005)

Finally, there were differing views on whether the RDS was an essentially inward-looking, parochial document, where the Republic of Ireland was treated, according to one respondent, as 'white space' on a map, or a useful point of departure from previous plans which set the basis for improved border coordination. There appears to be truth in both viewpoints. Certainly there was some consultation with civil servants from the Republic as part of the preparation process, a dialogue which continued with the development of the NSS for publication in the Republic in 2002 and has gathered momentum since then.

Citing continuing political sensitivities about territorial links with the Republic of Ireland, and the need to ensure cross-party buy-in, Ellis and Neill (2006: 133) conclude that the RDS 'makes only the feeblest attempt to place Northern Ireland in its island context'. The difficulty for those involved in the negotiations was that, as one former civil servant told us, 'it is quite difficult in Northern Ireland to find that political balance between acknowledging an adjoining jurisdiction and appearing to be subservient to it' (Interview NI2, planning consultant, 2005). There are enormous tensions still, particularly among unionists, over being seen to lay the path open to later unification of the two countries. The result is that political feasibility can sometimes work against using the consultation processes of planning to broker agreement on contentious cross-border issues. These political sensitivities appear to have lessened by the time the first five-year review of the RDS was published in 2008, with the review document much more direct and confident in its approach to cross-border collaboration than its predecessor (DRD 2008).

Among its achievements the RDS also set out a broad international context which was innovative in terms of UK planning at that time, as was its explicit championing of the ESDP as a source of inspiration. Within the relevant chapter outlining this wider context, a short section (pp. 32–33) is devoted to strengthening selected cross-border activities, including transport infrastructure, aspects of environmental management, and encouraging energy connections 'to create an all island energy market'. How such policies will be achieved and how they might reflect wider decisions on, say, economic development activities is less clear. When it comes to cross-border implementation, sensitivities remain, though as we shall see there are signs of change in the air.

Summarising RDS achievements

I think I would summarise by saying a good start with a document accepted by the whole of the community . . . but after a promising start the delivery has proved fraught with greater problems than perhaps anyone anticipated. Dissension . . . difference of view . . . cracks have appeared in it . . . We have to try harder in a number of important areas . . . on the environmental side . . . on infrastructure side and the cross-sectoral connections . . . down to the local level and up at the national . . . all facets could be improved.

(Interview NI6, former civil servant, 2005)

Spatial planning of the style advocated by the ESDP involves a call for greater consultation, policy integration, sustainable development and balanced, polycentric spatial development. Using this framework to summarise the achievements of the RDS is salutary. The consultation processes for the RDS provided a good example of spatial planning practices, carried out in unusual circumstances and playing a wider role than normal in brokering a shared sense of territorial identity around which spatial planning processes could be constructed. On policy integration progress to date has been less than exemplary however. In terms of vertical coordination, little progress can be expected until the planned local government reorganisation and the accompanying devolution of powers to this level. At the moment, Northern Ireland manages to be not only one of the most over-governed parts of the world in terms of its complex governance structures, but also one of the most highly centralised. In terms of horizontal, or cross-sectoral policy coordination, progress has been almost painfully slow. The fragmentation of departmental responsibilities allied to continuing periods of Westminster rule post-devolution during the key period after the plan was published were not helpful, though it is possible that following the resumption of power-sharing devolved government matters may yet improve. In that respect, the move towards a Programme for Government and an explicit Investment Strategy for the region have both been helpful, particularly those released following the resumption of devolved government in 2007. Though neither pays strong heed to the RDS explicitly, just a mention of hubs and gateways guiding the release of land for employment sites, nonetheless both carry within them strong commitments to addressing regional balance and addressing past imbalances in infrastructure. For instance, *Building a Better Future: Programme for Government 2008–2011* (Northern Ireland Executive (NIE) 2008a: 16) makes no mention of the RDS, but it does comment that 'We recognise the existing regional infrastructure disparities. We will work to address them and to ensure that we deliver a more balanced regional outcome.'

On sustainable development, it is fair to say again that the RDS sets the tone for subsequent strategies, notably in the region's subsequently published sustainable development strategy, but also in the Programme for Government. While the Programme for Government sets economic development as its priority, with addressing equity issues running parallel, sustainable development and addressing environmental concerns are also prominent. Other signs of change include recent moves to address the issue of dispersed rural housing (see below). Finally, on balanced development it is still difficult to point to major achievements specifically stemming from this policy, although new road investments provide a pointer as do attempts to consolidate rural development around existing settlements. More positively, however, the RDS has introduced a shared understanding of key issues for the whole region, and arguably helped in the process of turning policy-makers from a largely inward-looking, parochial gaze, to one much more focused on an all-island perspective. Given the small size and location on the island of Ireland, how to address the legacy of border issues in creating truncated hinterlands, settlement hierarchies and transport corridors is one of the key challenges facing policy-makers, and it is this issue that we turn to in the next section.

North West Ireland and the Derry–Letterkenny Gateway

The emergent process for cross-border planning in North West Ireland is taking place in the context of a major reversal in fortunes between the Republic of Ireland and Northern Ireland. For much of the post-war period, the economy of the south was seen as sluggish, marked by massive out-migration and high unemployment, while Northern Ireland benefited from an initially buoyant manufacturing sector around Belfast, not least shipbuilding, and substantial state subsidies from the UK government (Anderson and O'Dowd 1999a; Harvey *et al.* 2005). However, by the 1990s things had reversed dramatically. The political instability and civil society unrest surrounding the Troubles made the North less attractive to many private investors and with sluggish economic performance, the economy became increasingly dependent on the public sector. By contrast from the early 1990s to 2008 the Republic of Ireland's economy boomed, as Chapter 3 revealed. The country offered a stable political climate and an attractive financial environment, in particular a favourable corporate tax rate, attracting considerable inward investment, notably high-tech and pharmaceutical industries from the United States. With 4.2 million people in 2006,[4] the Republic of Ireland is about two and a half times more populous than its northern neighbour but its economy is nearly four times as large – Gross Value Added (GVA) in the Republic of Ireland was £102 billion (150 billion Euros) in 2006, while that in the north was just £24.5 billion in 2005.

There is a distinctive east coast bias in both population and economic growth across the island. In Northern Ireland the focus is on the Belfast Metropolitan Area, with over 1 million people living within 30 miles of the centre of Belfast. There are also some signs of an emerging economic corridor between Dublin and Belfast (Yarwood 2006), in the context of growing cross-border cooperation, notably involving the Newry-Dundalk 'twin city'. This success, however, only serves to highlight the growing prosperity gap between the east coast and the more peripheral parts of the island, including the North West region (ILEX 2005) which is the focus of the remainder of this chapter.

Despite its relative lagging position, it is important to note that the North West region has a growing population. The City of Derry has a population of just over 107,000, which grew by 5.1 per cent over the period 1995–2005, an average rate of 0.5 per cent per annum. County Donegal in the Republic of Ireland, with a population of 137,575 in 2002, grew at a similar rate, 5.8 per cent, over the ten-year period 1992–2002.[5] Since 2002 though the rate of change appears to have accelerated – the Draft Donegal County Development Plan (Donegal County Council 2006a) indicates that the county's population had reached nearly 147,000 in 2006. Most of this growth has occurred around Letterkenny, where population has grown at a rate of 1.7 per cent per annum. Within the Republic's part of the Letterkenny–Derry corridor then, in recent years the rate of population growth has been some three times greater than that across the border.

Reflecting on this trend, Paris (2006: 233) notes that planning officials recorded an increase in planning applications of 300 per cent in 1999–2000 in County Donegal with 'considerable growth in cross-border purchase of second homes [and] extensive cross-border investment activity [in housing]'.

Housing approvals in the period 2000–2004 totalled 20,800 (Donegal County Council 2006a), with the Greater Derry housing market now incorporating the border areas of County Donegal (Paris 2005, 2006; Murtagh and Kelly 2006). While some research has been done on these issues, it is still not entirely clear what the level of cross-border commuting is, nor how important second home ownership and speculative tourism rental properties are in driving the housing boom. What is clear however is that people's everyday practices have rapidly changed as a consequence of the demilitarisation of the border. What is less clear, perhaps, is whether these trends will continue in the same direction, now that the high growth levels in the Republic have started to falter.

Spatial planning in Northern Ireland's western border area

> [Things are different in the west because of] the way that local politicians and the local business leaders in particular grasped spatial planning . . . and they did it for ulterior motives . . . They're all keen spatial planners up there . . . they're keen spatial planners because the RDS gave the North West and Derry a position that it had never before had. So there is that enthusiasm for spatial planning in the North West at the local level that you don't get anywhere else in the north. It really is quite bizarre but refreshing . . . Although they say themselves they're into the spatial planning concept to get something.
> (Interview NI13, civil servant, 2006)

Aiming for a balanced approach to development across the province, the Regional Development Strategy (DRD 2001), for the first time in a national policy document, recognised the role of Derry as a regional centre. Prior to this mainstream thinking had reflected Peter Hall's view that the region could claim to have only one city region, Belfast (Hall 1999, cited in Murtagh and Kelly 2006), with Derry regarded as separate physically and culturally but economically dependent. This may have been a reasonable assessment at the time, but the growing porosity of the border with the Republic required a major rethink as Derry's effective hinterland was suddenly boosted. Partly informed by such changing economic realities, partly by the political imperative to address regional imbalances more fully than in the past, the RDS took a more positive view of Derry's role, including as a key objective of the strategy the need 'to strengthen the role of Londonderry as the regional city and transport hub of the North West' (DRD 2001: 81). This decision also reflects the wider RDS commitment to balanced growth across a network of cities and smaller settlements explicitly intended to improve equality of opportunity for people living in all parts of the region 'to meet the wider variety of development needs in a divided society' (DRD 2001: 44). Giving Derry an elevated status as a key strategic employment location also proved helpful in addressing a long-term sense of grievance within the city that it was being overlooked and losing out on public sector investment.

The Regional Development Strategy proposed that Derry accommodate a planned growth in housing of in the region of 13,000 dwellings up to 2015 (see Figure 4.2). This growth forecast was increased in the review of housing growth indicators in Northern Ireland (DRD 2006b), which identified a need for some 15,000 new houses for the Derry district in the period 1998–2015. While it acknowledges the importance of cross-border infrastructure issues in relation to Derry and Letterkenny (County Donegal) the RDS did not explicitly promote a cross-border city region or gateway, something which was to emerge the following year in the Irish National Spatial Strategy (see below).

The Derry Area Plan is essentially an 'old-style' local land use plan, adopted in 2000 after many years in preparation, and prior to the publication of the final version of the Regional Development Strategy. Perhaps more attuned to spatial planning approaches is the ILEX Regeneration Plan for Derry (known as ILEX, Derry has the only Urban Development Company outside mainland UK). This provides a broad spatial vision for regeneration in the city of Derry, focusing on two particular development sites, referred to as Ebrington (Foyle Banks East) and Fort George, together with the historic walled city.

A key development pressure in Northern Ireland concerns the recent growth in single unit rural housing. The more relaxed approach to the development of houses in the countryside in the region is quite marked compared to the rest of the UK. Recent research has suggested that permission has been granted in Northern Ireland for nearly three times more single dwellings in the countryside than in the whole of England and Wales together (National Trust 2004; Ellis and Neill 2006), a fact which was frequently quoted at us in interviews. This relatively laissez-faire attitude to rural housing results in part from historical-cultural differences and partly from in-grained attitudes towards governmental intervention (Gallent *et al.* 2003; Scott 2006). There is a strong 'traditional' belief that rural people should be able to build housing on their land for relatives, something which officials were loath to tackle when one of the officially recognised problems in the area was out-migration. Local politicians too had little to gain from backing controls over one-off or speculative developments. Given this background, planners tend to see themselves as struggling against the tide, with one government official telling us that:

> We live in a society where there is no consensus for planning . . . and that is very different from the rest of the UK . . . In Ireland we still have a gross lack of consensus for planning . . . they still don't want governments telling them what they can and cannot do.

> (Interview NI13, civil servant, 2006)

Continuing development of dispersed housing in the rural areas, however, risked undermining both the sustainability credentials of the RDS and its commitment to balanced development, in particular the smaller rural towns, or 'hubs'. Recognising that implementation of the Regional Development

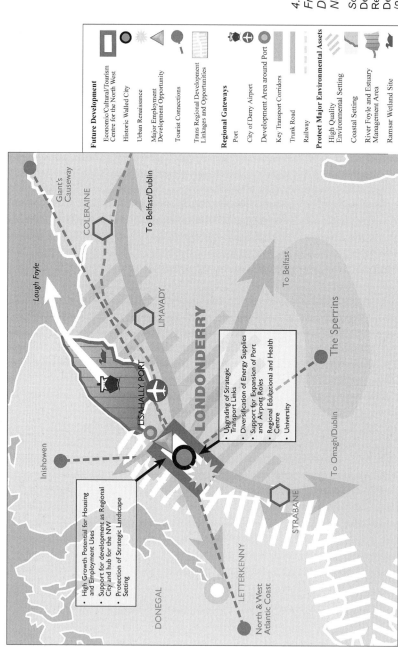

Future Development

- Economic/Cultural/Tourism Centre for the North West
- Historic Walled City
- Urban Renaissance
- Major Employment Development Opportunity
- Tourist Connections
- Trans Regional Development Linkages and Opportunities

Regional Gateways

- Port
- City of Derry Airport
- Development Area around Port
- Key Transport Corridors
- Trunk Road
- Railway

Protect Major Environmental Assets

- High Quality Environmental Setting
- Coastal Setting
- River Foyle and Estuary Management Area
- Ramsar Wetland Site

4.2 The Spatial Framework for Derry and the North West

Source: Department of Regional Development (2001).

Map labels:

Giant's Causeway

COLERAINE

To Belfast/Dublin

Lough Foyle

LIMAVADY

LISAHALLY PORT

LONDONDERRY

- Upgrading of Strategic Transport Links
- Diversification of Energy Supplies
- Support for Expansion of Port and Airport Roles
- Regional Educational and Health Centre
- University

To Belfast

The Sperrins

To Omagh/Dublin

STRABANE

Inishowen

- High Growth Potential for Housing and Employment Uses
- Support for development as Regional City and hub for the NW
- Protection of Strategic Landscape Setting

DONEGAL

LETTERKENNY

North & West Atlantic Coast

Strategy was being undermined by rapid development in the countryside, the Department of Regional Development has sought to tighten controls on rural housing. Following a period of consultation, draft *PPS14 Sustainable Development in the Countryside* was published in March 2006 (DRD 2006a). This document at one stroke removed the presumption in favour of development which had existed until then, a move that was controversial and challenged in the high court. Nevertheless a much stricter regime of development management is now in place on the northern side of the border, the explicit aim of which is to stem the tide of 'bungalow-blight' in the countryside. While *PPS14* was still only a draft, its provisions came into force immediately it was published, to prevent a flush of planning applications. A less restrictive draft replacement to draft *PPS14* was issued for public consultation in November 2008 as *PPS21*. At the time of writing (July 2009), the final version of the PPS is still awaited. During the course of the review the provisions remain in force, and the outcome of this review could have profound implications for development in both the northern and southern sectors of the North West region. A particular tension here, which we turn to next, is that the Donegal County Development Plan issued in 2006 opted to retain a presumption in favour of rural housing provision, albeit with some new restrictions (Donegal County Council 2006b).

Spatial planning in the Republic of Ireland's Border Region

The Irish National Spatial Strategy (Department of Environment, Heritage and Local Government 2002) identified for the first time a linked Letterkenny–Derry 'gateway'. This was one of the nine national gateways designated in the NSS to encourage balanced regional development, partly to address problems caused by economic overheating in the Greater Dublin area (see Chapter 3). It is the only gateway crossing the border with the north, presented as a mutually beneficial coupling of the two urban centres.

   The lead shown in the NSS, published a year after the RDS, in part reflects the accelerating political attention to cross-border issues in both administrations. However, it is also fair to say that cross-border cooperation does not generate the same political sensitivities in the Republic of Ireland as it does in the north, allowing the National Spatial Strategy to be more forthright in addressing border issues. Perhaps more importantly, both plans reflect a growing realisation of how quickly demilitarisation of the border had resulted in changed behaviour patterns for those who lived and invested in border areas, involving rapidly changing patterns of housing growth and commuting (Paris 2006). More than this, however, the changing political climate in the relations between the Republic and the UK opened up possibilities for a range of joint policy initiatives in areas of mutual concern, not least in tourism.

   In planning, changes were slower to take hold, and while there was some consultation between the two governments, the NSS and RDS were essentially developed separately, rather than as part of an integrated approach to 'all-island' planning (Murray 2004; Harvey *et al.* 2005). As Murray (2004: 240) notes, 'each strategy goes a certain distance but stops short in its own way of embracing the territorial logic of comprehensive spatial planning'. One of the issues we came across in many of our interviews was that while the strategies 'touched' in places, they were for the most part separate documents.

It is important to stress that the preparation of the strategies was a starting point, a useful break from the past in many respects, paving the ways for growing cooperation on strategic planning issues. For instance the regional planning guidelines for the Border Region (Border Region Authority 2004) began to develop further the concept of a Derry/Letterkenny linked 'gateway', incorporating proposals to 'support and promote strategic links with Northern Ireland in order to provide an effective interface between the two economies, capitalising on opportunities and removing impediments to cross-border interaction' (Border Region Authority 2004: 28).

Both regional planning guidance and the subsequent County Development Plan for Donegal sought to address the growth pressures around Letterkenny, with a proposed increase in population from a current base of around 15,000 to 35,000 by 2020 for the town (Donegal County Council 2006b: 11). The approach adopted in the County Donegal Development Plan draws heavily from both the National Spatial Strategy and regional planning guidelines, with an emphasis on developing strong urban centres, involving resisting urban-generated sprawl while still encouraging rural development. The National Spatial Strategy differentiated between such rural-generated demand for housing – which it says should be accommodated where it arises – and urban-generated demand, which it says should be restricted to specified areas allocated in development plans. This approach is premised on the idea of encouraging compact forms of development in selected rural towns and villages in order to promote a higher quality living environment. Despite the NSS statement, there is inevitably some ambiguity between what is regarded as rural- and urban-generated housing development.

The growth in loosely controlled rural housing development has become something of a cause célèbre in County Donegal and elsewhere in Ireland, with associated problems including poor design standards, intrusion on sensitive landscapes, contamination from septic tanks and long-distance commuting (Lynas 2004; McDonald and Nix 2005). The Donegal response to the rapid development of the Derry–Letterkenny area has been to introduce a new settlement strategy involving policies to restrict isolated development in the countryside, and directing new housing in favour of consolidating existing development nodes, mainly larger villages. While the general presumption remains in favour of rural housing development for those with an established 'need', this has been accompanied by a new regime, where development is permitted provided it does not breach certain criteria, including haphazard and ribbon development, unacceptable landscape intrusion, groundwater pollution and causing road safety concerns. In addition, established 'need' to live in an area is spelt out in some detail, to cover those who are an intrinsic part of a rural community, such as farmers and family, returning migrants, those working in the area, and those who have lived in the vicinity for seven years or more.

Urban-generated rural housing is identified as a particular issue for the Donegal parts of the Derry–Letterkenny corridor. In addressing the issue, Donegal planners have established another set of eligibility criteria for those wishing to develop in designated affected areas, such as parents living there at the time of birth, having lived in an area for seven years, or being an integral part of a community (farmers, teachers, those setting up businesses). For rural housing in general and urban-generated rural housing specifically, it remains to be seen how robust the new system is proven to be in practice, given the large number of 'escape clauses' inserted into the relevant sections of the plan. In intent at least, it represents a useful attempt to tighten control over one-off housing developments.

Referring to the views of a one-time president of the Irish Planning Institute, McDonald and Nix (2005) recall how:

> In an article entitled 'How We Wrecked Rural Ireland', MacCabe wrote: 'Go up any rural road and you'll find nests of bungalows all over the place. It is now out of hand and many planning authorities . . . have thrown in the towel.' Donegal and Kerry were 'beyond redemption' while Kildare was heading the same way.
>
> (McDonald and Nix 2005: 110)

Clearly Donegal planners would argue that the 2006 County Development Plan demonstrates that they have not yet thrown in the towel. But they must necessarily operate in a context where strong political support exists within central and local government for the rights of rural dwellers to build houses on their land (McDonald and Nix 2005) and more generally to encourage development in order to support rural services (Scott 2006).

Borders, border regions and north–south cooperation

The history of territorial struggles in Ireland leading up to the peace process in the 1990s undoubtedly exacerbated the impact that all state borders have on the economic and social life of regions bordering them. Truncating the city of Derry from much of its natural hinterland, until recently tight border controls, and mistrust between politicians either side reinforced the role of national territory. Borders separating nation states typically act as disjunctures to economic and spatial development, with border regions such as North West Ireland subject to different political, administrative, legal and fiscal jurisdictions which can act as barriers to cross-border activity and trade. Borders then can negatively affect regional economies by splitting economic catchment areas and by increasing transaction costs. Conversely, uneven fiscal regimes, for instance, differential petrol taxes, can promote some forms of cross-border activity. Many border regions though tend to be both economically disadvantaged and viewed as peripheral within the national spatial economy, an issue reflected in the remote North West of Ireland. However, with the demilitarisation of the border and the relaxation of controls during the 1990s, there has been a search in particular for new forms of economic interaction (Paris 2006), recognising the territorial logic of a North West cross-border region and the benefits to both communities of cooperation.

Following the Belfast Agreement cross-border cooperation has attracted new EU programmes and increased funding (Anderson and O'Dowd 1999a). Both the Republic and Northern Ireland have enjoyed Objective 1 status, bringing in large amounts of EU funding for structural readjustment programmes, though this funding stream is now being reduced. Additional funding was directed towards the peace process itself via the PEACE programme, which is unique to Ireland, while border regions have been major beneficiaries from INTERREG programmes. Physical and transport infrastructure projects feature prominently in these initiatives, together with relatively easy to agree initiatives such as cross-border cooperation on economic development and trade, cultural exchange and leisure facilities (Anderson and O'Dowd 1999a; Scott 1999).

In addition to the formal institutions established as a result of the Belfast Agreement, there has been a proliferation of local organisations involved in the Irish border regions. In fact local authority cooperation goes back a number of years; the North West Region Cross Border Group was established in the 1970s, with Murray (1998) suggesting that there were some 500 bodies cooperating on a north–south basis in 1998, covering research institutes, trade bodies, business groupings and NGOs. While all positive initiatives in terms of breaking down previous barriers to cooperation, the proliferation of institutions has led Murtagh and Kelly (2006: 242) to argue that 'the overload of structures has created a confusing and competitive governance map', making it difficult to see where or how decisions are made. Though variable in their aims and their impacts, it is fair to say that some of these cross-border groups have become highly effective lobbying groups, forcing the two national governments to take seriously the issues faced by border regions.

One of the intriguing features of border cooperation has been the leading role played by the private sector (Anderson and O'Dowd 1999b: 692). In the North West Region the chambers of commerce on either side of the border came together to identify and address shared problems, including deficits in infrastructure provision which were held to be restricting opportunities for economic development (Colin Buchannan and Partners 2003). Acknowledging the spatial nature of many of these issues, unusually for a grouping of business interests, the chambers have strongly promoted the concept of integrated cross-border spatial planning. A business representative explained how spatial planning was seen as a way of attracting more investment into the North West Region: 'We try to use the regional gateway and the concepts of the *Regional Development Strategy* as a means of levering in more private sector investment' (Interview NI12, business stakeholder, 2006). What is interesting here is that spatial planning is seen by the business community as a positive mechanism for promoting the west of the region. Following this lead, local governments have joined together to establish joint cause across the border, notably lobbying for improved road infrastructure

(Irish Central Border Area Network (ICBAN) and North West Region Cross Border Group (NWRCBG) 2006). Interestingly both the lobby documents noted in this paragraph were part-financed by the EU. Also interesting is that governmental actors saw such initiatives as helpful in various ways:

> because in many ways that type of cooperation, economic and otherwise, provides the cornerstones for on-going . . . within the Good Friday Agreement, those sort of ad hoc groups both sides of the border provide the political impetus to engage.
>
> (NI16, former civil servant, 2006)

The principal actors in the formal cross-border institutions are the civil servants in the relevant government departments in Northern Ireland and the Republic. Together with their ministers they determine the form and extent of cooperation in each of the areas designated for cooperation in the Good Friday Agreement. Initiatives are underway in all of these areas but not without problems caused by jurisdictional and fiscal differences; for instance, differences in corporate tax rates affect industrial location, while differences in housing taxation greatly affect housing markets in the border areas.

Since the publication of the two national spatial strategies the momentum for cross-border infrastructure development has rapidly gathered pace. The new National Development Plan for Ireland (2007–2013), for instance, commits the Irish government to substantial expenditure on infrastructure in the border regions both north and south of the actual border. Priorities identified in the National Development Plan include:

> The implementation of an integrated spatial planning strategy for the Gateway; further improvement in road links to the region; enhancing the capacity and resilience of energy support networks; strengthening telecoms infrastructure throughout the region; development of the City of Derry airport; cross-border collaboration in the development of the skills base in the region; and improvements in access to health and educational services on a cross-border basis.
>
> (Irish Government 2007: 97)

These proposals received a guarded welcome in Northern Ireland, where the money was welcomed warmly, but not without concerns on the part of some unionist politicians that such moves were 'raising the prospect of reunification of the island by economic stealth' (Bowcott 2007). The resumption of devolved government in Northern Ireland has seen growing signs that the border region issue merited substantial investment, using both internal and external funds. For instance, the *Building a Better Future: Programme for Government 2008–2011* (NI Executive 2008a) notes that:

> We cannot tackle the challenges we face alone. To help us deliver on our priorities, we are committed to fostering and promoting our

North/South and East/West linkages, through day to day contact between the relevant administrations, and through the North South Ministerial Council and the British Irish Council. In these contexts, we will continue to take forward mutually beneficial and practical co-operation with the British and Irish Governments and other administrations.

(NI Executive 2008a: 20)

The rationale for international cross-border working is further spelt out in *Investment Strategy for Northern Ireland 2008–2018* (NI Executive 2008b: 11), which argues that: 'Co-operation in developing infrastructure, where appropriate, will help ensure more efficient planning and joined-up delivery of key projects, resulting in better value for money, economies of scale in public investment and better deals from financial markets.'

As might be expected, the main emphasis to date has been on transport and tourism projects, particularly new roads and continuing support for Derry Airport. With Derry just 40 minutes' drive away from Belfast International Airport, Derry Airport makes little sense other than in a North West region context. On rail, the issues are similarly difficult. There is currently a very slow and circuitous route between Belfast and Derry, which was supported in the RDS but very soon after proposals were mooted for closing down some or all of the route. By contrast the North West Chambers of Commerce would like to see the line made into a fast route with an extended connection into Letterkenny. Likewise, there are discussions about extending gas pipelines from Derry into the Republic. Cooperation in such infrastructure initiatives seems the only logical way forward now, but there is still a lack of a clear institutional framework for this in the North West.

Health infrastructure has recently emerged as a major concern in the North West. The issues here are inherently spatial – parts of the North West are remote from major urban centres, and in some parts of the Republic, particularly remoter areas and some border regions, facilities in Northern Ireland are more readily accessible than those in the south. In the context of the rapid population growth in the Letterkenny area, some of it driven by movement from Northern Ireland, there appears to be considerable use of cross-border facilities among the new generation of cross-border commuters and second home owners, not always legally:

> Again you hear anecdotal stories about people using their local knowledge about where the best service is . . . Now they are only anecdotal stories . . . but if they exist it is important to understand the dynamics of that . . . to help us plan well for medical services in these areas . . . Can we deliver better medical services in border areas by doing so jointly . . . absolutely!
>
> (Interview NI13, civil servant, 2006)

Considerable problems exist in searching for a solution to this issue, not least in relation to funding since Northern Ireland has a universal health service free at the point of delivery, while the south does not, so interchangeability of entitlement is not possible (Harvey *et al.* 2005). Interestingly enough, European funding via the INTERREG programme is proving influential at this early stage of cooperation, with a programme called CAWT setting up pilots for improving cross-border cooperation, from people accessing out-of-hours general practitioner services in Derry from across the border, to hospitals sharing information on addressing kidney disease.

There have also been important tensions in recent decisions about where to locate major new investments in hospitals, and whether to make these decisions based on national territorial concerns, or in the context of the wider North West. For instance, in Northern Ireland

> the strategic plan for health here again didn't start off with the RDS . . . with priorities established regionally . . . The big debate was where the hospital was going to go between Enniskillen and Omagh . . . and again it wasn't about which is the better infrastructure? . . . Which is the better catchment? . . . Where does this make best sense in terms of spatial planning? . . . So again there was a spatial issue to be debated, that was never really rehearsed.
>
> (Interview NI8, academic, 2006)

In the end Enniskillen got the go-ahead in 2005 to start building a new acute and emergency services hospital, while Omagh facilities are to be substantially upgraded. The Investment Plan (NI Executive 2008b) for the region does not make specific links to gateways or hubs, or to cross-border health issues. Instead it makes considerable play of new facilities being built so that most people would be within 45 minutes' access for emergency, acute and maternity facilities, and all within one hour, implying an alternative spatialised vision for accessing hospital facilities.

Meantime plans to concentrate expertise in certain aspects of cancer care within the Republic have led to major public debate about proposals to reduce the level of coverage in the North West, with patients expected to travel further in the future, to Dublin or Belfast, rather than Sligo. The plans provoked considerable local controversy, even though they were presented as rational in terms of health and spatial planning, being supported by many in the medical profession:

> Maybe there's even evidence that the binary approach to provision of infrastructure is beginning to break down . . . In terms of hospitals . . . it's interesting that in the provision of specialist cancer care treatment in the North West . . . our own health strategy recognises that we can't really be fixed about where competency rests . . . or where facilities rest in terms of providing an advanced cancer care treatment facility in the North West . . . It's medicine that should provide that and what's in the best interest of patients . . . and it could be provided on a shared basis.
>
> (Interview NI14, Irish civil servant, 2006)

What is interesting is how the debate subsequently evolved in a spatially informed way, with the Irish government's (2007) National Development Plan investment proposals for north–south cooperation including two items relating specifically to health:

- Comprehensive studies on health and education co-operation to be over-seen by the responsible Departments and agencies, North and South;
- Maximising the potential for cross-border cancer services, building on the project to provide services for Co Donegal.

(Irish Government 2007: Executive summary, p. 20)

The NDP also sets out specific plans for each of the Republic's 'Gateways', including Letterkenny–Derry. Proposed expenditure includes a commitment to provide: 'Improvements to the stock of healthcare and social infrastructure such as regional hospital and specialist care services on a shared basis between Donegal and facilities in Northern Ireland' (Irish Government 2007: 31).

So while cross-border healthcare issues were not initially conceived in terms of the national spatial strategy, the solution to it is being sought in part through the spatial planning apparatus, including the spatial strategy being prepared for the North West, which we turn to next.

Towards a spatial strategy for North West Ireland

Cross-border cooperation on strategic spatial planning had been taking place in a low key sense since work started on the two national strategies, involving an informal network of key actors in the two administrations. This work was then taken forward at a more formal level through the British–Irish Governmental Conference, with the two governments commissioning work to look at the integration of the National Spatial Strategy and Regional Development Strategy, which inevitably pointed to gaps and the potential to do better (International Centre for Local and Regional Development 2006). This was followed up in May 2006 when the Intergovernmental Conference gave a commitment to a new cross-border North West Gateway Initiative, which would include a non-statutory integrated spatial plan and development framework focusing on the Derry-Letterkenny gateway – consultants were commissioned to prepare the plan.

Both inside government and outside there is strong support both sides of the border for a North West Spatial Strategy, in part recognising the need to address the infrastructure underspending of the past and also the need to address the specific problems and new opportunities associated with the border regions. The plan itself will be a non-statutory policy instrument, but hopes are high that it will be influential in shaping the future investment strategies of both governments. It was commissioned from private sector consultants, who were encouraged to think creatively, building from previous studies rather than replicating them.

That's the whole point in what we're trying to do in the North West is actually to look at the North West taking the border away . . . That's not making a political statement, it's about looking at the North West and how it works . . . you come up with different conclusions when you remove the border . . . turning things round so that people are actually looking at each other and recognising the cross-border dynamics that do exist.

(Interview NI13, civil servant, 2006)

Already signs of change in attitudes to the border are permeating the official spatial plans of both north and south, where both governments are currently reviewing and revising their earlier national spatial strategies. In the north, the interim review of the RDS published in 2008 shows a key diagram where clear links are made to the Republic's National Spatial Strategy (see below), unlike the earlier key diagram in 2001. It also contains a specific policy on improving links with neighbouring regions in the south (DRD 2008: 27).

While the logic of planning for social and physical infrastructure provision on a cross-border basis is irrefutable, a comprehensive approach to spatial planning in the North West region must also address more complex issues such as how to manage the location of new housing development and employment sites, with both sensitive political issues in the region. Not surprisingly then a number of issues arose in our interviews that suggest *implementing* such a strategy will not be without its problems, not least in housing which has become a major cross-border issue.

Paris (2006: 206) suggests that the rapid development of housing in the North West area during the early years of the twenty-first century 'resulted in some of the fastest growing electoral districts in the Republic of Ireland being located immediately across the border from Derry in County Donegal'. This has created enormous localised pressure on infrastructure, in particular roads. Our interviews also revealed widely held concerns that rapid housing growth in the Derry–Letterkenny corridor was promoting unsightly urban sprawl and haphazard rural housing development (Figure 4.3), associated with under-provision of basic services and infrastructure. Typical comments included:

Donegal is just a disaster . . . I was up there last week on the west coast . . . it was just obscene . . . and the people building houses there are mostly English-speaking northerners . . . It's just . . . do-what-you-want!

(Interview NI8, academic, 2006)

[I]f people in Donegal are happy with bungalows in every other field . . . that's up to them. We don't want that but that's our business.

(Interview NI12, business stakeholder, 2006)

*4.3 Fields of bungalows, near Letterkenny, Donegal. One of our respondents told us:
'The joke round here now is that bungalows are our main cash crop'.*

They've just let it rip [in Letterkenny] . . . It's just horrendous . . .
there's just one long traffic jam coming down the hill in the morning
. . . It's outrageous.

(Interview NI9, academic, 2006)

The issue is fundamentally a cross-border one because so much of the
housing growth in the Republic is said to be fuelled by people moving in
from the north. There are many reasons for this. In the immediate aftermath of
the demilitarisation of the border at least, housing was relatively cheap on the
Republican side of the border and a relatively lax attitude existed to allowing
housebuilding in rural areas, while house sales were not liable to stamp duty,
unlike the north, and attracted no domestic tax. The system of control on new
rural housebuilding in Northern Ireland, while more relaxed than that in mainland UK, was considered to be tighter than that in the Republic, even prior to
publication of draft *PPS14: Sustainable Development in the Countryside*
(DRD 2006a) and the removal of the presumption in favour of rural housing
development. Our interviews were mostly held before the formal publication
of Donegal County Council's proposals to restrict certain types of housing
development in rural areas.

Part of the problem which exists is that the changes in behaviour are so
dramatic and recent that not a lot of firm evidence exists about the nature and
scale of cross-border movement, not helped by the differing data collection
timeframes on the two sides of the border. Despite the efforts to fill this gap,
as one central government planner told us:

> when you start to look at the housing market in the North West you end up very quickly in the world of anecdotes. It's quite difficult to really understand that, yet it's an important dynamic because people do make life choices about where they are going to buy a house based on prices of the houses . . . the stamp duty they have to pay . . . the rates . . . all those issues. Many, many people live on one side of the border and work on the other side.
>
> (Interview NI13, civil servant, 2006)

In similar vein, no one yet quite fully understands the underlying causes of the economic boom in the Letterkenny area, which appear to be a mixture of 'catch up' with the rest of the Irish economy, differences in tax regimes in the two countries, and possibly also the benefits of becoming part of the hinterland of the city of Derry. It is difficult to see evidence yet of Derry benefiting much from Letterkenny's growth. Given such issues, it is difficult to see how the cross-border spatial plan in itself will be able to address major spatial development imbalances without wider government changes. As one civil servant told us in understated fashion: '[Fiscal] decisions that are taken in Number 11 Downing Street or in Dublin have potentially quite big impacts on the context of the border' (Interview NI13, civil servant, 2006).

Hard borders, soft spaces?

> So I think you're going to find the border geography completely reframed . . . instead of seeing a border with north and south you're going to see a much blurrier zone in which nationalist politics is going to shape a much more positive agenda.
>
> (Interview NI18, academic, 2006)

This chapter reveals that even in Northern Ireland where planning is widely held to be hierarchical and rigidly bureaucratic, the new spatial planning is bringing about massive changes in thinking and practice. It is possible to argue that the various cross-border collaborations of local government, and the recent decision to provide strategic planning for a new international cross-border region, are both classic examples of soft spaces. While fuzzy boundaries seem to be less of a feature, we can see how some of the most clearly articulated challenges to the status quo are coming from the thinking carried out in these mechanisms which cut across rather than align with traditional planning boundaries and thinking. But it is worth emphasising that part of the reason for this lies with the path-breaking work of the Regional Development Strategy in 2001. For it is this which in effect empowered local actors to come together to imagine a new future for the west of Northern Ireland, where it was more than a shadow of Belfast and instead part of a new 'gateway' linking Derry and Letterkenny. It is this rather than the generic ESDP conceptual language which begins to challenge the dominant influence of Belfast in planning for the future of the region.

The political challenge is interesting. The planned reduction in the number of local government units in Northern Ireland from 26 to 11 within the next few years would see a much larger city region local government body for the Derry region. Under the public administration reforms, the responsibilities of new local government bodies will be broader and their capacities stronger than the present-day local authorities. Given the predominantly nationalist politics of the west of the region this could be very significant indeed in opening up the opportunities for greater cooperation between County Donegal and the new Derry local government. While undoubtedly viewed with concern by some, for others it is a major political opening. Sinn Féin, for instance, published its Charter for the North West in February 2007 (www.sinnfein.ie/pdf/nwcharter. pdf), which makes much play of the potential of spatial planning to improve the lot of those who live in the region, calling for a statutory integrated spatial plan which was fully consulted upon and binding on the two governments. It also calls for a fully integrated approach to regional healthcare, and for a regional cancer facility for the North West. Regional politics may turn out to drive or impede the integration process – but it will certainly be evident at every twist and turn.

Politics aside, while it is the intention of those involved to provide an innovative framework for spatial development in the North West, as with previous spatial plans at national level, the real proof of its success will come in turning the new vision into reality. Competition for development is certain to continue and, unless there is some equalisation of rates of property taxation in the two countries it is difficult to see how the tide of development towards the south can be checked, particularly in view of the tightening of planning controls in the north. Indeed many in County Donegal would not want to check development there; economic development tends to be seen as universally beneficial, and while there has been a reaction against housing sprawl in rural Donegal, there is still a political will for more development, as evidenced by the planned doubling of the size of Letterkenny. How the spatial plan for the North West Region addresses these key urban development issues remains to be seen. What it can do without controversy though is improve the quality of future development in the North West, ensuring that the development of physical, social and economic infrastructures takes account of the realities of what is now a permeable border, not least in terms of housing and labour markets.

5

Spatial planning in a devolved Scotland

Introduction

This chapter explores spatial planning in Scotland, arguably the administration where the UK's devolution agenda has gone furthest. Scotland has always had a different planning system from the rest of the UK, so in some respects it has had a head start in establishing its autonomous credentials. Nonetheless devolution has given new impetus to creating a distinctive Scottish approach to planning, changing both the parameters and procedures for regulatory and forward planning. In broad terms this has seen a widening role for planning, granting it a form of metagovernance function for better policy integration, delivered principally through a new national spatial plan – the National Planning Framework – and legislative change.

The Scottish case study presented here centres on policy at Scottish national level and the subnational policies developed for the two city regions centred on Edinburgh and Glasgow in Scotland's 'central belt'.[1] This focus was adopted because:

- The two city regions provided interesting examples of areas with very different socio-economic conditions and institutional histories with regard to strategic spatial planning: Glasgow and West Central Scotland is regarded as having a history of innovative metropolitan-area planning (Wannop 1995; Lloyd and Peel 2005; Goodstadt 2007), while the literature is less positive about Edinburgh and its hinterland's approach (Turok and Bailey 2004; Bramley and Kirk 2005).
- Spatial and economic strategy in Scotland under the Labour administrations of 1999–2007 focused, rhetorically at least, on cities as the 'drivers of the Scottish economy' (e.g. Scottish Executive 2002, 2004a),[2] and particularly on the central belt which became increasingly conceived of as a bipolar metropolitan area (Bailey and Turok 2001).
- Within the two main cities the waterfront areas of each city were examined as they constituted two of Europe's largest regeneration projects, and were

prioritised as the two 'premium spaces' in Scotland's attempts to attract and retain economic investment (Scottish Executive 2004a).

This spatial focus enables an examination of both the impacts of devolution and strengthening city regionalism and of how a potential shift from land use planning to spatial planning is being worked out in the Scottish context. It is particularly valuable in helping understand how new practices emerge and are shaped by institutional history at different levels of governance.

The national socio-economic context

With a population of 5.1 million and a GVA of £86 billion in 2005 (Scottish Government 2007), Scotland is the largest of the devolved administrations and it also has the largest land area. A high proportion of the population is concentrated around the two cities of Glasgow (population of Greater Glasgow 1.75 million) and Edinburgh (population of Greater Edinburgh 1.5 million) in the central belt. Outside the central belt the cities of Aberdeen and Dundee are the only substantial urban agglomerations in an otherwise sparsely populated and predominantly rural landscape.

   Even prior to devolution, the Scottish Office had a good deal of autonomy from Whitehall, while the Scottish Parliament created in 1998 has legislative powers over all matters that are not reserved by the UK Parliament, which

5.1 Scottish Parliament building, Edinburgh

include planning (Figure 5.1). Following devolution the Scottish government embarked on a modernisation programme, although as a more recently established and smaller bureaucracy than Whitehall there was greater emphasis on joined-up service delivery than on interdepartmental policy coordination (Scottish Executive Policy Unit 2000). Following the 2007 elections when the Scottish National Party (SNP) formed a minority government, quite radical changes to the institutional architecture of the government were implemented with departments merged so that just five cross-cutting central departments now exist: Finance and Sustainable Growth (including spatial planning), Health and Wellbeing, Education, Skills, Culture and the Arts, Justice, and Rural Affairs. The SNP's budget priorities are identified as health, education and tackling crime.

The Scottish planning system

The Scottish system has always been separate to that in England and Wales and although generally policy has tended towards convergence with that in the rest of the UK (Allmendinger 2003), the Scottish development plan system also remained distinctive (Cullingworth and Nadin 2006). Scottish local government was also different from that in England, with a two-tier system of regional authorities and local councils until 1996. While regional authorities were abolished in 1996 and replaced by a unitary system of local government, joint working on structure plans was maintained in six areas, including former regional authority areas such as the Glasgow and Edinburgh city regions (Cullingworth and Nadin 2006). A review of strategic planning in Scotland was initiated in 2001 which suggested that, with the proposed National Planning Framework, there would be no need for a higher tier of development plans over much of Scotland. The consultation paper *Making Development Plans Deliver* (Scottish Executive 2004b) and the following *White Paper: Modernising the Planning System* (Scottish Executive 2005) proposed a system of strategic development plans for the four main city regions (Glasgow, Edinburgh, Aberdeen and Dundee) with local development plans elsewhere. This pattern of development plans was incorporated into the Planning (Scotland) Act 2006, which also gave statutory status to the National Planning Framework (NPF), itself published in 2004 (Scottish Executive 2004a).

Executive responsibility for planning in Scotland rests with the Planning Directorate of the Scottish government, which since May 2007 reports to the Minister of Finance and Sustainable Growth. The National Planning Framework is prepared by a team in the Planning Directorate, while Strategic Development Plans are to be prepared by groups of local authorities designated by ministers. Local planning is a function of individual unitary authorities established in the local government reorganisation of 1996. Relations between the national and local tiers are considered to be reasonably positive, in part because of regular meetings, creating a positive culture of collaboration between local and national officials on strategic planning issues.

lanning Framework

preparing a National Planning Framework emerged in *A Review*
Planning (Scottish Executive 2001) and the intention to go
...ஆ with preparations was announced in 2002. The European Spatial
Development Perspective (ESDP) provided a context for and helped steer the
preparation of the NPF. According to Purves (2006: 111), 'The national spatial
framework was seen as a vehicle for addressing the implications of Scotland's
geographical position in Europe and the opportunities and challenges which
that represented within the context of devolved government, European

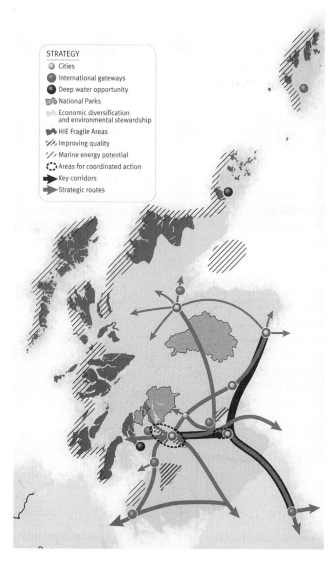

STRATEGY
- Cities
- International gateways
- Deep water opportunity
- National Parks
- Economic diversification and environmental stewardship
- HIE Fragile Areas
- Improving quality
- Marine energy potential
- Areas for coordinated action
- Key corridors
- Strategic routes

*5.2 National
Planning
Framework 1 key
diagram*

Source: Scottish
Executive (2004a).

enlargement and the global economy.' More than this, however, the centrality of a European discourse within Scottish planning practice appears to reflect a shift by the devolved Scottish administration to position itself in Europe as a separate country, distancing itself somewhat from the UK government.

From the outset the NPF was expected to perform a role beyond traditional land use planning, creating a framework for strategic decisions to be taken by the Scottish Executive and to guide other stakeholders in theirs (Figure 5.2). The 2004 Plan attractively laid out ten 'key elements' focused on economic, social and environmental issues, with a heavy dose of infrastructural concern: energy, water, transport, ICT and waste all feature as key elements in their own right. The draft NPF2 is also very much focused on infrastructure questions. For those involved, the preparation of NPFs has helped build agreement around a long-term spatial vision for Scotland (Purves 2006).

Preparation of the original NPF was largely an executive-led rather than politician-led exercise and it was intended to be advisory, having a light touch, rather than be directive (Peel and Lloyd 2007). The rationale for this approach was spelt out for us by one of those involved:

> there are some who feel that we should have a more directive NPF that people must comply with . . . and I'm not keen on that . . . I prefer working with consensus and dialogue. I think it currently works quite well . . . and we have some extensive buy-in from the local authorities.
> (Interview S1, government planner, 2005)

While recognising the benefits of having a national development framework, the lack of direction on issues such as housing numbers was commented upon by several of our interviewees, including those who felt it should have been more comprehensive and used to assign housing targets. More generally there was a concern that:

> The NPF suffers from that tentativeness . . . We're promised that the next one will have a harder edge to it . . . it will start to identify priorities . . . start to make some choices . . . where things should go, and perhaps where things shouldn't go . . . From the narrow house-building perspective, what we've always said to the Executive is that we would like to see some broad guidance about housing growth.
> (Interview S18, housebuilder, 2006)

As one of those centrally involved argues (Purves 2006: 121–122), there have been plenty of critics of the plan, but for all this it has been generally well received within Scotland and also on an international stage as an exemplar of successful spatial planning. As with most other national spatial plans, critics have highlighted the lack of clear mechanisms for moving from plan to implementation, particularly in terms of linking to the investment plans of infrastructure providers. In addition, the level of response to the consultation process was low, which Purves (2006) attributes to low levels of understanding of the likely importance of the first NPF, but which some of our interviewees attributed to the limited efforts made to engage with stakeholders. In many respects the first NPF received similar types of praise and criticism to that found in Wales, with the successes seen to be largely about improving the levels of awareness around an agreed spatial development agenda among other government departments, notably those involved in economic development and transport.

The status of the NPF changed as a result of the Planning Act 2006 which makes it a statutory document and requires it to identify priorities for the long-term spatial development of Scotland. The National Planning Framework 2 (Scottish Government 2009) designated fourteen national developments, mostly strategic transport infrastructure improvements, but with others related to energy grid proposals, one related to drainage, and one relating to the 2014 Commonwealth Games. The NPF2 document then is shaping up to play an increasing role in coordinating the provision of infrastructure in Scotland, reflecting some of the experience under NPF1. Although integrated policy is a recurrent theme, inevitably there are structural issues in achieving this. For instance, the separation of transport policy (Scottish Executive) from transport delivery (Transport Scotland) and the establishment of Regional Transport Partnerships with boundaries which are not coterminous with strategic planning areas add layers of complexity when it comes to integrating spatial planning with transport.

The central belt: the socio-economic context

The economies of Edinburgh and Glasgow performed well in the early 2000s (see Table 5.1). Edinburgh's economy was particularly successful and labour market participation rates, for example, reached levels not previously thought possible here. This success has, however, brought its own problems not least in relation to issues traditionally situated squarely within land use planning's purview, such as housing supply and affordability (for more on this, see Docherty and McKiernan 2008). A further consequence of a tight housing market has been increasing commute lengths, as people struggled to match

Table 5.1 Key economic statistics, Scotland

	Edinburgh	Glasgow	Scotland	UK
Population (2005)	458,000	579,000	5,095,000	60,238,000
Economic activity rates (2005)	77%	66%	75%	78%
ILO unemployment (January 2008)	4.8%	7.3%	5.0%	5.2%

Source: Scottish Executive (2007); Office for National Statistics (2008).

housing and employment locations. Edinburgh's infrastructure needs have been very much to the fore in recent spatial planning debates, notably involving transportation and the provision of water services to new development. In short, there has been a concern that the effects of Edinburgh's economic success are not being dealt with as well as they might be, particularly where they impact on neighbouring municipalities in the city region, with spatial planning considered partly responsible. Unlike Glasgow there was no strong tradition of city region cooperation to draw on in moving towards metropolitan region planning.

Glasgow can be regarded as Scotland's only true metropolitan area: the travel-to-work area encompasses some 2 million people, one-third of the Scottish population. The city region has the fixed infrastructure of a metropolis connecting the centre with adjacent areas and a number of satellite settlements. To some this suggests a greater need for strategic spatial planning, drawing from the substantial institutional history in this area (see Goodstadt 2007). Glasgow's economy performed well in the first few years of the twenty-first century, building on the foundations of an urban renaissance begun in the late 1980s. This stabilised and turned around several decades of extreme population loss. The City had, however, a persistent problem of 100,000 long-term unemployed and an inclusion discourse surrounding this issue was very evident in policy debates. The dual city idea was thus very apparent here, in contrast to Edinburgh where the sheer strength of the economy had lifted many back into the labour market.

The rest of this chapter explores the Scottish case to shed light on the book's overall themes. It first examines the national picture in Scotland and how devolution has led to furthering difference in spatial planning systems and practices between Scotland and the rest of the UK. It then looks at the subnational scale in depth. Finally, conclusions are drawn as to the future for Scottish planning and what the case tells us with regard to the book's main concerns.

Rescaling Scottish governance

Filling in the nation state

The National Planning Framework represents a major 'filling-in' of the national level. However, despite its development and the production of a raft of new policy documents, spatial planning changed little in the period 1999–2008 in terms of the relative powers of local and central administrations. Other policy sectors with strong links to planning exhibited far more change. For example, transport policy and provision experienced a great deal of devolution from Westminster to Edinburgh, but this was no 'double-devolution' wherein powers cascaded down to local government also. Despite the creation of Regional Transport Partnerships, transport as a sector effectively 'recentralised', focused on the Scottish Parliament rather than on the UK Parliament. Local authorities too had limited transport powers and funding, and this was little changed (see also MacKinnon *et al.* 2008). For some this was problematic, with the perception that spending is: '98.9 per cent within the control of the Scottish Executive . . . we [locally] have literally peanuts to spend on transport' (Interview S23, regional planner, 2006). Given the large increases in funding for transport nationally, this represented a significant 'filling-in' of the state at the Scottish national level and was proving highly influential in shaping future development patterns and planning policies (see case study below). Similarly, water infrastructure was firmly in the control of the national government as privatisation in this sector had not gone as far as in England. Organisational and funding difficulties meant that this proved to be a significant problem for local actors in realising their planning goals (also see later).

The Planning Act 2006 was interesting for its attempt to change the hard institutional infrastructure to drive policy integration. It did this through requiring strategies in selected policy areas to pay attention in their work to the production and implementation of spatial plans. Agencies in health and transport, for example, were required to line up their actions and their spending plans with the national and subnational planning frameworks. This is clearly potentially a major force for policy integration, but how it works in practice proved not so simple, an issue which is explored in the case studies below.

Filling in the city region

The policy focus on cities in Scotland post-devolution gathered pace throughout the early twenty-first century. Given that Scottish cities are typically governed by a number of local authorities this focused attention on local authority collaboration for some form of city region or metropolitan-scale planning. The designation of four city regions in 2004 was one culmination of this thinking. These were to be governed in a way modelled on the approach taken in Glasgow-Clyde Valley (GCV) following the abolition of Regional Councils in Scotland in 1996. Here, the eight local authorities set up a strategic executive body to undertake a number of functions including land use planning. By contrast, some other strategic bodies had no permanent executives. Strategic spatial planning at the city region level thus gained authority as part of, and partly as a result of, an emphasis on cities and their importance as economic drivers in Scottish policy generally. The setting up of Regional Transport Partnerships also contributed to a filling-in of governance arrangements between the national level and local authorities.

Fluid scales of intervention

Devolution to, and the filling-in of, the city region scale did not prevent national government from intervening in specific spaces locally. In Edinburgh, the Scottish Executive led the production of the West Edinburgh Planning Framework (WEPF), arguing that central government intervention was necessary given the scale of the challenge in this part of the city. Some interviewees suggested that such intervention was only necessary as 'Edinburgh Council was not really geared up to deal with that [the scale of the issues]' (Interview S2, national planning body, 2005). Certainly the structure plan could have gone further in defining a vision for this area but, as we will explore further in this chapter, the Lothian authorities were seen by government planners as unwilling or unable to address the issue in a timely way through the structure plan.

It was assumed in the NPF that the Executive would get involved in other places of national significance but this did not happen. In the Clyde Valley, also designated as an area of national significance in the NPF, the social and intellectual capital developed during the production of the Structure Plan meant that national intervention was resisted. So, the Executive appeared to act pragmatically in areas where there were issues in the national interest and where the capacity to deal with them by local players was absent or there was a lack of willingness to deploy such capacity. Processes of filling in and hollowing out are not then quite as simple as they first appear. Clearly the Scottish Executive retains the power to intervene and the bases for doing so were confirmed in legislation in 2008. However, the power to resist also exists locally, if the potential to tackle problems arising there can be demonstrated.

This vignette highlights some of the complexities surrounding the fluid scales and scope of planning in Scotland. In the next section we detail some of the processes behind strategic planning and some of the objects of planning attention in such work.

Strategic spatial planning in Scotland's central belt

In the west of Scotland there is a long history of public sector collaboration in strategic planning (Wannop 1995; Goodstadt 2007). This was one explanation for the eight authorities in west central Scotland continuing to collaborate after the abolition of Strathclyde Regional Council in 1996, though the Glasgow-Clyde Valley area is smaller than that of Strathclyde. In planning, a permanent executive, the Glasgow-Clyde Valley Structure Plan Joint Committee (GCVSPJC), was set up to develop a structure plan and deliver its objectives. The committee's efforts in relation to the Plan and other initiatives have been much lauded in the planning profession and its operation provides the model for Scotland's future city region planning as envisaged in the Planning Act 2006. The work of the committee provided much of the focus for this case study.

Glasgow-Clyde Valley is then an area with a long institutional history of collaboration to build on. An interesting question concerns why GCV took the path it did in building this strategic capacity. Some of the answer lies in the issues detailed earlier, in relation to its truly metropolitan nature, for example. Part of the reason also lies in the greater consensus among local authorities that the key issue facing the city region was to go for growth and to capture funds from the EU, UK and Scottish administrations.

In contrast, in the Edinburgh-Lothian City Region (ELCR) there was less common ground in dealing with growth and its externalities. Here, the four local authorities had less institutional capital to draw on in dealing with such questions with tensions apparent between them, leading to a perception that 'because of the relationships between some of the authorities . . . [growth management] is not quite under the control it should be' (Interview S23, regional planner, 2006).

The main area of scrutiny in this chapter are the structure plans for the two city regions centred on Edinburgh and Glasgow and activity associated with them. The Glasgow-Clyde Valley structure plans analysed here include the one adopted in 2000, alongside three alterations that have been published since and a subsequent replacement plan, rewritten but very much a development of the 2000 Plan, which was approved by Scottish ministers in 2008. The 2000 Plans all focus on urban regeneration. Such activity is centred on a spine running through the conurbation, loosely centred on the river Clyde. This overturned an emphasis in previous decades on growing peripheral parts of the conurbation through new towns and edge city business parks. Complementing this were smaller regeneration initiatives focused on town centres and neighbourhoods and an emphasis on promoting a green infrastructure network for the conurbation involving public spaces and linking green corridors. Subsequent alterations to the Plan introduced the Ravenscraig area (a former steelworks) as a regeneration priority and extended the Clyde regeneration area. For those involved, the 2000 Plan and those following are notable for building a widely based partnership which sought to produce broad strategic priorities and to move away from what might be thought of as traditional prescriptive regulatory controls, leaving these instead to local plans (Goodstadt 2007). To ensure implementation followed the broad strategic priorities set out in the structure plan, local plans were largely produced in tandem, with seven of the eight local authorities producing local plans within a year of the structure plan.

The Edinburgh-Lothian Structure Plan under scrutiny here was adopted in 2004 and prepared by the Edinburgh-Lothian Structure Plan Joint Liaison Committee. It was less clear about its strategic spatial priorities. This lack of clarity reflected not only the diversity of the area's needs, but also a lack of agreement among the local authorities on urban growth and growth management, a disagreement that was also evident 'among the development industry, among communities, among almost everyone really, about the spatial strategy' (Interview S18, housebuilder, 2006). This problem of institutional coordination may get worse as the Planning Act Scotland 2006 has enforced a widening of the city region structure plan area to take in the councils of Fife and the Scottish Borders, to become operative in 2009. The relationships between these local authorities and the existing structure plan ones were also considered by some to be disjointed. Adding to the sense of moving ahead before full negotiation had taken place was that the authorities moved quickly to get their local plans approved prior to new city region governance arrangements coming into being, effectively committing themselves to their own priorities before they might get hide-bound by any joint agreements.

The chapter now turns to look at how planning has acted as a locus for policy integration in Scotland.

Policy integration in the Scottish territory

The Scottish governance line usefully highlights how vertical linkages were used to translate material from one spatial scale to another without need for further exploration. Thus, the European Spatial Development Perspective provided context for the National Planning Framework but consulting it was not considered necessary in the production of subnational plans. Instead ESDP aims were assumed to be reflected in the NPF, and it was this latter representation that was translated locally. Interestingly, the ESDP did become part of argumentation that sought to elevate the Edinburgh-Glasgow bipolar metropolitan area into a higher order of settlement in a pan-European economic space. This process was thought by one stakeholder to be a two-way flow of information and influence, with the ESDP shaped by actors in Scotland as well as these actors taking their cue from it, in part due to the personal links between the key Scottish players and their counterparts in Europe.

Vertical integration between the NPF, structure plans, local plans and local regeneration initiatives such as the Clyde Waterfront appeared good in the central belt, particularly in the west, reflecting a close working relationship between many planners who cohered into a typical policy community (Marsh and Rhodes 1992). Thus while a hierarchy was acknowledged, it was clear that ideas moved up and down it accordingly:

> [the NPF] did pick up with our priorities and pushed them through into major cabinet statements . . . it tried to create a balance between the major priorities that were emerging from the bottom-up [and from top-down].
>
> (Interview S23, regional planner, 2006)

The Clyde Waterfront regeneration, for example, was a local initiative that was taken on board by the Scottish Executive, which now recognises it as a major opportunity in the NPF and in the National Regeneration Strategy. A waterfront development strategy is being developed in collaboration between the Scottish Executive, Scottish Enterprise and the four local authorities centrally involved.

> So what we have in the plan is now carried through into the Scottish Executive's regeneration policy statement. And from the policy statement we are having Clyde Gateway as a national URC [Urban Regeneration Company]. And Clyde riverside . . . that's also going to be a URC. So the government has picked these up . . . That wouldn't have happened without this phalanx . . . of us and all the other agencies pushing for the major priorities and major projects.
>
> (Interview S23, regional planner, 2006)

In the Edinburgh and the Lothians, on the other hand, it was evident in the regeneration of the Edinburgh and Leith Waterfronts that there was a lack of dialogue and coordination between the agencies involved:

> I think the feeling in Edinburgh is that the market has been sub-
> stantially overestimated . . . It started because it [the Edinburgh and
> Leith Waterfront], was the only place you could build on . . . it's
> beginning to falter because the scale of demand isn't there . . . And
> the support in the local plans in terms of design and infrastructure
> isn't there to the extent that it perhaps is in Glasgow.
>
> (Interview S18, housebuilder, 2006)

In the Edinburgh metropolitan region it was clear that problems arose from a lack of dialogue and coordination between local authorities, attributed in part to personality and political differences between politicians in the different areas. Many local authorities were performing future visioning exercises but there was a need to ensure more consistency across these visions: the 2004 structure plan granted a great deal of flexibility for local plans to go in different directions, which was sometimes to the detriment of more strategic planning goals. From a national perspective, 'the structure plan and local plans . . . conform . . . but I think the extent to which the different councils then pursue different agendas is evident' (Interview S1, government planner, 2005).

This flexible process did have its drawbacks in the absence of a clear national steer in some policy areas (see the NPF discussion above). For example, in terms of new housing provision local authorities were collectively planning for many more new units than the Scottish Executive. This created particular difficulty when coordinating infrastructure provision, especially in the case of water where Scottish Water's dependence on national funding meant that whatever demand was assumed locally, there would be funding only for the number deemed necessary by the Executive. It was not surprising therefore that actors within and beyond the immediate planning policy community wanted planning to exhibit a greater degree of certainty in thinking about future provision.

That said, in general we found a greater degree of integration and cooperation in Scotland than in some of our other cases. Priorities were decided mutually, reflecting the 'governance village' in Scotland which in turn reflected the scale of the polity here vis-à-vis that centred on Westminster. As a result the interaction between and within policy scales was far more apparent than in many other places. Thus priorities derived from the local level, among a tightly integrated local policy community, were adopted nationally. As one person explained to us, 'the government has picked these [Clyde Gateway and Clyde Riverside] up . . . that wouldn't have happened without this phalanx . . . of us and all the other agencies pushing' (Interview S23, regional planner, 2006).

But the 'village' could also act to help pursue and legitimise a more nakedly political, clientelist, form of decision-making. Major decisions on investment in planning and infrastructure in the central belt did not always seem to take their cue from the NPF, or from the decision-making systems put in place to help make choices between schemes (Scotland on Sunday 2006; Docherty *et al.* 2007). The village has many positives, however. Priorities, territorial and otherwise, are known and shared, even among national ministers. It also explains how things get done in the sense that ministers are often looking for issues to champion, often derived locally, in a way they do not do so much in Westminster.

Spatial planning as integrator

At national level there has been progress on bringing different policy communities together around a spatial planning agenda, although some interviewees see a continuing difficulty here, largely in relation to investment programmes, a long-standing issue for planning: 'there is an issue about whether the silos in the Executive . . . are doing enough to engage with that [integration] agenda. It is a case at the smaller detailed level of aligning spending programmes' (Interview S16, local planner, 2006).

But links between policy sectors were improving, not least since the Scottish Executive has committed to an approach for improving the level of integration between spatial decision-making and major capital investment. While the NPF helped the Executive to perform this role in coordinating between planning and other policy sectors, some saw this as limited with little dialogue and mutual shaping of policy area priorities, such that '[the NPF] feels very much like a cut and paste job between each executive department' (Interview S22, environmental NGO, 2006). This said, it should be acknowledged that this is a young institution mobilising a new policy mechanism, so we might reasonably expect greater sophistication in future iterations.

Certainly getting public sector policy agendas coaligned was seen as a first step in a better integration of policy and delivery, involving a continuous massaging of networks. Again the scale of Scotland relative to England made this easier, since the major agencies, particularly in the public sector, knew each other personally and understood each others' respective organisational agendas. This has helped in developing priority areas for intervention such as the two waterfronts, for instance, such that priority areas have 'grown organically over a number of years until they reached the significance of being strategic and national scale priorities' (Interview S16, local planner, 2006).

This consultative emphasis was extended beyond the Executive and the wider public sector. Such an emphasis at times seemed overly corporatist, but there is no doubt that it helped actors to pursue common agendas, with the Executive said to have an open door policy, including for landowners and developers, creating a largely invisible network of interactions. Such openness was talked of very positively by most of our respondents and appeared to represent a step change from previous levels of engagement. The drive for greater participation from stakeholders does, however, have a downside, at least for some of those expected to respond to successive consultations: 'I made an estimate of how many consultations the Scottish Executive alone had sent us . . . it was hundreds . . . nine hundred and something. And that's just the Scottish Executive' (Interview S14, commercial stakeholder, 2006). Certainly, in debates about the Planning Act some stakeholder groups were arguing that now they felt over-consulted and were keen to see action and not just consultation.[3] There was a degree of irony here in that the Planning Act was part driven by a desire for both greater community engagement and delivery.

In GCV we found evidence of the considerable work being done to join up policy, with partnership working strongly in evidence. This approach engaged other policy sectors traditionally close, but not as close as they might be to planning, for instance, utility companies which have sought to make active inputs into planning processes, relating to their asset base, spare capacity and pinch points, as an aid to those deciding on future development patterns. Efforts at network building appear to have developed sufficient social and intellectual capital to overcome many traditional barriers and contributed to the development of a spatial planning that broke free from a narrow land use focus, something appreciated by national policy-makers: 'they [the GCV SP Team] have worked hard to bring an integrated view . . . from the local enterprise companies . . . from the local health boards' (Interview S3, civil servant, 2005). It should be added that this work was perhaps both necessitated and made more difficult by the greater degree of complexity in west central Scotland than other areas, including the ELCR, due to the sheer numbers of stake-holders.

Information sharing was then vital to the successful *delivery* of the Structure Plan. How this was done depended on a permanent team of staff, which was lacking in ELCR. Structure and local plans were co-produced and as part of structure plan development, statements of 'common perspectives' were drawn up with relevant stakeholders in particular policy areas. Out of these Joint Action Programmes were developed with responsibilities for delivery allocated. This ongoing effort meant that the Plan was not just a static document, it began and maintained a process of delivery among a wide range of stake-holders, driving an integration process as it did so.

Such action planning was a prominent feature in Scotland. Planners themselves were often called managers, rather than officers, perhaps reflecting coordinative and delivery, rather than regulatory functions. The new legislation requires strategic plans to be accompanied by action plans which might develop this action orientation further.

More locally, the city region scale networking above was often replicated, both across scales and to other policy communities. For instance,

> in the Glasgow [Waterfront] case I think it [development] was driven more successfully by the planning system . . . than in Edinburgh . . .
>
> The structure plan [was important] but where I think Glasgow scores is that Glasgow City Council has driven that process on . . . particularly through its most recent local plans . . .
>
> I think they are good examples of proactive plans that promote development and give a pretty clear steer on what the City is wanting in terms of design framework and development principles and so on.
>
> (Interview S18, housebuilder, 2006)

In contrast, the Edinburgh Waterfront took longer to come forward in any significant way. This discrepancy in approach partly relates to issues around infrastructure, such as difficulties surrounding the provision of a tram system in Edinburgh. Other stakeholders confirmed that plans appeared to be less well articulated in the East because of the less well-joined-up policy process.

This is not to say that there is a deep consensus in the Glasgow city region; for instance, one environmental group was of the view that 'the structure plan has been very effective in papering over the cracks where local authorities have taken slightly divergent views' (Interview S22, environmental NGO, 2006). However, there is enough institutional social capital for authorities to get some way beyond horse-trading and pork barrel politics to develop a plan that can deliver something more than the sum of the individual authorities' activities. This process has been aided by the renewed attention to urban regeneration and brownfield development in recent years which deflects growth pressures away from wealthier suburban authorities. That said, while the urban renaissance, pro-growth approach had brought forward development, some of it was not considered to be of a great standard in terms of design or in terms of transport provision, again suggesting that all was not perfect with the Glasgow-Clyde Valley model.

A more regulatory approach was in evidence in the Edinburgh-Lothian structure plan. This approach partly reflected the nature of the challenge in the city region, which was to manage and redistribute urban growth and its externalities. However, as a consequence of failing to deal with strategic priorities, ELCR was having a lot of problems controlling growth as a consequence of the lack of an agreed and coordinated approach among the local authorities. The structure plan was effectively sidelined. Having a good plan thus appeared to matter as local authorities struggled to deliver projects and to coordinate development within their boundaries so as to deliver strategic objectives both within their areas and across the wider city region. In this context, the strategic vacuum meant that it felt to some as if the development industry was able to set about cherry picking sites. Development in other words was developer-led rather than plan-led when it came to the wider city region scale.

The approach of the core city in the city region is also important in such instances. For some developers it seemed that '[in the Lothians] you get the sense that Edinburgh is the dominant partner [and] is trying to push some of the negative effects [of growth] elsewhere . . . and they're not dealing with the integration of some of these issues as well as they might' (Interview S18, housebuilder, 2006) (and see Gore and Fothergill 2007: 64). By contrast, the institutional capital and the development of mature political relationships in GCV was generally felt to be much stronger, such that '[some authorities] who are not sharing in the heavy development . . . say okay . . for the betterment of the whole metropolitan region those need to be our priorities . . . nobody has broken line' (Interview S23, regional planner, 2006).

In general terms, there was a broadening of spatial planning's focus with greater connections made to policy areas and policy networks beyond planning. One notable area lay in connections to health agendas which were a prominent driver of wider public policy in the central belt. In the Glasgow city region in particular this attention was driven by the area's position at the bottom of many European health league tables. The creation of health partnerships helped cross-fertilise policy agendas, including planning, and such agendas were often married to others. First, to very significant social inclusion discourses, themselves long-standing drivers of regeneration projects in GCV. Second, alliances were made with an environmental policy nexus, such as the Green Network Partnership Board in Glasgow-Clyde Valley where participation from the four health boards and the Healthy City Partnership drove forward the area's green infrastructure proposals which became part of a National Development in NPF2. This activity also found its way into the GCVSP and subsequent activities of the Structure Plan Team.

Coordinating infrastructure delivery

A key element in spatial planning performing an integrating role lies in its ability to coordinate development with infrastructure. In recent times the UK has struggled to deliver effective infrastructure and to align such efforts with planning strategies. Given the large-scale investments required for substantial housing and commercial development initiatives and the associated risks associated with implementation, caution from infrastructure providers in reaching out beyond their immediate policy communities is not altogether surprising. In an era of tightened public finances and heightened media scrutiny, managers are keen not to create under-utilised capacity and equally not to be left exposed to accusations of failing to invest in improved capacity where it is required. As such their need to manage the high risks associated with providing large-scale, expensive infrastructure programmes is always likely to impact on the ways in which they engage with planning's agenda.

The provision of water and transport infrastructure to serve new development has proved to be particularly difficult, especially in areas of major growth. In relation to transport, privatisation processes and institutional and regulatory change have led to a very fragmented institutional environment. The resultant complexity does not help land use planners to get new development served by transport. As more powers were handed to the Scottish Executive, this problem eased a little, and larger amounts of money for transport in Scotland also helped (Docherty *et al.* 2007). But at national level fragmentation is perpetuated by a split of functions where policy remains in the Scottish Executive, but delivery lies, and even here not exclusively, with Transport Scotland. This implies a degree of separation and the need for more institution building work within the transport policy sector, even before links to other sectors are considered.

Subnationally, the creation of Regional Transport Partnerships (RTPs) appeared to be a missed opportunity for territory-focused integration, with their authority undermined by limited powers and funding. In addition, RTP boundaries were not coterminous with strategic planning boundaries, adding to the coordination required to join up strategies.

The Scottish Executive's transport appraisal guidance recognises the need for integration with land use, which constituted one of five objectives against transport proposals which need to be appraised. But transport stakeholders challenged land allocations and there was a concern that a hierarchy in which planning has power over transport bodies could lead to frictions, particularly if it meant planners taking decisions on whether to go ahead with individual transport projects. The outputs of RTPs and their relationships with plans is thus an ongoing concern to be negotiated in the development of strategies. This involves a maturing set of relationships and there will inevitably be issues, not least in the early years. The tensions at present were certainly very clear in some of our interviews:

> I expect we will include their [Structure Plan] priorities in ours [transport strategy] . . . although I have to say there's no certainty we will do that . . . but I would be very surprised if the solutions we come up with don't reflect what's already in the Structure Plan.
> (Interview S19, regional transport body, 2006)

In relation to water, the infrastructure provider, Scottish Water, had something of a *bête noire* status among the Scottish development industry in the early 2000s, something which emerged strongly in some of our interviews: 'the biggest single frustration for all sectors of the development industry . . . it's been a colossal issue . . . a complete shambles' (Interview S18, housebuilder, 2006). Communication has helped to determine the relationships between the two policy sectors and overcome misconceptions, with the water company frustrated that they felt planners were coming up with large-scale schemes for which they expected the water company to supply capacity for in advance of the plan. While this is, of course, one legitimate model of infrastructure provision, it hasn't been dominant in the UK for several decades. But out of a difficult period has come some sort of resolution:

> A lot of local authorities are saying they will now use the information we've published to temper their strategies . . . saying that 'we can see you have got a lot of capacity over there' . . . which is a potential opportunity. But as a business we're not going to dictate where planning should take place.
> (Interview S17, infrastructure provider, 2006)

This is integration as a coalignment of strategies, rather than full-scale policy integration but represents a useful step forward. Similarly, the Glasgow Strategic Drainage Plan showed limited integration in terms of the range of stakeholders but environmental, planning and water agencies cooperated extensively to model future demands and coalign their respective strategies.

The degree of integration was affected by timescales however, and the different drivers in each policy sector. So while Scottish Water planned on a four- to eight-year basis, local plans operated on a five-year programme and structure plans were on a twenty-year cycle. The result was a gradually changing emphasis, so that initially 'we had the idea of a plan-led system . . . plan-led investment . . . and what we've come down to is plan-informed investment' (Interview S17, infrastructure provider, 2006). But this seemed more realistic and positive, provided momentum can be maintained to keep up the dialogue. The Planning Act 2006 recognised the issue by obligating Scottish Water to integrate its plan with the planning system, but this stopped short of requiring a coaligning of investment plans with spatial planning priorities. There was the danger of lip service being paid to spatial planning priorities therefore, an issue compounded by the complexity of Scottish Water's regulatory position: it is answerable to four different regulators and so planning must take its place among the organisation's immediate audiences and constituencies.

Limits to integration

In general terms the integration challenge had led to a neater alignment of policy rhetoric and paper strategies, but it was in implementation that differences emerged, with a frequent refrain in our interviews being that infrastructure issues in particular remained a problem. The result was said to be a certain professional 'arrogance' about having good plans, tempered by a realisation that implementation of the plans remained problematic. This attitude was confirmed by a stakeholder very much on the inside of plan production: 'we plan and we plan and we plan . . . we're actually very good at it . . . but we have no interface whatsoever with implementation . . . we don't then seriously take it into delivery and implementation' (Interview S23, regional planner, 2006).

In using spatial planning tools to deliver built environment outcomes, clearly there are limits to the degree to which all strategies can be fully integrated at all times across all scales. Two issues are worth highlighting here. First, in relation to timescales, as highlighted above, coaligning policy agendas is made more difficult by the timing of strategy production in different policy areas. Economic development policy is generally recognised as being reasonably well integrated with land use planning, but some short-termism was in evidence and priorities at national level appeared to change rather quickly. This had the effect of putting them out of step with planning priorities. In addition, there is a layer of community planning in Scotland which was intended to help with joining up policy but which works on much shorter timescales and this can also cause frustrations.

Second, and more theoretically, the complexities of strategic planning in action are recognised by actors, many of whom readily acknowledge that with so many different bodies involved there is always going to be some disconnection, and that may not of itself be a bad thing. The more issues that come into the discussions the more fraught discussions can become, as the different rationales of planners and others come into play, as evident in cases such as where 'the health board . . . say to us why can't you plan development where we've got spare capacity in a medical centre? But . . . if you map all those . . . you might find everyone living out at Dumbarton!' (Interview S16, local planner, 2006). But the sharing of this knowledge and the value of it shouldn't be underestimated. Again, many of these relationships are new, or at least modified in the light of devolution, and interviewees, while highlighting the realpolitik of an integration agenda, noted that this might change as partnership working becomes more deeply embedded in governance culture. So for the time being, there is an acknowledgement of the tensions involved in giving up immediate internal 'power' in pursuit of some abstract notion of the wider collective good:

> we, like many other organisations, are not very good at giving up control . . . we say we want these thing to be aligned . . . but aligned around what we want . . . so we are going to need a more mature approach to partnership than we've got at the moment.
> (Interview S20, economic development agency, 2006)

Conclusions: from land use to spatial planning?

Healey (2006) asserts that the UK's new spatial planning agenda assumes a governance landscape that does not yet exist. This notion is part proven but also contested in this case. Devolution gave impetus to Scotland's long-standing differences in planning policy and practice from much of the UK. The Scottish polity has taken spatial planning seriously, as evidenced nationally in new legislation and the attention given to mechanisms such as the NPF. There is also evidence of learning from places such as Northern Ireland. However, planning was particularly influential in places where it had local political support and long-standing commitment. In such places this attention led other policy sectors to take spatial planning more seriously, or consider it where they had not done so before. The rest of this concluding section returns to the book's central themes of integration, rescaling and the potential shift to spatial planning.

First, with regard to integration, forward planning mechanisms have drawn in other policy sectors around a discussion of territorial futures. Planning was both a repository of activity generated in other governance arenas, but also part of a wider process of co-production and coaligning of strategies. It did, perhaps understandably, often struggle to be the driving, primary force in shaping the context for other sectors such as transport. In this changes to the hard institutional infrastructure helped promote coordination, such as Scotland's Planning Act 2006. But creating such arrangements implies changing the soft infrastructure too. There are limits to this. In pursuing greater integration, aligning public sector priorities is seen as a 'first step' but this is a considerable issue in itself. Just maintaining existing degrees of coordination requires great attention, but developing it further to encompass other stakeholders magnifies the difficulties inherent in this project, especially given the inevitable turnover of key individuals. But here there is a departure between former critiques of the planning system and current practice. In the past planning was much criticised for having limited control over investment, while over-playing its potential to shape places through regulatory powers alone (Vigar *et al.* 2000). What is emerging in Scotland is a greater emphasis on dialogue, on the coalignment of strategies for mutual benefit. This does, of course, have limits to the level of integration it is likely to achieve, not least in failing to solve the difficulties associated with infrastructure investment, but this collective effort in achieving a kind of 'power to act' rather than planning assuming a 'power over' role seems to be a very useful step forward. Many planners want an obligation on actors from other policy sectors to engage with planning at a variety of different points and various pieces of legislation have gone some way to enshrining this principle for sectors such as water and transport. But the soft institutional infrastructure, such as administrative routines, cultures and practices, is what will make such legislative requirements actually work and legal provision does little but force people to pay attention to each other's strategy with little real integrative effort. The existence of a permanent team in GCV to design and implement a strategic city region plan is one way of helping drive a spatial planning agenda beyond 'one-off' plan productions. This in turn requires high-level political commitment and associated funding.

Second, in relation to rescaling, we see various changes to the institutional infrastructure with a filling-in of the national, regional and city regional scales. The city region in particular proves to be a good fit for some issues. For instance, in transport, it provides a locus for simultaneous cross-sectoral and multi-scalar partnership, but it is not appropriate for other issues such as waste. But the creation of new institutions has often not been accompanied by a parallel hollowing out elsewhere in the polity. It thus often adds to what is an already congested governance landscape. The spatial planning project is seen as a legitimate way of dealing with this through bringing together policy agendas as it 'recognises the interdependence of . . . things' (Interview S20, economic development agency, 2006). But it requires others to pay attention to what happens in planning arenas and this requires political support for the spatial planning 'project'. Without this, 'soft' institutions and spaces, while helping to escape statutory straitjackets, imply a high level of inter-agency agreement and cooperation. The necessity of consensus in such arrangements could undermine the development of a challenging strategic vision in the absence of high-level political buy-in of the type evident in the Thames Gateway (Chapter 8). In many ways then, the Scottish experience with 'soft spaces' is very different from that encountered elsewhere in this book, and indeed it defies the idea of a simple separation of hard and soft spaces of governance, as the evolution of Scottish thinking around city regions amply demonstrates.

More broadly, the need for such integration is partly driven by the fragmented governance landscape and capacity reduction in many parts of the public sector, even in a comparatively well-endowed public sector in the UK context. This leads to our final theme of land use to spatial planning. While the tools of the planning system remain the same the capacities and outlook of public agencies are different to the past. The public sector typically has less potential to deploy the tools of direct development and investment and relies a great deal more on the private sector to help deliver urban development. That said, there are the actual constraints on public sector action and those perceived by actors in the public sector, which are in turn framed by public discourse. Scotland has shown itself to be more traditionally social democratic in its policy outlook than in England (Keating 2005). But any differences with England with regard to the pursuit of economic development were marginal with each framed within a wider context of neoliberal urbanism that shapes what are desirable levels and types of intervention by the public sector. One way in which this was manifest was in a reliance not on partnership per se but in the balance of power within such partnerships, with the private sector in a driving role. Another lay in the form of economic growth being pursued which was often not much tempered by environmental or social considerations:

> When the chips are down economic growth has the highest priority . . . and it's not sustainable economic growth, it's just economic growth.
>
> (Interview S2, civil servant, 2005)

Spatial planning as an integration project is then a reflection of wider discourses in government and beyond.

Finally, with regard to a shift to spatial planning, tensions are keenly felt when planning's visionary role comes up against its regulatory functions. They need each other; but there are tensions: 'they [citizens] look at every aspect of what we do to see if there's [the] slightest mistake or gap that they can exploit. The end result is that we have to be very careful of going through all the procedures' (Interview S13, local planner, 2006). And this constraint acts as a barrier to the emergence of a visionary, opportunity-making spatial planning as it reinforces a path dependency among planners, which led some at least to conclude that

> we have a generation of planners . . . who find it incredibly difficult to move away from land use planning . . . they talk about spatial planning but what they're really on about, because they are comfortable with it, is land use planning.
>
> (Interview S13, local planner, 2006)

This retreat to land use planning typically revolves around the playing of some traditional games within planning such as land allocations. These allocations are structured by the demands of the quasi-legal elements of the system and the need for some certainty in land markets. The missing element, evident in the Edinburgh Waterfront development debates, for example, is a failure to piece such considerations back together again in the context of a place-shaping agenda. In this case how to marry conflicting quantitative demands in

city regional strategies with the needs of specific local place-making opportunities through action area master plans. In essence, how do planners
become more reflexive and flexible about some of these quantitative elements
when faced with more qualitative demands – what sort of development might
be appropriate in a particular place to depart from established policy and
practice, for example? So there is some conflict between the struggle for the
maintenance and creation of place qualities and some of planning's other
functions, although these should not be seen as insurmountable: in GCV this
problem has been overcome by dropping almost all regulatory criteria from the
structure plan (see Goodstadt 2007).

Finally, what does this tell us about planning's capacity to shape better
places? In this chapter we have seen two very different approaches to city
region and local scale planning. One is tightly organised with plans co-
produced at various scales to achieve a commonly held set of objectives. The
other situation is more fragmented across scales and agencies. Do these
different approaches yield differing outcomes? The answer is yes. The real
differences lie in the coordination and delivery of policy, which contributes to
achieving urban development and coordinating the distribution of the costs
and benefits of it. That said, it is hard to say that better quality places have
resulted from a greater capacity to plan. The lack of influence of planning over
infrastructure delivery and the pressure of market forces both act in ways that
mean planning has to retain a critical awareness of its limitations as well as its
potentials. We return to these issues in Chapter 9.

6

The Wales Spatial Plan and improving policy integration

The Welsh experience of spatial planning post-devolution is intriguing in many respects, not least in the way the Wales Spatial Plan (WSP) is expressly positioned as a vehicle for policy integration and its invention of new Welsh regions. This chapter looks at the Welsh Assembly Government's approach to policy integration through the lens of *People, Places, Future: The Wales Spatial Plan* published in 2004 (Welsh Assembly Government (WAG) 2004e). According to its introduction:

> This first Wales Spatial Plan is about reflecting honestly and clearly the way a whole range of activity and investment occurs across our particular geographic space and using our knowledge to shape the future. It aims to ensure the Welsh Assembly Government's policies and programmes come together effectively with the workings of local government, business and other partners across Wales, to enable a truly sustainable future – one that works for all the different parts of Wales. It sets a strategic, integrating agenda for the next 20 years.
>
> (WAG 2004e: 3)

The Welsh Assembly's pursuit of a distinctively Welsh approach to spatial policy is widely acknowledged (Harris 2006; Harris and Hooper 2006). This is evident, for example, in the decision to produce only high-level guidance, with limited spatial specificity in the 2004 Wales Spatial Plan, plus a decision not to use the plan to allocate future housing growth figures between local authorities. In addition, the plan opted to avoid local authority or other sub-national administrative boundaries already in existence in favour of creating six new areas (or subregions), defined with fuzzy boundaries. In effect the WSP created new planning spaces for Wales that were unrelated to any previous planning spaces. Fuzzy boundaries are not in themselves unique, but the combination of fuzzy boundaries with high-level policy and a lack of strong direction on issues such as housing does add up to a distinctive approach unique to Wales. For its supporters, this approach is radical and innovative, breaking out from previous patterns of planning practice, while for others serious questions emerge about whether the new approach would be effective in shaping future development in Wales.

In this chapter we first outline and contextualise spatial planning in Wales before exploring two specific policy issues. First, the merits of using fuzzy boundaries are examined, looking at the newly created Welsh areas. Second, there is a case study of cross-border planning across in the West Cheshire and North East Wales subregional spatial strategy, another new planning space, which extends the discussion in Chapter 4 about planning across political boundaries.

Wales: setting the context

With a population of 3 million and GVA of £40.9 billion, Wales is smaller on both counts than all the English regions bar one, North East England. The main centre of population is in south east Wales, with the Cardiff city region having a population of some 1.4 million (Morgan 2006). Smaller concentrations of population occur in the north east, and in the industrial areas of the south coast and valleys, including the city of Swansea. The uplands in central Wales and the far west coast are sparsely populated and act as natural barriers to travel between North and South Wales. The major communications routes tend to be east–west, with those along the North Wales and South Wales coasts also providing international routes linking Ireland with the UK and Europe.

Despite close geographical connections with England, Wales, with its own language and culture, is distinct from the rest of the UK, and devolution represented a victory for those concerned to ensure that its national identity is consolidated and strengthened. It is important to emphasise in this context that Wales is a new nation which enjoys a strong historical cultural identity, while within its boundaries there is considerable diversity and local distinctiveness. In this context, all of the emerging strategies for Wales are in a sense feeling their way to a sense of national consciousness and consensus which celebrates rather than obliterates local cultures and identities. As Harris and Hooper (2006) note, this means that the Wales Spatial Plan can be read differently by various audiences, who each see in it particular commendable attributes and shortcomings, whether it be too much or too little emphasis on moving towards a stronger territorial identity and politics. It is notable then that the 2004 Plan explicitly rejects a 'one size fits all' approach in favour of developing local understandings of what the issues are, while remaining remarkably silent on key aspects of Wales' diverse cultures and identities, for instance, with little mention of issues involving the Welsh language (Harris and Hooper 2006).

The momentum for devolution in Wales grew more slowly than in some parts of the UK, with support only achieving critical mass relatively recently. The Welsh Office and the post of Secretary of State for Wales were not created until 1964: prior to that, Welsh affairs were dealt with by the Home

Secretary (Cullingworth and Nadin 2006). Although a welcome first step, the creation of the Welsh Office was not widely regarded as successful in generating distinctive policies for Wales, with many Welsh public sector institutions part of or mirror images of English institutions. While both Scotland and Wales rejected devolution in their respective 1979 referendums, in Scotland momentum in favour of devolution grew much more decisively than in Wales (Glasson and Marshall 2007). The 1997 referendum in Wales was won by only a very narrow margin, in effect providing a challenge for the new Welsh institutions to succeed in order to bring more people behind the devolution project.

Following on from the referendum, the first elections were held in May 1999, with receipt of devolved powers by the new assembly in July 1999. Unlike the Scottish Parliament, the Welsh Assembly has limited funding, possesses only executive functions and currently does not have powers to make primary legislation, only secondary and subordinate legislation. In planning, such secondary legislation has an important role through, for example, setting out the General Permitted Development Order and Use Classes Order. The Assembly can also issue its own national policy guidance, which has a significant role to play in shaping local planning outcomes and processes. Further legislative authority can be gained through Legislative Competence Orders which have to be approved by the Assembly, Secretary of State for Wales, both Houses of Parliament and the Queen in Council. Nevertheless, for now, Welsh planning legislation originates within the UK government apparatus, even though responsibility for a wide range of policy sectors was devolved to the Assembly, including economic development, housing, local government, tourism, planning and transport.

Politically, the first two terms of government in Wales were Labour-dominated, involving a coalition with Liberal Democrats in the first term. The broad intent of the first two administrations focused on economic development, social justice and sustainability, along with fostering a strong Welsh identity, set out in *Wales: A Better Country* (WAG 2003).[1] Things changed in the third term (post-May 2007) and now Labour leads a coalition government with Plaid Cymru, the Welsh nationalist party. The *One Wales* document, rapidly produced by the incoming coalition government, committed it to investigating the possibilities of full law-making powers within the context of the Government of Wales Act 2006. There is also a commitment to creating a Commission to examine finance and funding, including tax varying powers. The coalition government did not introduce wholesale restructuring of government departments, so these remain very similar to the pre-2007 structure. The executive arm of the Welsh Assembly is called the Welsh Assembly Government.

Historically there has not been a formal regional tier of governance within Wales itself; indeed until devolution the principality as a whole was categorised as a 'standard region' in the UK context. The Welsh Assembly Government has though established four regional offices (North, Mid, South East and South West Wales), dealing primarily with economic development, transport and education. These are purely administrative regions which are not reflected in planning policy. As we noted earlier, the Wales Spatial Plan focuses instead on the six 'functional' subregions identified in Figure 6.1, whose boundaries were not coterminous with any existing administrative or political unit.

Local government in Wales was reorganised in 1996, abolishing a two-tier system of county and district councils and replacing it with a single tier of 22 unitary authorities. The Welsh Assembly Government has so far decided not to pursue a major restructuring of local government, acknowledging some of the upheaval costs this would incur. Instead it has sought to develop improved coordination systems for local services under its Making the Connections programme (WAG 2004b). Pursuing this approach it commissioned the Beecham Review (2006) *Beyond Boundaries: Citizen-centred Local Services for Wales*, which praised the achievements since devolution in improving aspects of service delivery, but found that counterproductive local competition, limited local leadership capacity and inefficiencies in delivery

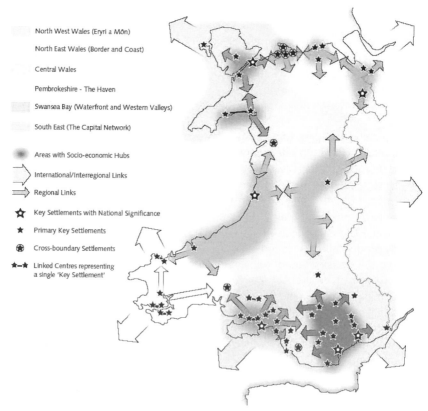

6.1 Wales Spatial Plan key diagram, illustrating fuzzy regions
Source: Welsh Assembly Government (2008).

were all preventing major improvements. Rather than restructuring local government the review argued that artificial sectoral and geographical boundaries needed to be addressed through greater cooperation and emphasis on service delivery. It then made various recommendations for promoting greater cooperation among local authorities, which the WAG is now following up, adopting an innovative citizen-centred approach to service delivery (Morgan 2007; see below). The Beecham Review made reference to the Wales Spatial Plan agenda for using subregions operating above local authority level, suggesting that ministers responsible for each of the WSP Areas should widen their remit to include overseeing the mechanisms for promoting local area cooperation.

Pursuing the integration imperative

The model of national government in Wales is sometimes referred to as being 'state-centric' (Cooke and Clifton 2005; Goodwin *et al.* 2006), not least as the new administration has sought to strengthen the role of the National Assembly. One of the key themes running through the early administrations was the need for joined-up policy-making, including an emphasis on working better across the public sector and with other bodies in the private and voluntary sectors. Given our comments in Chapter 2 about the politics of integration being a mechanism that can either bolster a central steer over policy affairs or foster diversity, there is an inherent tension in this 'integration' agenda, which can variously be perceived as about promoting open partnerships and as ensuring adherence to a centralist agenda. A complicating factor in the case of Wales is that Cardiff remains at the heart of national policy-making, while a powerful distrust exists of the capital in parts of the country's political establishment (Morgan 2006). Responding to such tensions the decision has been made to decentralise many of the Welsh Assembly's staff away from the capital, so that eventually 60 per cent of civil servants are based elsewhere (Morgan 2006). Running alongside this 'decentralisation' tendency has been a clear centralisation imperative which has seen a number of previously arm's-length public sector bodies such as the Welsh Development Agency and Learning for Wales brought directly into government.

Many of the WAG's reforms have centred on a strong commitment to collaborative government, bringing together the diverse institutions involved in public sector governance to pursue common objectives:

> The Government has a radical vision of a Welsh public service, sharing common goals and working across functional and organisational boundaries. We will use the opportunity conferred by devolution to bring together the different elements of the public service in a more integrated way – to create greater dynamism, with more efficient and effective service delivery. The merger of a number of ASPBs [Assembly Sponsored Public Bodies] into the Welsh Assembly Government is a significant step towards the achievement of a Welsh

public service. The Welsh public service covers local government, the NHS, national bodies sponsored by the Government, national parks, universities, colleges, schools and others. These organisations with different purposes, constitutions and accountabilities, and involving business and voluntary sectors in delivery, can be brought together by the shared values of social justice, equality, sustainability and a sense of community.

(WAG 2004b: 6)

The main WAG strategy documents all tend to assert a strong commitment to integration with other policy strategies and to embracing a holistic rather than purely sectoral approach (see e.g. Figure 6.2). This is spelt out most clearly in the documentation for the WSP (see below) and sustainable development. Wales has a statutory requirement to publish a Sustainable Development Scheme showing how it will promote sustainable development. The first scheme, *Learning to Live Differently*, was adopted in 2000, and a revised scheme, *Starting to Live Differently*, was published in 2004 (WAG 2000, 2004c). The *Sustainable Development Action Plan*, identifying priority actions for the period 2004–2007, was also published in 2004 (WAG 2004d).

In pursuit of common objectives and shared values, the National Assembly has adopted a 'policy integration tool', developed with Forum for the Future. This tool is intended to ensure that new policies and strategies are assessed against the Assembly's wider objectives with its legal commitment to pursue sustainable development. The policy integration tool, formally the 'Government Integration Tool', is an appraisal framework which initially at least assessed policies and strategies against the seven core objectives of the Welsh Assembly Government set out in *Wales: A Better Country* (WAG 2003):

- promoting the economy
- action on social justice for communities
- action on our built and natural environment
- strengthening Wales' cultural identity
- ensuring better prospects in life for future generations
- supporting healthy independent lives
- promoting openness, partnership and participation.

The Integration Tool approach has found favour elsewhere among the devolved territories, notably in Northern Ireland. In many ways it gives teeth to the wider government commitment to integrated policy by ensuring that on paper at least all the strategies are aligned and do not contradict each other. It is early days however to see whether all this strategic work makes its way into distinctive policies on the ground. So in the case of the first sustainable development scheme, the formal report on its effectiveness congratulated the Welsh Assembly on its efforts to mainstream sustainable development, while noting that there was little evidence of change happening on the ground

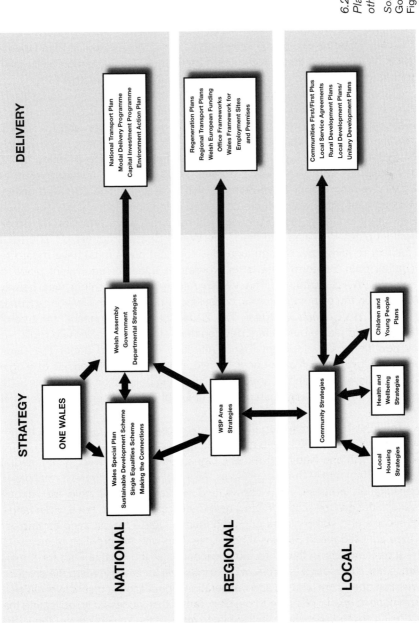

6.2 *Wales Spatial Plan: connections to other strategies*

Source: Welsh Assembly Government (2008: Figure 11).

(CAG Consultants 2003). Others have also criticised the high-profile activities of the Welsh Assembly Government on sustainable development, echoing concerns that the strong rhetorical commitment to sustainable development is not always reflected in individual decisions on issues such as tourism development (see later) and renewable energy (James 2004; Haughton *et al.* 2008).

The Welsh planning system and the Wales Spatial Plan

It is clear from the ministerial introduction to the Wales Spatial Plan Update 2008 (WAG 2008) that it is regarded by the new administration as its main vehicle for policy integration, and it is to this subject that we now turn.

Planning in Wales is subject to the same primary legislation as England, though from the 1980s through to devolution, the Welsh Office had progressively taken over responsibility for secondary legislation and for issuing national planning guidance. Despite this, policy development relied heavily on English practice such that prior to devolution planning practice in the two countries was very similar (Powell 2001). With its unitary system of local government post-1996 some Welsh local authorities prepared unitary development plans while others continued with earlier local plans. The 2004 Planning and Compulsory Purchase Act made separate provision for development plans in Wales and made the Wales Spatial Plan (WAG 2004e) a statutory requirement, though local development plans must have regard to it rather than 'conform' (the latter wording is used for equivalent plans in England: WAG 2008: 7). The Welsh Assembly Government was heavily engaged in the planning reforms, consulting widely through *Delivering Better Plans for Wales* (WAG 2004a). The 2004 Act retains a unitary structure of development plans, but unitary development plans themselves are replaced by new Local Development Plans. Although established under the same primary legislation, Welsh Local Development Plans will consist of single documents, a less complex approach to planning policy than the multiple suite of documents approach characteristic of Local Development Frameworks in England.

The Welsh Assembly began its consultations on a national spatial framework for Wales in 2001, with a draft plan published for consultation in 2003 (Cullingworth and Nadin 2006: 97). Consultation was viewed as an integral and important part of the plan process. As such, in addition to the formal paper consultation process, road shows and workshops were held for various stakeholder groups across Wales, deliberately structured to get a wider range of sectors and stakeholders engaged than is typical for planning strategies. Once adopted the WSP was then followed up with the creation of multisectoral partnerships to flesh out the implications of the Spatial Plan for the six Areas that it proposed (see below). The intention for those leading the process was that open consultation and deliberation would allow a distinctively Welsh approach to spatial planning to develop, rather than necessarily replicating the models adopted elsewhere. In this sense many of the key policies of the WSP are expected to emerge organically through debate and being tested against local stakeholder opinion rather than developed first by a cadre of professional planners. The Wales Spatial Plan was prepared by a small unit located centrally outside the Assembly's Planning Division, with a strong political steer from the minister responsible and reporting to a cabinet subcommittee. The final version, *People, Places, Futures: The Wales Spatial Plan* (WAG 2004e) was published at the end of 2004 following agreement by the full Assembly. This was replaced in 2008 by the Wales Spatial Plan Update (WSPU: WAG 2008).

According to Harris and Hooper (2006: 141), one of the aspirations of the Welsh Assembly Government in preparing the Wales Spatial Plan had been to politicise the Welsh territory. Partly this was about developing thinking about Wales as a national territory and also about developing a stronger policy apparatus for dealing with distinctiveness within the country, most evident in the work on creating six new Area identities. Recognising that Wales is not a cohesive functional region, with parts of the country relating better functionally to adjacent parts of England than to each other, there was felt to be a need in the first iteration of the Plan to focus on producing something distinctly about Wales, inducing a degree of introspection, so that unlike in Scotland, there were only limited efforts to position Wales in Europe (Harris and Hooper 2006). At one level this is a slightly harsh reading. Comparison with the Yorkshire and Humber RSS, for example, shows that it too makes few explicit links to Europe. Moreover the WSP does attempt to deal with the global drivers of economic change and was one of the first to use ecological footprint analysis to assess the impacts of Wales on other areas. The WAG has also been involved in various European networks on planning and sustainable development issues. Possibly responding to the critics the 2008 WSPU is somewhat stronger in this respect, not least in adopting ESDP concepts in the Area summaries, notably with the adoption of the notion of hubs and the emphasis on improving connectivity between them. The Area sections also mention how they connect to neighbouring areas and mention trans-European transport networks where relevant. Nonetheless, Harris and Hooper's view that the 2004 WSP failed to articulate a strong sense of how Wales operates within a wider European or global context still holds when looking at the 2008 Update.

The WSP makes much of its role as a tool for cross-sectoral integration:

> Making sure that decisions are taken with regard to their impact beyond the immediate sectoral or administrative boundaries; that there is coordination of investment and services through understanding the roles of and interactions between places; and that we place the core values of sustainable development in everything we do.
>
> (WAG 2004c: 3)

The policy integration agenda is in many senses both stronger and more distinctive than the WSP's spatial dimension, leading Harris and Hooper (2006:

139) to argue that the WSP is best seen as 'a practical mechanism for sectoral policy integration . . . the objective of policy integration dominates the plan'. Links to land use planning are limited, resulting in a 'Spatial Plan' which for its critics has little to say about either spatial development or traditional planning themes.

The published version of the Wales Spatial Plan purposefully avoided certain controversial planning issues typically found in spatial plans, perhaps most notably with the absence of clear guidance on locating future housing growth. The key to this was the clear intention that to begin with the WSP would serve as a high-level strategy which would guide future development without being too prescriptive. In many ways this reflects a learning process, echoing the Irish and Scottish Spatial Strategies about the value of high-level strategic direction allied to a strong desire not to end up embroiled in heated debates about detail. As one of those involved told us, this was a clear choice on the part of those involved:

> The political direction here . . . and the one that is better for the long-term is to say we're not going down a 'you must' route, we'll go down a collaborative route that shows people the benefits of why they need to work together. So there is still some desire from the planning fraternity for the Spatial Plan of Wales to be regional planning guidance . . . and we're not going down that route . . . we've made that explicit . . . it's about trying to take a better view and guiding actions . . . it is a visionary . . . incremental approach. Setting the vision and then getting people to talk about it.
>
> (Interview W1, civil servant, 2005)

Much of the early work of the plan, including its consultation period, was focused on developing consensus around the strategic priorities for the broad plan and the nature of its six Areas, including agreement on how to take this approach forward to the next stage of more detailed strategic guidance (Harris 2006). This very much reflects the view of the Welsh Assembly Government that it should be seen more as a process rather than as a fixed end-point strategy, with the 2004 document seen as a building block, establishing both credibility and also general agreement on a direction of travel.

For Glasson and Marshall (2007: 116), however, the 'actual vision is very broadbrush, as is much of the overall plan which is more of a descriptive stocktake than a forward looking strategy'. They go on to argue that as it stands, the WSP was unlikely to be sufficient to guide local planning and decision-making. Not surprisingly then, the high-level nature of the WSP approach with its lack of specifics also caused some concern among our interviewees, and was a recurrent theme in the consultations for the WSP Update (see DTZ 2008; see also WAG/RTPI Cymru consultation workshop summaries, www.rtpi.org.uk/item/1617). However, for those involved in producing the plan, these 'omissions' reflected a desire precisely not to be a standard 'spatial plan', with all the tensions and delays felt to be associated with that. In this sense the process of brokering agreement around broad strategic priorities was of value in itself as part of a first round of work on a national spatial plan, while also playing to local sensitivities of not wanting to see an overly detailed set of prescriptive policies imposed from the top-down.

Breaking out from the expectations around producing a traditional 'plan' was also seen to be important in getting buy-in from a wide range of stakeholders within government and beyond. Seeing the WSP as a thoroughgoing attempt to spatialise the corporate thinking and working habits of the Wales Assembly Government, and its partners, it represents a radical departure from practice elsewhere. In this context it was not surprising that the concerns about the lack of links to traditional planning issues in our interviews came mainly from planners and the development industry, while others were more receptive to the approach adopted in the WSP. It should be added that most planners also saw merit in the high-level strategic approach; it was just that they worried about where it left them when it came to developing their own plans. This was an issue that came out strongly during the WSPU consultations. In formal terms the WSP is a statutory document for the government, but it is not considered a statutory document within the planning hierarchy, rather something that local development plans must have regard to, and as such is part of the 'test of soundness' for LDPs. For local planners, the WSP was not proving to be a major hindrance to their work:

> Well, there is a statutory obligation to have regard to it . . . but the level at which it's pitched . . . I don't think will cause any particular problems for us . . . At that level it allows you to do virtually anything you want to.
>
> (Interview W10, local planner, 2006)

The key to understanding the WSP and its critics is to realise that those who are most vocally in opposition frequently want it to be something other than what it has set out to be and, unsurprisingly, it is found wanting. By contrast those who support it tend to be those who take the WSP on its own terms, as an ongoing process for brokering agreement in the context of a new territorial government which needed to build consensus rather than impose a particular political agenda for development. In this context we found civil servants broadly supportive of the WSP's ambitions to provide a government-wide integration tool with an evolving spatial agenda. In essence, the WSP was one of a series of strategies that helped provide a context for the decisions of individual departments:

> So we need to provide a more integrated and diverse economy. I think the spatial plan is a good focus for that . . . if you'd left it to the economic developers we'd be running around in circles building small factory units everywhere.
>
> (Interview W6, civil servant, 2005)

Seen from the bottom-up, local authorities tend to welcome the plan cautiously, mainly as they sought to negotiate the implications for them of having to work in new 'subregional' groupings rather than focus on their own boundaries. We return to this theme later.

The consultation draft of the Wales Spatial Plan Update set out an upbeat assessment of the achievements to date of the Spatial Plan, which it claimed 'is now a key consideration in the development of national and local policies. In short it has become an important integrating tool for decision-makers at local, regional and national level' (WAG 2008: 1). While this statement did not make it into the final version, it presents a clear statement of what the Plan's supporters believe. The final version of the Update document retains the upbeat assessment of the achievements during the first few years of the Plan, pointing to the work of the Area partnerships (see below) and also the way in which the WSP areas had been used to inform the decision-making of a wide range of other sectoral bodies, notably for transport and European structural funding.

But the official summary of the consultation responses (DTZ 2008) reveals a range of concerns that broadly echo those we encountered in our interviews about the 2004 WSP. First, that the main impacts to date were on governmental processes, influencing the plans of others. Implementation on the ground was not yet seen to be coming through. Second, there is a broad acceptance that the WSP's approach is the right one for Wales, focusing on high-level strategic issues and allowing subregional partnership work to fill in the details. But allied to this is a constant refrain that the plan is pitched at such a level of generality that it has found consensus at the expense of not setting out distinctive policies that will find their way through to implementation. Third, the evidence base for the plan was felt to be weak relative to a more standard planning exercise, reflecting the views of some of our interviewees that it in some ways opted to sidestep the evidence gathering in favour of building consensus around the kind of objectives for the plan that its stakeholders felt able to sign up to.

> It wasn't an evidence based evaluation . . . it was almost opinion testing – 'can you sign up to this?' Rather than 'does the evidence point to this as a realistic way forward?' To my mind it has largely been unencumbered by evidence . . . it's been 'are these the issues we're facing and do you think this is the right set of topics that concern you?'
>
> (Interview W14, academic, 2006)

Fourth, the strategy was felt to be dominated by economic development and with insufficient attention to environmental concerns, including green infrastructure (see WAG/RTPI Cymru consultation workshop summaries, www. rtpi.org.uk/item/1617; see also DTZ 2008). The implication here is that the WAG's statutory responsibility to promote sustainable development remains unconvincing in the WSP, which contains many references to sustainable development but lacks substantive policies to back this up.

In summary then, the WSP approach is distinctive and it needs to be evaluated against both its own internal remit and wider expectations. As a spatial planning document, it is strong on consultation processes, and as an aspirational document on policy integration, though it remains to be seen whether it actually performs well on this count. As a 'spatial' strategy document, the distinctive approach taken meant that initially it was not strong, but the Update shows how much work has been undertaken in the intervening period, largely living up to the promise to deliver the spatial detail once further local consultation work had been undertaken. This involved partnerships working in each of the six subregions, to develop local frameworks which were then put out for consultation as part of the 2008 Update.

It is worth emphasising here that the agreed 2008 Update is now the statutory WSP document, retaining the broad elements of the 2004 Wales Spatial Plan and giving formal status to the work on developing strategic frameworks for each of the six Areas or subregions, which we turn to next.

New spaces, fuzzy boundaries and the new subregions of Wales

Looking from the outside-in, Wales can appear unified . . . but when you cross the border . . . we're as parochial as they get. We have issues of getting local authorities to work properly together . . . issues over who gets the funding . . .

Using a spatial process to let us identify what are the priorities across Wales . . . is trying to lift the debate above the parochialism if you like.

(Interview W6, civil servant, 2005)

The six Areas identified in the Wales Spatial Plan were for many a contentious creation, as they represented entirely new spaces for planning policy and indeed for government policy more generally.[2] Moreover they were deliberately defined with fuzzy boundaries so that the areas merge with each other and overlap. Part of the initial concern was about how these areas were chosen and their unifying characteristics decided, while the fuzzy boundaries also left some people confused about which localities 'belonged' in which Area – an outcome that some felt was deliberate as it allowed a greater degree of policy flexibility on the part of the WAG. By contrast, for those responsible for the WSP the appeal of the new approach was precisely this destabilising of existing identities and breaking away from thinking around local government boundaries. In effect the new Areas were, initially at least, a form of 'soft space' governance, which allowed new thinking to work through into the planning process.

The approach adopted also opted for fuzzy boundaries, based on the argument that the new functional subregions needed to reflect that housing markets and journey to work areas are not precisely delineated in practice, that they do in fact overlap, and that policy should be flexible enough to accommodate diverse practices. Local authority boundaries not only failed to reflect such functional realities but were also seen as representing a barrier to thinking through how people really lived their lives. For all the apparent advantages of the new approach, there have been concerns about whether the Areas adopted for the WSP were meaningful or acceptable outside the spatial plan context, since: 'several key agencies operating throughout Wales maintain that the functional areas defined in the plan lack sufficient clarity to be accepted as genuine functional areas' (Harris and Hooper 2006: 144). What is meant here is most clearly evident in the Central Wales Area, which covers the entire central part of Wales, including much of the west coast and borders. This was the one area that tended to be mentioned in interviews as lacking any great functional cohesion, instead seeming to represent the remaining parts of Wales after the other functional spaces had been identified. It may also be that this links to the criticisms aired during the WSPU consultations that the Plan was not strong on rural issues generally. The WSPU deals with such concerns by adopting a hub and clusters approach, identifying sub-areas within each Area that seem to have functional linkages and the potential for spreading growth from major towns to surrounding areas.

The Area approach has been actively pursued in the period since 2004. Area networks have been set up for each of the six Areas, with high-level committees chaired by a minister and involving senior executives from relevant agencies meeting twice yearly to oversee progress (Figure 6.3). Interim policy statements were issued during 2007 and published on the Assembly website, then incorporated into the 2008 WSP Update. The Update was put out for consultation in early 2008 and formally adopted in summer 2008.

In the foreword to the interim statement on the North East Area study, Sue Essex, the minister who had initially led work on the Wales Spatial Plan,

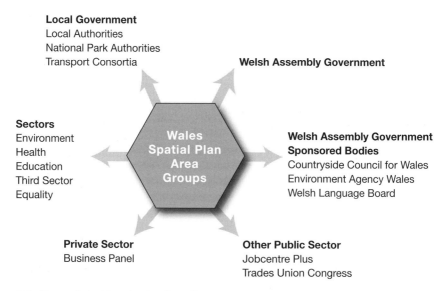

Local Government
Local Authorities
National Park Authorities
Transport Consortia

Welsh Assembly Government

Sectors
Environment
Health
Education
Third Sector
Equality

Wales Spatial Plan Area Groups

Welsh Assembly Government Sponsored Bodies
Countryside Council for Wales
Environment Agency Wales
Welsh Language Board

Private Sector
Business Panel

Other Public Sector
Jobcentre Plus
Trades Union Congress

6.3 Key stakeholders for the Area Groups
Source: Welsh Assembly Government (2008).

outlined the purpose and nature of the area documents, explaining that priorities for action were being determined by the groups in each of the spatial plan areas:

> In order to turn the Spatial Plan into reality, my Cabinet colleagues and I set up and continue to provide leadership to Spatial Plan groups in each Spatial Plan area. These groups have been meeting regularly and working collaboratively to determine what the local priorities for action should be. The Spatial Plan Groups include the Welsh Assembly Government, Local Authorities, the voluntary, equality, environment, education, business and health sectors.
>
> (http://new.wales.gov.uk/about/strategy/spatial/
> northeastwales/northeastinterim/areavision/?lang=en)

Given the lack of coterminosity with any existing political boundaries, the fact that each of the area spatial planning partnerships was chaired by a Welsh Assembly minister helped ensure political buy-in, though this also meant that the WAG very much steered the process. Each area also has a dedicated member of the central spatial planning team allocated to it. For local planners in Wales the resulting area frameworks were helpful in filling in some of the spatial detail that was felt to have been lacking in the earlier WSP, while avoiding the pitfalls of prescription. However, the response by the Town and Country Planning Association (TCPA 2008) to the WSPU consultation process suggests that the level of detail is now getting close to the point where a formal public examination might be required, if the WSPU was to inform the content of local development plans (TCPA 2008). We are less convinced on this point, since the level of spatial detail on specific policy issues remains very limited.

Fuzzy boundaries did cause some initial consternation among local authorities, not least as some found themselves having to work with the partnerships of two or three Areas, creating resourcing issues. In addition, the TCPA (2008) argue that fuzzy boundaries can lead to uncertainty and a lack of transparency. Looking at the concept of fuzzy boundaries from the perspective of the WAG, there are clearly some advantages. Avoiding specificity allows for manoeuvre, particularly over a diverse political, economic and cultural landscape. As such the WSPU 2008 highlights this as one of the distinctive features of the spatial vision in the plan: 'Fuzzy boundaries: The Spatial Plan areas are not defined by administrative boundaries. This enables partners to work together on common issues in a flexible way, and some may be involved in more than one Spatial Plan Area Group' (WAG 2008: 28–29).

Nonetheless, a degree of firming up of boundaries over time is evident, with boundaries being equated to administrative areas for statistical analysis purposes. So while the Areas still overlap with each other, their boundaries are perhaps becoming slightly less fuzzy in practice and local authorities have learnt to negotiate fuzziness in ways that suit their needs. The result is that the six Welsh areas themselves still resemble a form of 'soft' governance space in the sense that they are not coterminous with other institutional boundaries, though as other organisations adopt this organisational framework (see WAG 2008) this may change.

In the WSPU consultations during 2008, the bulk of the comments at area level concerned the region known as South East Wales Capital Network, in effect the Cardiff city region. The politics of attempting to work at the scale of the Cardiff city region have been analysed in some detail by Kevin Morgan (2006). As he points out, to understand the underlying tensions involved it is essential to be aware of the wider national politics of the dominant role played by Cardiff in political life and in Welsh economic growth, plus the cultural issues associated with young Welsh-speaking people moving out of rural areas into the capital. Overlaying this is the personality politics involved between local politicians and the Welsh Assembly, with some long-standing tensions evident. At the local level, thinking of a wider Cardiff city region immediately touches upon the sensitivities around the considerable prosperity around parts of Cardiff, particularly to the coastal zone, as opposed to the continuing social problems in the former coalfield areas.

Out of these tensions and much political debate an acceptance has gradually emerged that the city council area, with just 315,000 residents, is too small to command a strong presence on the international stage, whereas a city region of 1.4 million could fairly claim to demand attention. The decision to create a Capital Network Area in the WSP proved helpful to those trying to promote a form of city regionalism for Cardiff. Recognition that the new area contained its own distinctive sub-subregions (City and Coast, Heads of the Valleys, Connection Corridor) also probably helped the idea gain acceptance, highlighting the different needs of parts of the newly created 'city region'. As Morgan (2006) notes, however, there were tensions from the start of this process, not least over its would-be governance arrangements, which remain unclear. The WSPU fleshes out the initial concept for the Capital Network and begins to provide a clearer strategic context for the work that is proposed. This is strong on the need to use future investment in the area to address the spatial inequalities that exist within it. Central to achieving the vision is improving the transport links between the various centres within the city region and also between it and adjoining areas. However, according to the report on the consultation process (DTZ 2008), the implicit approach here to manage growth in Cardiff and redirect it to other areas raised some concerns, particularly within the private sector. Related to this were concerns that an imbalance in allocating new employment sites and housing might unbalance the city region and impede its future growth.

What is interesting for the purposes of this section is that it was the WSP which provided the vehicle around which this debate around city regionalism started to coalesce, allowing a detailed debate about what kind of approach to city regionalism was locally appropriate and to work through some of the tensions and necessary compromises that Morgan's work refers to.

Arguably, we begin to see here that the WSP approach of bringing stakeholders together to develop Area frameworks was helping to broker a contested rescaling of policy thinking in a way that, for some at least, was felt to be locally sensitive and appropriate. As one civil servant told us about the Area work in general:

> Of course at times there are frictions between certain parties, but on the whole it's a sign of the success that we've got hundreds and hundreds of people across Wales working on this . . . giving it more detail . . . developing it into action plans . . . So I think it is quite a distinctive approach . . . I wouldn't say necessarily that it is right for anywhere else . . . but ultimately we feel it is the right way for Wales.
> (Interview W15, civil servant, 2006)

Directing growth and achieving sustainable outcomes

Allocating future housing around Wales

As we noted earlier, the WSP is a statutory document of the Welsh Assembly Government, but it does not legally form part of the statutory planning system, with Local Development Plans (LDPs) simply having to have regard to it, a weak phrasing. There has been no legal testing of the relationship between the WSP and LDPs, with no LDP that we are aware of to date failing the 'soundness test' because it failed to have regard to the WSP. The advantage of the statutory/non-statutory approach adopted in Wales is that it allowed the Spatial Plan to have the credibility of general statutory status, while not being a formal part of the planning system allowed it to be developed more speedily and helped sidestep factions forming for and against its contents. For instance, not having to deal with statutory matters such as housing allocations allowed the WSP to be approved without a formal public examination.

While acknowledging that there were reasons for the lack of prescription on housing allocations to local authority areas, the development industry was generally looking for greater national guidance. Accustomed to housing being a core strategic issue in English regional planning, the development industry had expected a similar approach in Wales, something which would provide them with the opportunity to contest proposed housing numbers at a strategic level. For developers there are potential costs to the Welsh approach, as they envisage having to debate the scale of housing growth at each local development plan's public examination (in England the numbers are determined in the RSS, so local debates are focused on site issues). Certainly our interviews revealed that housebuilders generally preferred the certainties of the English system at this stage, though attitudes may change as people get used to the approach being developed in Wales.

While greater detail is emerging in subregional planning studies, which will include housing projections, civil servants in Wales made clear to us in interviews their continuing opposition to prescribing housing numbers, explaining that although they issue housing projections these are essentially trend based and do not have to be taken into account by local authorities.

Instead Assembly officials aim to work collaboratively with local authorities on the apportionment of housing numbers, drawing on local knowledge of circumstances and accepting that trend-based projections are not always accurate.

This reluctance to prescribe housing numbers could have unforeseen consequences though, for instance, if local aspirations for a higher level of housing growth lead to a higher cumulative total than national projections predict. The problem with this approach is that it makes it difficult to make decisions on where to direct investment for supporting infrastructure. At present, the signs are that rather than overestimating housing numbers the opposite might be happening, with one national planner conceding that in parts of Wales 'the combination of housing numbers in Local Development Plans is coming up with less than the Assembly's projections, so the collaborative work is trying to encourage them to increase numbers there' (Interview W15, civil servant, 2006). The jury is still out at this early stage on whether the Welsh approach will work. Given its smaller size and the national emphasis on improving joint working across government agencies at all scales, this is something of a litmus test for how Wales can show that it can produce a distinctive policy regime.

Bluestone development, Pembroke

Another potential litmus test for many people concerns whether the WSP provides adequate guidance when it comes to taking controversial decisions over commercial developments. Friends of the Earth Wales included the case of the Bluestone development in the Pembrokeshire National Park in its list of shame for how they argue the Welsh planning system has failed to meet its sustainable development mandate (James 2004). Bluestone is a short-break leisure village partly in the Pembrokeshire National Park which was given the go-ahead in 2004 despite a series of legal challenges by the Council for National Parks. It is variously estimated to be a project worth £45–110 million, capable of housing 2,500 people, generating an estimated 600 direct jobs and a further 200 indirect jobs (the case for the development is most clearly set out in WAG 2006, a press release). The development was presented as a much needed boost to tourism in an area in need of jobs, a sustainable tourism project with green credentials and a commitment to creating year-round, high-quality jobs. While the development proposal preceded publication of the final Wales Spatial Plan it was being considered at the time that the Plan was being drafted and debated in public.

Pembrokeshire is located at the far south-west corner of Wales and is an area of relative economic disadvantage. In WSP terms it is part of the 'Pembrokeshire – The Haven' Area. The area relies heavily on employment in tourism, with a key policy issue being how to transform the tourist sector from one essentially providing short-term low-value employment into something supporting more permanent, higher value employment (Midmore and Thomas 2006). The Bluestone development proposal was seen by some locally as a catalyst for bringing about this shift in the quality of tourism development, but by others as a threat to the environmental qualities that attract tourists to the area. It had economic and social implications beyond the immediate locality, its impact touched upon a wide range of policy sectors and it had clear spatial implications. In other words it was exactly the kind of development proposal that the Wales Spatial Plan ought to be helping to shape. As far as local planners in the National Park and County Council were concerned, however, the Wales Spatial Plan had little if anything to say about this kind of project. Neither was there a local spatial policy context:

> You wouldn't find a pre-emptive planning policy trailed through the planning hierarchy. I would be very surprised if Pembrokeshire had any pre-emptive policy on the desirability of that sort of development in the National Park. As such it's not a sector governed strongly by spatial planning logic.
>
> (Interview W13, academic, 2006)

Planners recommended refusing the proposal, but both the National Park and Pembrokeshire planning committees granted approval (see James 2004; Milne 2005). Tourism officials at the local and national level were for the proposal, while the WAG had already approved substantial funding support in principle for the project should it go ahead, leading some to claim a conflict of interest (James 2004). The eco-emphasis of the proposal plus claims that it would generate all-year-round employment and help revive the local tourism industry resulted in considerable political support for the development in Pembrokeshire. The case against the development was essentially that it was too large and would have environmentally detrimental impacts, and as part of it was in a national park, it set an undesirable precedent. The Assembly Government refused to call in the proposal, arguing it was not of sufficient significance, yet the case ended up going through the Courts of Appeal and the House of Lords (James 2004; Milne 2005).

The result was confusion. Different parts of the system appeared to have come to different judgements on the relative merits of the proposal and how this fitted in with the Wales Assembly Government's understanding of sustainable development. As with many major tourist developments involving inward investment, Bluestone appears to have been considered on its own merits with little attention to emerging spatial policy at national or local level. The WPSU 2008 section on Pembrokeshire and the Haven retrospectively provides a broad context for future tourism development in Pembrokeshire, referring to the need for more high-quality provision (with Bluestone specifically cited as an example), while also protecting those aspects of the environment that draw tourists into the area.

In terms of coordinated policy delivery then, the Bluestone development proposal was supported by the Welsh Assembly, despite conflicts with some of its environmental policies. It is not clear that the planning process played much of a role in shaping this nationally important debate, other than providing the legal basis for appeal. In essence the decisions were based on political judgements about the need for economic development in the area, irrespective of written policies supporting environmental protection. The Spatial Plan has now retrospectively begun to address the issue, but its ambiguous wording still leaves considerable scope for interpretation, and it is in any case a non-statutory document within the context of the planning system.

The issue here comes back to our concerns about the way in which 'integrated' policy-making can become a steamroller that stifles debate within government and to an extent beyond. So the final decision over Bluestone may well be the right one for the area, but it suggests that professional planners were interpreting sustainable development as an integrative device where environmental issues were of strong importance in the local context, while others felt that the social and economic dimensions were what mattered most. This may have been many things, but it was not carefully balanced debate and integrated policy-making, not least as some arms of the WAG had already committed themselves to the project prior to the planning application. As one local academic argued:

> There is an issue of whether these sorts of organisations are open to the sort of coordination spatial planning calls for, or whether it's integration behind the objectives they want to lead on . . . Different agencies integrate around different things . . . so whose agenda is at the core of the integrative efforts of the Welsh Government?
> (Interview W13, academic, 2006)

Taking this argument further, when it comes to sustainable development multiple interpretations are possible, some more environment driven, others potentially more sensitive to economic matters. At the very least it is not clear that the WSP process led to a distinctive understanding of sustainable development being brokered through the consultation process. The result was that when it came to examining controversial projects in the absence of a clear steer within the planning system, or from the WSP process, the policy vacuum allowed a pragmatic decision to be made which privileged powerful economic development interests. Interestingly, another development that argued its sustainability, the Lammas Eco Village also in rural Pembrokeshire (though not in the National Park), has been resisted by local planners on the grounds of environmental impact including traffic generation (see Maxey *et al.* (2006) and the website www.autonomousgeographies.org). Lammas involved 9 residential units over 31 hectares and little net increase in employment while the Bluestone development comprised 335 lodges over 202 hectares, 5,000 day visitors and 600 jobs. However, it was the relatively small-scale, low-impact Lammas proposal that was refused because it was not 'sustainable' and generated 'too much' local traffic. It goes without saying that unlike the 'flagship' Bluestone development with its substantial contribution to traffic generation, the WAG has not rushed in to support the small-scale Lammas project politically or financially. The whiff of hypocrisy hangs over Pembroke.

West Cheshire and North East Wales: a cross-border subregional strategy

Our main 'governance line' for Wales involved North East Wales, where we were interested particularly in the growth tensions associated with this area given its proximity to the English city of Chester. North East Wales is one of the new spatial planning areas in the WSP, though our central concern here is how it intersects with the neighbouring areas in England. In many senses the interests in boundaries here echoes those introduced in Chapter 4, such as how spatial planning attempts to deal with the difficulties posed by political and administrative disjunction, not least concerning regulatory arrangements. While the border between England and Wales is not a national border in the sense that it separates sovereign states, it increasingly represents a political boundary between the diverging policies of the Welsh Assembly and those of the UK government relating to England.

The West Cheshire and North East Wales area possesses considerable economic dynamism and cross-border interaction already, creating pressures on the planning systems of the two jurisdictions, while until recent joint work there was a feeling that possible synergies were being neglected. The 'discovery' of the new cross-border region has been an important political awareness-raising exercise for all concerned. Thinking of North East Wales on its own, it is a largely rural area. However, in the context of a 'Wrexham-Deeside-Chester' hub, as the WSP prefers to call it (Figure 6.4), or a Chester city region as it could easily be thought of, it becomes part of a large and economically dynamic city region with all the potential and growth problems that this might suggest. This was soon recognised by those involved:

> This cross-border work was a real eye-opener for both politicians and officials in Cardiff . . . Looking at North Wales within its boundary is not particularly exciting economically . . . but when you look at this economy across the border, it's actually more powerful than you have in South Wales going across the border to Bristol . . . in terms of its performance.
>
> (Seminar, civil servant, 2007)

These cross-border links are outlined in the Welsh WSPU section on North East Wales:

> For Flintshire, Wrexham and Denbighshire, the cross-border linkages to the wider area of Chester and West Cheshire are crucial. The opportunity in this border area of North East Wales is about harnessing its special characteristics not only to benefit North East Wales but the wider geography, east and west. It will be a place where the strengths of prosperous areas are enhanced and the benefits of economic growth are maximised through linking areas of opportunity with areas in need of regeneration.
>
> (WAG 2008: 70)

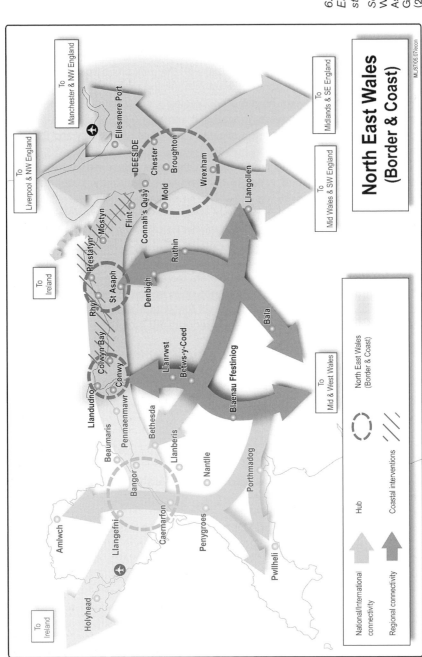

6.4 North East Wales strategy

Source: Welsh Assembly Government (2008).

Recognising the strong economic links in particular, public bodies both sides of the border have now been working together for a number of years. Consultants were commissioned to undertake a study of the area (G.V.A. Grimley 2004) and more recently, a non-statutory subregional spatial strategy, West Cheshire/North East Wales subregional spatial strategy has been adopted by the local authorities, the Welsh Assembly Government and the North West Regional Assembly (but not the North West Regional Development Agency, which refused to sign up to it formally). Objections to the plan came from both sides of the border. A key concern at the consultation stage was that the draft put forward was said to be largely focused on economic issues, relegating social and environmental issues to residual importance or simply as a constraint on development, something clearly set out in the consultation response by the Royal Society for the Protection of Birds (RSPB 2005). The RSPB also highlights its concern about what it refers to as 'creeping validation', as ideas become 'accepted' in this non-statutory plan which is not subject to a formal examination in public on either side of the border, as a normal plan would be.

The adopted strategy defines the new region as encompassing a core area of Chester and Ellesmere Port and Neston in England and Wrexham and Flintshire in North Wales, together with a wider reference area including Denbighshire, the Wirral and Warrington. The area is broadly speaking relatively prosperous, with low levels of unemployment and a growing population. There has been a strong flow of people moving out of Chester, the largest centre of employment, to live in North Wales (G.V.A. Grimley 2004), to the extent that much of Flintshire comes within the housing market and journey to work area of Chester. In effect, the Welsh border counties are providing space for housing to meet demands generated in England, while conversely Chester is providing employment for residents living in Wales.

A particular planning issue in the subregion is the strong and tightly drawn green belt around the city of Chester. This has been strongly enforced, partly as a North West Regional Assembly and Northern Way policy to direct growth towards the core city regions of Liverpool and Manchester, and partly to conserve the historic character of Chester itself. The unintended consequence of this constraint policy has been to generate a spill-over of local demand beyond the green belt boundary of Chester, with particular implications for the border counties in North Wales. The result has been a massive growth in commuting, as the constraints on local housing supply mean that more people are opting to commute into Chester from further afield, including Wales where property is often cheaper. Over time this ripple effect has spread through neighbouring Flintshire into Denbigh. In effect the subregional strategy is an attempt to better manage this process for those on either side of the border. It is, however, not viewed by all as a politically neutral act. For some it is a threat to the Welsh identity, as English people are attracted to live in and commute from Wales, something we return to later.

While both the subregional spatial strategy and the WSPU 2008 argue for focusing economic growth on the Chester, Wrexham, Deeside and Ellesmere

Port hub as an economic driver for the subregion, the North West regional spatial strategy public examination panel concluded that there should not be further regionally significant economic development in Chester. The overall regional spatial strategy policy is instead to concentrate growth on the inner parts of city regions in the North West and Chester is on the periphery of the Liverpool city region. The Panel Report put forward the view that:

> We consider that the location of further regionally significant economic development at Chester would be likely to result in additional commuting and traffic congestion.
>
> (Shepley and Hurley 2007: 90)

Moreover, the panel resisted pressures to increase the housing provision in Chester, arguing that it would damage the green belt and the historic character of Chester. As we have already noted, housing constraint in Chester is likely to result in further pressures for development in areas like Flintshire and Denbigh in Wales. This in turn is likely to increase rather than reduce commuting into Chester, unless economic growth is suppressed in which case it could have a significant impact on the economic prospects of the subregion, particularly on North East Wales.

This case study illustrates the problems of cross-border spatial planning when there are different regulatory practices, where a decision taken the English side of the border based on a regional approach to spatial policy can have important implications for an adjoining area. In this sense the formal North West Regional Spatial Strategy will not only decide what happens at the subregional scale in England, but also influence spatial policy across the border in Wales where, in the absence of strategic direction, the amounts of new development will be determined in local development plans. So it will be down to local decisions to establish how much of Chester's growth can be accommodated in Flintshire and Denbigh, although clearly these decisions will themselves have wider impacts.

As we noted earlier, there have been some objections to the way in which the joint subregional strategy was prepared and its position within the statutory planning apparatus. The Celtic League (2008) got involved in this debate rather belatedly,[3] but nonetheless provided a useful overview of why some people read events as acts of territorial political incursion rather than passive or even collaborative planning:

> The West Cheshire North East Wales Sub Regional Spatial Strategy is intended to provide a non-statutory framework for cross-border cooperation and development between North East Wales and West Cheshire over the next 15 years, since it came into effect in 2006. Even though the Welsh Assembly Government is one of the partners of Strategy, the economic entity of a North East Wales and West Cheshire sub region, its [sic] aims to create is likely to influence the

Wales Spatial Strategy in terms of planning, development and regeneration for the North East Wales area . . .

Moreover, public consultation for the strategy seems to have been very limited and it is also unclear just how the Strategy is open to public scrutiny and/or objection at all. Cross-border cooperation may be all well and good economically, but when English counties and businesses are able to exert an influence over important local decisions such as housebuilding, then something has gone seriously wrong.

. . . The redevelopment of North East Wales by English minded councils and business and commercial interests will be bad news for the Welsh language, identity and culture and could create a corridor of immigration (or colonisation) into the Welsh speaking heartlands (the Fro Cymraeg) of North East Wales. . . .

The Celtic League has written to the First Minister of the Welsh Government (see below) to express its concerns and to ask some very pertinent questions.

Dear First Minister Rhodri Morgan

North East Wales and West Cheshire sub region

I am writing to you to express our concerns about the existence and functioning of the above sub region, which has culminated in a non-statutory sub regional spatial strategy for North East Wales and West Cheshire.

Our concerns stem from the potentially damaging influence that this spatial strategy could have on the Local Development Plans (Unitary Development Plans) for these areas of Wales, where decisions regarding planning and regeneration can be made with little consideration for Welsh cultural and linguistic identity. If the Wales spatial plan and the North West spatial plan is to be overseen in the context of this West Cheshire/North East Wales sub region strategy then there are obvious issues for how the territorial integrity of Wales can remain intact. . . .

Admittedly the spatial strategy is non-statutory, but in our opinion it nevertheless seems to have influence on the town and country planning system in Wales, which have no Regional Spatial Strategies. Therefore there is an issue of accountability here and we would like to know how the Strategy went through a validation process and what recourse, if any, the public have to lodge objections to the Strategy and how those objections will be heard by an Independent Inspector?

We look forward to receiving your comments.

Your sincerely

Rhisiart Tal-e-bot General Secretary

(Celtic League 2008)

We reproduce this at length not to endorse it,[4] but because it highlights some important issues about the role of soft space governance and non-statutory planning processes in the new spatial planning. What the Celtic League argument highlights is that neither the WSP nor the cross-border subregional strategies are formally part of the Welsh planning hierarchy and neither of them is subject to a formal public examination. Much of the thinking in the sub-regional plan has understandably been fed into the 2008 WSPU. In fairness both subregional and national spatial strategies were subject to public consultation processes, with the WSP and WSPU consultations seemingly well publicised. But the problem remains that local spatial development policy will be determined through local development plans which should have regard to the WSPU which in turn incorporates the broad work of the North East Wales/West Cheshire subregional strategy.

Conclusion

Taken overall the Welsh Assembly Government has reworked policy across new scales of spatial planning governance in a novel and distinctive way. It manages to be a 'corporate plan' with a spatial dimension, in effect running parallel to the statutory land use planning system. This is its distinctive take in many ways – rather than an evidence-based, expert-led analysis of what is needed for the future spatial development of Wales, it instead sets up a process for thinking about the future whose emphasis is on the process of consultation rather than simply producing a plan to a set timetable and format. Its main achievements are perhaps in changing corporate thinking and building consensus at this stage, though with the 2008 Update it has begun to fill in spatial detail. In many ways similar to our conclusions for Scotland, one of the achievements in Wales has been in creating a process for the co-production and coalignment of strategies across government and related institutions, in the process creating a wider audience for spatial planning. The process of building a strong policy community where spatial issues can be debated at different scales is no mean achievement. This case study also reveals more than any other how spatial planning can be imagined as something linked to but also separate from the formal statutory planning system. Spatial planning emerges here as not an 'evolution' from regulatory planning, but as a parallel process with wider aims in changing corporate thinking and practices.

The national scale of spatial strategy-making plus the six new Welsh areas or subregions are important because they introduce new spaces for spatial planning in Wales, neither of which forms part of the statutory planning process, other than the statutory requirement that local development plans have regard to the Wales Spatial Plan. There is a real issue about whether this distinctive approach has actually led to a set of documents which is any better than those we look at elsewhere in this book in producing visionary plans which are likely to lead to better developments on the ground. In many respects it is still too early to make a clear judgement. But given that so much of the work of the Wales Spatial Plan is presented as fairly high-level strategic statements, it is difficult to see where difficult decisions have so far been grappled with and distinctive or decisive new policy directions determined. In other words there is a distinctive approach to producing the Plan, which has much to commend it, specifically in the context of Wales as a newly devolved territory. But it is less easy to see much evidence that it has achieved anything beyond the integration of various paper strategies plus a stronger sense of common purpose in terms of a more corporate approach to the future development of the territory of Wales. This partly reflects the limited devolution package still operating in Wales, which has limited discretion over funding and legislative change.

A number of significant issues emerge from the experiences of national spatial planning in Wales. The first concerns the tension between prescription and flexibility inherent in any multi-tiered planning system. Debates over rescaling and the drivers of change discussed in Chapters 1 and 2 highlighted the need for more effective forms of economic governance. However, the issue of scope and struggles over policy sectors was also highlighted as being integral to the changing nature of scale. Economic development and competitiveness were privileged over environmental issues in the Bluestone case which perhaps reflects how such struggles are being played out at a national level within the Welsh Assembly. Wales is not unique in seeking to facilitate developments that will improve employment opportunities. What marks this case out though is how little the Wales Spatial Plan had to say about a nationally significant development such as Bluestone and how, despite its primary purpose as a document for policy integration, the decision on Bluestone was contrary to other national strategies on environmental protection.

The second issue concerns the role that national plans and strategies should take in creating certainty and balancing national and local concerns. The Wales Spatial Plan has taken a different stance on identifying the spatial implications of its policies through the fuzzy boundary approach. While this may be necessary to create 'useful uncertainty' and allow some coherence to be overlaid onto a diverse situation it has had the downside of creating a vacuum on housing issues. Part of the reason for the introduction of Regional Spatial Strategies in England was to introduce greater certainty on housing development targets for local authorities and communities, leaving decisions over location to local planning authorities. In Wales the process is now being undertaken outside of the Wales Spatial Plan process, which might help meet future housing needs in the broad subregion by overcoming certain local anti-development tendencies, but this is not without causing ructions over the nature of Welsh identity and the emergent territorial politics of the border area.

We conclude with something of a hypothesis, namely that a high level of generality in a plan, as opposed to providing spatial specificity, allows consensus and the appearance of integrated policy-making, but that this in effect simply transfers the decision-making process over difficult issues to other arenas, whether these be political, legal or otherwise. Alternatively, providing spatial detail is a way of creating tensions, slowing down the plan-making process and alienating some stakeholders, but it does allow decisions to be made within the planning arena around an agreed strategy. Neither is perfect, nor right for every territorial situation. But what the Wales case study does is flush this tension out into the open.

7

English spatial planning and dealing with growth in the Leeds City Region

This is the first of two chapters on growth management issues in English regions, with this chapter focusing on Leeds in Yorkshire and Chapter 8 looking at London. Although both are covered by the same national planning framework for England, they represent very different regional contexts as London enjoys a form of regional democratic accountability for planning issues which does not yet extend to other parts of England. This chapter looks at Leeds because it provides a good illustration of some of the current pressures in the planning system to think about city region issues, including the key spatial planning challenges around infrastructure provision. Leeds is particularly interesting because it has emerged as one of the most remarkable urban success stories in England since the late 1980s. Part of the industrial heartland of West Yorkshire, noted historically for its wool and engineering industries, more recently it can reasonably claim to have established itself as a major financial services centre, second only to London in England. For neighbouring authorities, the growth of Leeds has been both a blessing and a curse. On the positive side the city has developed a large functional hinterland, with substantial growth of commuting to Leeds city centre in particular. While the new jobs are welcome for those within commuting distance, the growth of Leeds also brings problems for its neighbours, in terms of house price growth and affordability for local people, and loss of greenfield sites to new housing developments. A key issue for Leeds is that the government expects housing to be resolved at local authority level, while it is actively empowering regions and city regions as preferred scales of governance for economic development and, most tellingly, bids for government investment. This leaves local authorities with responsibility for dealing with difficult development decisions, without having much influence on the essential decisions around infrastructure investment needed to support successful development. It is in this broad context that this chapter examines the pressures for a rescaling of the politics of development in favour of a Greater Leeds area, known as the Leeds City Region.

The remaking of Leeds as a successful urban economy has not been accidental. For over two decades the city's leaders have sought to reposition it as a leading city both within the region and within Europe, aspiring to match the success of cities such as Barcelona (Haughton 1996; Haughton and While 1999). In particular Leeds grasped the opportunity offered by the dismantling of the West Yorkshire County Council to promote itself as a centre for service sector growth and as the regional city for Yorkshire and the Humber, for instance, its efforts to brand itself as a 24-hour city and retail centre in the mid-1990s. With growing evidence of success, apparent in terms of new jobs and a massive building boom for commercial and residential properties in the city centre, the city's leaders set out to find common cause with other large cities to present its case for governmental investment, not as a 'basket case' economy in need of major resuscitation, but rather as a major engine of economic growth, albeit with some problems of social exclusion. Leeds was a member of the influential lobby group Core Cities from its formation in 1995, a group involving some of the most powerful English provincial cities (Newcastle, Leeds, Sheffield, Manchester, Liverpool, Birmingham, Nottingham and Bristol). The Core City Group has consistently promoted the concept of city regions as economic drivers of their regions.

But the story tucked away behind the apparent economic success of Leeds is its limited positive impacts on those most in need within the city. This is something local leaders are all too well aware of, and indeed notions of a 'two-speed' city very much play to the success of the city's leaders in attracting government funds for regeneration in its run-down areas (Haughton 1996). But with more than a decade of growth to build on, there is much to suggest that the lessons learnt have not necessarily been the right ones. In a linked pair of articles Leeds University academics have outlined the considerable expansion of new building in the city centre, for both commercial and residential usages, including a recent rush to build skyscrapers (Chatterton and Hodkinson 2007; Hodkinson and Chatterton 2007). They argue that much of the city centre boom in residential apartments has been problematic, reliant on a largely speculative rental market, with high vacancy rates and very limited social infrastructure to support residents, meaning the new city centre flats have proven attractive mainly to short-term residents who quickly move on. Local council estates are being demolished and rebuilt with private housing, with some provision for social housing attached. But in effect there is a displacement effect going on here, where the poor are being moved around the city to make way for the new residential spaces close to the city centre, many of which will be second homes or speculative purchases rather than homes to live in (Chatterton and Hodkinson 2007; Hodkinson and Chatterton 2007). The much-vaunted 24-hour city initiative of the 1990s has brought about a rise in 'entertainment' in the city centre, but far from a civilised European-style café culture. At night-time, the city centre has become awash with large, drunken groups moving between large, corporatised pubs and clubs, driving out those in search of a different type of cultural experience. As with the Greenwich Millennium Village's attempts to create a European-influenced apartment-living neighbourhood, it has been a very partial, very English approach (see Chapter 8). In many ways it is an exemplar of how the government's particular take on business-led regeneration leads to lopsided development which caters to select groups and corporate investors in pursuit of their money, but which is not commercially, socially or environmentally sustainable into the long term. In this context, the move to a city region scale of policy-making thinking ought to have afforded the opportunity to inject fresh thinking into how to address some of the problems of Leeds' growth.

This chapter then examines the way in which spatial planning for Leeds and its surrounding areas has sought to address growth management problems, notably how to plan strategically for new housing. First, though, we must set the scene by providing a bit more about the recent spatial planning experience in England, elaborating on some of the broad themes introduced in Chapters 1 and 2.

Spatial planning in England

England is the largest and in many respects the most complex of the UK territories, due not least to its greater population size (50.5 million) and the scale of its economy (GVA £861.6 billion in 2004, out of a UK total of £1,033.3 billion: Phillpots and Causer, 2006: 218). But most importantly for our purposes England has become increasingly politically complex, partly as a consequence of the asymmetrical nature of UK devolution, leaving England as the only substantial territory without its own bespoke form of territorial government (Jones *et al.* 2005; Keating 2005). More than this, the consequence of the delegation of powers to the Mayor and the Greater London Assembly and the abortive attempts to introduce elected regional assemblies elsewhere, has created uneven regional democratic institutional representation across England. The eight English regions outside London have nonetheless experienced a considerable strengthening of their regional institutional frameworks, with the introduction of Regional Assemblies, which have strong representation of co-opted councillors as a means of improving their democratic credentials, plus Regional Development Agencies (RDAs) which, though business led and business oriented, do have local councillors and other 'community' representatives on their boards. Regional Assemblies are important as they have formal responsibility for preparing Regional Spatial Strategies, which include Regional Transport Strategies, plus overseeing a variety of other regional strategies, including for housing, and providing a formal 'scrutiny' role over the activities of RDAs. RDAs are important as the main conduit for government efforts to promote economic development across the English regions, over time managing to argue successfully for greater funding and discretion in how they can spend this. Government Offices for the Regions are also argued to be an essential link between regions and central government departments. One of the consequences of the creation of this new regional institutional landscape has been a parallel regional 'rescaling' of many of the activities of the various stakeholder groups which seek to influence the policies of the new bodies (Haughton and Counsell 2004).

Despite such advances in regional institutional structures, the absence of a strong English territorial governmental machinery is something which still regularly attracts critical political and media commentary, typically whenever one of the devolved nations flexes its new-found independence with an eye-catching new initiative. However, the failed referendum in the North East in 2004 revealed that there was little appetite to introduce a formal elected regional scale of politics, and there appears to be little or no pressure for an all-England assembly or parliament either. The result of this is a series of asym-metries in the new regionalism, where English political affairs at national level are dealt with by UK government departments, which are also responsible at varying levels for setting the context for the whole of the UK, leading to occa-sional confusion about whether a policy directive is specifically for England, England and Wales, or for the UK as a whole. At the moment national planning for England is done in a Whitehall government department, which must also take into account the need to provide a broad tenor if not quite a framework for the planning systems of the devolved territories, with Wales still formally dependent on the Westminster government for primary planning legislation. There is no single spatial strategy for the UK, and while the devolved admin-istrations in Northern Ireland, Scotland and Wales have all produced territorial spatial strategies, there is no unifying equivalent for England.

England's economic expansion in recent years has been strongly focused on the south-east corner of the country, where economic growth and the physical development needed to support it are a continuous political point of contention. Indeed the development politics of the south east are always a strong influence on reforms to the planning system. Green belt politics in particular are heavily shaped by the strong support for them in parts of the south east, where green belt is seen as a powerful tool for resisting the impo-sition of unwanted new housing in the countryside. One consequence of this London-centricity in English planning policy is that some central government announcements can easily be portrayed as insensitive to the needs of the north (see below, on the Sustainable Communities action plan). More impor-tantly, perhaps, the anti-development lobby of the south east and beyond has been particularly powerful at the level of county councils. In the English system of local government, there is a mix of two-tier authorities (county councils and local authorities) and unitary authorities. The unitary system is most frequently found in urban areas. In planning terms, unitary authorities provided both the broad strategic and detailed local plan in a single unitary plan, while in two-tier authorities the county councils provided the broad strategic framework for planning (structure plans) and local authorities provided the detailed local plans.

To understand recent English reforms in which county councils were largely stripped of their planning powers, it is important to understand that many of the county councils have been in opposition to central government pressures requiring them to build new housing at a faster rate than they claimed their areas could cope with without encroaching onto politically sensitive green belt areas or greenfield sites more generally. The most important recently completed English planning reforms have been the 2001 Planning Green Paper followed by the Planning and Compulsory Purchase Act of 2004. These established a new two-tier system of spatial planning for England that operates at the regional and local scales (Regional Spatial Strategies and Local Development Frameworks respectively). Local Development Frameworks, prepared by local planning authorities (district councils, unitary authorities, metropolitan districts and London boroughs), replaced the previous mixed system of local plans, unitary development plans and county-level structure plans. Regional Spatial Strategies were upgraded to become 'statutory', where the previous system of Regional Planning Guidance, though increasingly influential, had remained non-statutory. In addition, sustainable development was introduced as the statutory purpose of the whole planning system, with greater scope for stakeholder engagement in the plan-making system also introduced. The main rhetorical reasons given for the reforms emphasised that they would streamline the system, allowing it to be both quicker and more responsive to changing market conditions. There is little doubt though that political motives also played a part in the rescaling away from counties in favour of a stronger regional tier of planning.

Regional Spatial Strategies are prepared by regional planning bodies (RPBs), usually the Regional Assemblies, then formally issued by central government on the advice of the relevant Government Office of the Region (Marshall 2002; Haughton and Counsell 2004; Pearce and Ayres 2006). The exception is London, where responsibility for developing and publishing the London Plan rests with the London Mayor (see Chapter 8). Regional Planning Bodies are typically a group of local authority planners and local councillors working as a subgroup of the regional assembly, with the regional assembly having a small group of core staff plus secondees from local authorities and elsewhere to help them in preparing drafts of the RSS. As such RSSs are essentially prepared by the local and regional actors who constitute the RPBs, but the final say rests with central government which necessarily colours their content. There is an interesting tension, if not fault-line, which runs through this process, whereby central government professes disappointment that many RSSs lack distinctiveness, are short on spatial direction and duck difficult decisions, so it exhorts others to do better while retaining final responsibility itself! Part of the problem is that the regional planning system is not backed by an elected regional government, instead relying on co-opted local councillors to work through the Regional Assemblies and Regional Planning Bodies. The result is that a degree of local turf protection pervades the system, making it difficult to broker decisions based on the greater regional good rather than avoiding upsetting individual local governments and their sensitivities. To cope with their democratic deficit, RPBs are understandably expected to have in place systems for widespread consultation, plus scrutiny by Public Examination over several weeks in front of an independent panel, and an iterative process of sustainability appraisal (Counsell and Haughton 2006a).

Some of these tensions would have evaporated if central government had been able to take forward its plans to devolve greater powers to elected regional bodies, which would have included regional responsibility for issuing regional spatial strategies. However, in the aftermath of the failed referendum in the North East such moves have become unthinkable for the foreseeable future, resulting in a period of reflection on how best to move forward. In 2007 in a consultation document reviewing subnational arrangements for economic development (HM Treasury 2007), the government proposed amalgamating RSSs into single 'integrated regional strategies' to be prepared by Regional Development Agencies – the unelected regional assemblies would be abolished. For many this could prove problematic (Baden 2008; Marshall 2008), not least since RDAs are unelected, business-led quangos very heavily focused on economic growth. In effect it shifts responsibility from one type of weak non-elected body to another type of unelected body, one not known for its sensitivity in dealing with dissenting voices.

Central government

Central government responsibility for planning has shifted departments four times in successive departmental reorganisations since New Labour came to power in 1997. For the period covered by the present research, the main responsibility for planning matters lay initially with the Office of the Deputy Prime Minister (ODPM) and was subsequently transferring to a newly created Department of Communities and Local Government (DCLG), widely known as Communities. Given this book's central interest in the politics of integration, it is worth noting that for a short period many of the main related functions were brought together in one super-department between 1997 and 2000, the Department of the Environment, Transport and the Regions. However, amidst concerns that this department was becoming too much for one Secretary of State to manage, many functions have since been separated off in subsequent departmental reorganisations. For instance, much of the work on transport planning now lies with the Department for Transport (DfT), for environmental planning and sustainable development with the Department for Environment, Food and Rural Affairs (DEFRA), and for heritage planning with the Department for Culture, Media and Sport (DCMS) (Cullingworth and Nadin 2006). Functional integration into one super-department had initially been seen as a way of improving policy coordination by addressing interdepartmental rivalries and communications issues, while more latterly the approach has been to build 'integration' more centrally into the mechanisms of government (see below).

It is important to emphasise that planning has come to be seen by government as a key policy arena for addressing certain national political priorities and as part of its agenda for better integrated policy (see Chapter 2). Most notably perhaps, planning has attracted attention for its alleged negative impacts on housebuilding rates, national competitiveness and economic growth. While the Blair and Brown Labour governments' planning reforms have clearly addressed a broader agenda than just these concerns, at the heart of recent reforms appears to be an attempt to make planning more business friendly, at one level a continuation of previous Conservative governments' efforts to ensure that planning does not act as a constraint on economic development. But there is a clear break with previous practice, not least the assertion of a central role for sustainable development in planning policy, with sustainable development now a core objective of the planning system (ODPM 2005b). It is also notable that planning is very much seen as an important tool in the government's policy repertoire for addressing climate change. As we noted in Chapter 2, there has been considerable debate over planners' use of sustainable development, including whether it has been subverted from a well-intentioned mechanism for achieving 'balanced' sustainable development, to one where economic development imperatives always seem to hold sway, while planners over-estimate the value of urban compaction policies as a sustainability tool at the expense of alternative approaches (Haughton and Counsell 2004; Counsell and Haughton 2006b; Gunder 2006).

The issues here are complex (see Haughton and Counsell 2004), but in summary, proposals for new housing developments on greenfield sites almost invariably meet local resistance from the existing residents of an area, which can then create a political backlash in which politicians lose their seats. This is particularly true in England, especially in the south east. There are powerful national lobby groups such as the Campaign to Protect Rural England (CPRE), RSPB and National Trust who ensure that oppositional voices are heard at a regional and national level too. Faced with official projections of substantial future increases in the demand for new houses as population grows and lifestyles change, the UK government has been left trying to find places to build them in the face of entrenched rural opposition. As we saw in Chapters 3 and 4, the issues are different in Ireland and Northern Ireland, where opposition to rural housing has been less vocal and indeed there is a strong rural lobby that argues that rural housing should not be discouraged in the context of welcoming back former emigrants wishing to return to their family roots. Government planners by contrast see the costs of providing scattered housing in terms of expensive or poorly provided infrastructure (water, energy, roads, schools, clinics, shops) and limited public transport, leading to car-dependent sprawl which is typically aesthetically poor quality and as such intrusive on rural landscapes.

For both the UK and Irish governments the main answer is seen to be promoting 'urban compaction' or consolidation, where the emphasis is on directing the bulk of new housebuilding into existing urban areas where the supportive infrastructure and community fabric either already exists or can be provided most cost effectively. In England this has seen the introduction of a series of targets into the planning system for the proportion of new housing being located on 'brownfield' sites, that is those sites previously developed on, for instance, abandoned factories or railway sidings, plus targets to increase the residential density of new developments, in effect more homes per hectare. This has become justified by a 'sustainable development' rationale, which says this approach is more 'sustainable' as it recycles abandoned land, saves greenfield sites from development, and promotes the use of existing urban infrastructure. If mainland European cities can be attractive places to live, with high-density, mixed-use neighbourhoods, the argument goes, so can English cities (Urban Task Force 1999).

The problem with this approach is that it has been used to force through some fairly poor-quality urban developments without adequate social and green infrastructure, in effect a form of town cramming which is insensitive to existing qualities of place, the desire of many people to live in homes with gardens and not flats with balconies, and the need for good urban parks and other urban spaces to make high-density living attractive (Evans 1991; Breheny 1997). The result is some unattractive new developments, too often involving substantial residential complexes packed tightly into small areas adjacent to busy main roads, with noise and air pollution for those who live in them. With national and local governments typically unwilling to pay for creating and maintaining public parks and similar open spaces, and developers willing only to provide those forms of public space palatable to buyers, too often the result has been poor-quality neighbourhoods. The twin refrains of national planners therefore are the need to build more houses more rapidly, with improved neighbourhood quality of life, always justified by the rationale that this must happen as it is sustainable, without seriously considering alternatives that might be more sustainable, such as well-designed new communities in rural areas. Spatial planning with its emphasis on place-making issues becomes a central plank of the government's efforts to reassure citizens that it is possible to develop good-quality urban spaces, and in the process achieve what is known in sustainable development terms as a 'win-win' situation, where economic, social and environmental benefits are all achieved in true integrated fashion. What we begin to see already though is an affirmation of our earlier comment (Chapter 2) that spatial planning is essentially a political process, rather than a neutral technical exercise dominated by professionals. Those days, if they ever really existed, are long gone.

Within government at least two paradigms collide in seeking to influence the evolution of planning practice, those who prioritise an 'integrated' approach to sustainable development, which can of course be read as a politically inspired reading of sustainability, and those who prioritise an economic growth agenda, mainly those in the economy-oriented departments. The latter are driven by a narrow agenda for developing planning's role, based on the need to focus on generating wealth and jobs, in the expectation that these will 'trickle down' to help meet the government's social and environmental agendas. So running alongside the rhetorical shift towards a greater engagement with sustainable development, the minutiae of the operation of the planning system have increasingly come under scrutiny from central departments such as the Treasury and what was the Department of Trade and Industry (now the Department of Business, Enterprise and Regulatory Reform) (see also Glasson and Marshall 2007). Both of these departments have dedicated teams whose remit it is to influence the planning system principally in support of the national competitiveness agenda. Treasury-led moves to improve the performance of planning have resulted in a string of policy reviews including (see Table 7.1): the *Review of Housing Supply* (Barker 2004); the *Barker Review of Land Use Planning* (Barker 2006); the *Eddington Transport Study* (Eddington 2006), and the *Subnational Economic Development and Regeneration Review* (HM Treasury 2007). These studies fed into the

Table 7.1 Major government reviews and White Papers, 2004–2007

Review	*Implications for spatial planning*
Barker Review of Housing Supply (2004)	Promotes a market approach to housing supply with increased investment in social housing and the introduction of a Planning Gain Supplement to capture some of the development gains
Local Government White Paper (2006)	Introduces a requirement for Local Area Agreements to deliver Sustainable Communities Strategies and for these to be coordinated with Local Development Frameworks. Also promotes Multi-area Agreements between local authorities across administrative boundaries in city regions and elsewhere
Lyons Inquiry into Local Government (2006)	Promotes a greater recognition of the role of local government in place shaping and citizen engagement
Hampton Review of Regulation (2006)	Looks at reducing the regulatory burden on business through a rationalisation of activities
Eddington Transport Study (2006)	Examines the links between transport and the UK's productivity and economic growth, promoting sustained investment in transport infrastructure and prioritising city centres, key intra-urban corridors and international gateways
Barker Review of Land Use Planning (2006)	Proposes that planning takes a more positive approach to economic growth, reducing delays and introducing new procedures for dealing with major infrastructure projects
Planning White Paper (2007)	Responds to the Barker Review of planning by promoting a more responsive planning system which integrates economic, social and environmental objectives. Introduces new procedures for dealing with major infrastructure projects, removing them from direct planning control
Review of subnational economic development and regeneration (2007)	Proposes abolishing regional assemblies and combining Regional Spatial Strategies with Regional Economic Strategies under the overall responsibility of RDAs

Planning White Paper and Planning Bill 2007, which, among other changes, aim to streamline the planning system, removing major infrastructure proposals from direct planning control and thus in theory speeding up their delivery (DCLG 2007), and introducing a new system of national policy statements. The 2006 *Pre-Budget Report* (HM Treasury 2006) identified reform of the planning system and investment in transport infrastructure as key measures for achieving productivity and growth, together with investment in 'sustainable housing supply'.

More broadly supportive of integrated regional planning, the Treasury with the Department of Trade and Industry (DTI), Department for Transport and ODPM (as they then were) introduced regional funding allocations for housing, economic development and transport (HM Treasury 2005; see also Ayres and Stafford 2008). This is the latest of a steady stream of Treasury initiatives to demonstrate greater regional sensitivity in budget allocations, in this case allowing regional partners to put forward their own suggestions for funding priorities (Ayres and Stafford 2008).

A wide range of other government departments is also included in the internal consultation network on changes to spatial planning: DEFRA, Department for Culture, Media and Sport, Department for Education and Science (DfES – this department has subsequently been reorganised and renamed), Department of Health, Home Office and Ministry of Defence. Enthusiasm for spatial planning appears mixed in these departments. In our interviews, DCMS, for example, saw clear benefits in developing its links with spatial planning both within central government and in the regions through Regional Culture Consortia. DfES, on the other hand, appeared less enthusiastic, suggesting that we should proceed without an input from them as planning was apparently not something they had much involvement with. The reluctance of the education sector to engage with planning issues was something which cascaded through the system to the local level, with one planner, for instance, telling us that 'education is a silo that is almost impenetrable' (Interview E14, London planner, 2005).

Outside the departments of state, the Cabinet Office also addresses issues impinging on planning, in particular through the Prime Minister's Policy Unit. The internal network of consultees on changes to central government planning policy includes the nine Government Offices for the Regions (GORs) in England, which track work carried out by Regional Planning Bodies on Regional Spatial Strategies and are ultimately responsible for issuing revisions of RSSs. The Regional Coordination Unit supports the GORs from the centre. Also involved, both nationally and regionally, are government agencies, such as the Environment Agency, Natural England, Highways Agency and English Heritage, which all employ specialist planning staff. Within DCLG itself, there are also crucial links between spatial planning staff and those engaged in work on urban policy, housing and neighbourhood renewal. We return to the issue of integration at central government level in Chapter 8.

Sustainable Communities action plan

The Sustainable Communities action plan was issued in 2003 and while not a statutory document, its contents and its follow-up have been very influential in shaping subsequent national and subnational planning policy and practice. The plan emerged as a response to the increasingly evident problems of a lack of affordable housing in the south east and housing market failure in parts of the Midlands and north. Dressed up in the language of sustainable development, the concept of creating 'sustainable communities' was first introduced in a speech by the Deputy Prime Minister in 2002, and further developed and translated into concrete policy proposals in the Sustainable Communities Plan (SCP) (ODPM 2003c).

The SCP designated four major growth areas in the south east of England – Thames Gateway, Milton Keynes/Northampton, Stansted/Cambridge and Ashford – and nine Housing Market Renewal Pathfinders for areas of housing market failure in the north and Midlands. These ambitious plans were naturally greeted with considerable media and professional attention, not least as substantial public money was expected to be allocated to the designated areas. In the north there was an outcry from MPs and local government councillors aghast at the implication that the north was an area beset by problems, pointing to the considerable growth potential of the north and arguing for help in promoting the north's role as an economic driver. Responding to this the government announced a string of other initiatives, including the Northern Way as a new mechanism for providing a coordinated economic growth strategy for all three northern regions (Yorkshire and Humber, North West and North East).

The Northern Way is interesting for the purposes of this chapter for several reasons. First, it is a good example of a newly created 'soft space' of governance, having no previous history as an administrative unit. Second, the Northern Way strategy put at its heart the idea that eight city regions existed which constituted the main economic drivers for the north (Counsell and Haughton 2007). These city regions were themselves a new invention, yet another layer of soft space governance, emphasised by the decision to portray them with fuzzy rather than clear boundaries. Finally, responsibility to develop the Northern Way strategy was given to the three RDAs of the north, sending a clear signal that it was essentially an economic strategy, not a spatial planning strategy. Nonetheless, the government made clear that it expected regional planning bodies to take account of the Northern Way approach in their spatial strategies. On top of this, the Northern Way and the city region partnerships that grew out of it became increasingly influential in developing bids for future public infrastructure spending, especially for transport. In effect then, spatial strategies, which rely for implementation on the delivery of infrastructure investment, became subordinate in part to the non-statutory, economic-oriented plans of the Northern Way. We will explore some of the tensions this created below when we look at the work going on around the Leeds City Region, one of the Northern Way's designated city regions.

As part of the wider Sustainable Communities initiatives successive government announcements introduced 'new growth points' and the 'Eco-Towns'
initiative (DCLG 2007). The growth areas, new growth points and Eco-Towns
collectively constitute an important part of the government's efforts to speed
up the supply of new housing, expected to accommodate up to 900,000 new
houses between them. Not surprisingly then, there is some debate on the
merits of work under the Sustainable Communities banner, with some hailing
it as a new agenda for planning, while others have decried it as a smokescreen
that allows the government to force through a massive housebuilding programme for the south east (Gallent and Tewdwr-Jones 2007). Both views
contain more than a grain of truth. At one level Sustainable Communities work
does embed within the various strands of documentation a broader vision for
planning, focusing on sustainability and quality of life issues. Alternatively there
is still considerable uncertainty about what the government means in its use
of the term 'Sustainable Communities', inspiring a rhetoric of aspiring to high
standards of place making while continuing to allow through the system considerable amounts of unremarkable development (Allmendinger and Tiesdell
2004; Gallent and Tewdwr-Jones 2007).

Not surprisingly then, 'Sustainable Communities' inspired initiatives, not
least the Northern Way and the reprioritisation of the Thames Gateway (see
Chapter 8), have provided sometimes uneasy but nevertheless critically important inputs into RSSs, both symbolically and in terms of attracting government
investment to support planning aspirations. It is perhaps telling that as the
Sustainable Communities work does not form part of the statutory planning
system it is not subject to the same level of public scrutiny as Regional Spatial
Strategies and Local Development Frameworks, with no requirement for
Sustainability Appraisal or Public Examination, for instance. Understandingly,
tensions have arisen where growth aspirations in Sustainable Communities
Plan initiatives conflict with different growth aspirations in emerging Regional
Spatial Strategies. This was particularly evident in the south east and east of
England regions where Regional Planning Bodies aspired to lower levels of
housing growth than the growth area studies promoted (see e.g. Hetherington
2004).

New policy tools within and running alongside planning

Planning has seen a new range of technical approaches introduced in recent
years, including Regional Planning Guidance/Regional Spatial Strategies,
subregional strategies and Local Development Frameworks, and an attempt
to speed up approval of major infrastructure projects by creating a parallel
planning system for them. Supporting these has emerged a range of new
policy instruments which have helped embed government priorities into local
planning practice, such as brownfield site targets, new housing number allocations, residential density targets, targets for time taken to approve planning
applications, and the sequential test, a system for ensuring that greenfield
sites are considered for development only after other options have been

considered first. Community involvement has also been strengthened and sustainability appraisal introduced as a way of ensuring that a more 'balanced' consideration is undertaken of whether strategies meet sustainable development objectives. The latter two in particular are broadly supportive of the government's adoption of some of the features of spatial planning outlined in Chapters 1 and 2.

This section though focuses on aspects of the wider governmental apparatus with which these tools must intersect. In particular as part of the push for better integrated central government policy, a range of related policy tools has been introduced, most notably those associated with the Treasury's public spending reviews, which allocate future government funding between departments. The new language of planning then has had to incorporate policy terms and acronyms, such as Public Service Agreement (PSA) targets, Local Area Agreements (LAAs) and Multi-Area Agreements (MAAs). In devising Public Service Agreement targets, central government seeks to ensure that its priorities are reflected throughout the public sector, so in effect they serve not only to focus attention on deliverable outcomes from public spending but also greater coordination across government departments. The various targets are intended to be broadly constituted, with planning expected to contribute to its own main target (PSA6), which covers things like housing supply, brownfield land and density targets, and speed of planning decisions, plus other targets. As more than one department might be required to play a significant role in achieving a particular outcome, provision is made for joint targets. For example, the 2004–2008 Spending Review (HM Treasury 2004) identified a joint target on regional imbalance (PSA2) for ODPM, DTI and the Treasury, requiring them to:

> Make sustainable improvements in the economic performance of all English regions by 2008, and over the long term reduce the persistent gap in growth rates between the regions, demonstrating progress by 2006.

This PSA2 target is important in the context of this chapter as it was one of the driving forces behind the Northern Way, which is intended to contribute to reducing differences in economic performance between the three northern regions and the more prosperous regions in the south and east.

Local Area Agreements are agreements on priorities between central government and Local Strategic Partnerships (LSPs). The LSPs are partnerships of public sector bodies and local stakeholders which are given the remit to produce Sustainable Community Strategies for their areas, a form of overarching strategy for an area which all the main service providers are expected to agree to. Local plans, or LDFs, are intended to be an integral part of the assemblage of local strategies, not least in providing spatial expression for them. Multi-area Agreements are a mechanism that allows neighbouring LSPs to come together across administrative boundaries to form joint agreements, usually on particular issues such as economic development. In the absence of a formal statutory basis for city regions they have been promoted as a tool for coordinating policy between local authorities at the city region scale (DCLG 2006a).

The Yorkshire and Humber Plan and the Leeds City Region

Spatial planning context

With a population of over 2.8 million, a workforce of nearly 1.2 million and a GVA of nearly £45.5 billion (Leeds City Region Partnership 2006), Leeds is the largest of the three city regions designated by the Northern Way strategy for the Yorkshire and Humber region. It contains about 48 per cent of the region's population and generates 60 per cent of its GVA. Two separate policy streams provide the main context for spatial policy in the Leeds City Region (Figure 7.1), economic development and regional planning, with transport an important linking concern.

In Yorkshire and the Humber, the three main strategies are the overarching 'integrated' regional framework Advancing Together, the Regional Economic Strategy (now in its third version) led by Yorkshire Forward, the RDA for the region, and the Regional Spatial Strategy. The statutory planning framework for the regions consists of the Regional Spatial Strategy and Local Development Frameworks, with the RSS also empowered to undertake sub-regional work as it deems appropriate. Under new arrangements introduced in 1998 (Haughton and Counsell 2004), the first substantial spatial strategy for Yorkshire and the Humber was published in draft form in 1999 as Regional Planning Guidance (RPG). Following public examination in 2000 the modified RPG was issued by government in 2001. The final RPG document though left many questions unresolved, most notably perhaps about the scale of housing growth required in economically buoyant areas such as the Leeds City Region. Four years later, and following the 2004 planning reforms, a draft Regional Spatial Strategy was published in December 2005 (Yorkshire and Humber Regional Assembly 2005) which aimed to address these issues. Housing growth emerged as one of the key issues at the examination in public in September/October 2006, leading to the Panel recommending a further increase in housing numbers in its report published in March 2007. Further increases again were proposed in the Secretary of State's Proposed Amendments (September 2007) and these were incorporated into the final plan (see below).

The Yorkshire and Humber Plan, which is the name given to the Regional Spatial Strategy, was finally published in May 2008 and has a horizon through to 2026 (Government Office for Yorkshire and Humber (GOYH) 2008). Apart from the housing allocations, it is largely uncontroversial, setting out a broad vision for the region's future and a series of supporting policy statements. In general terms our interviews found a level of contentment that the RSS process did not rock the boat too much, alongside a sense of frustration for exactly the same reason. In broad terms, there was a feeling that despite RSS

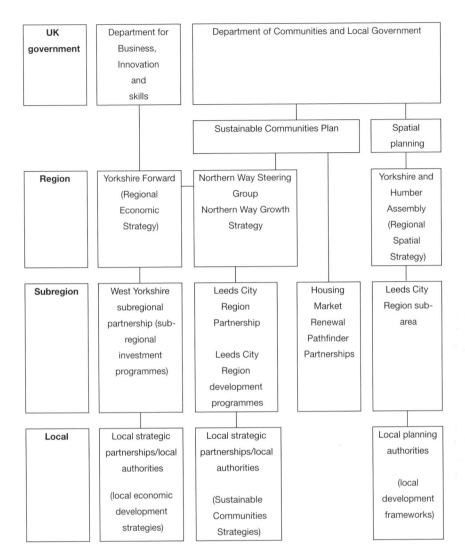

7.1 Different policy streams, Yorkshire and the Humber

Source: adapted from Counsell and Haughton (2006a).

becoming a statutory instrument, it was not clear how important it was in the overall system of multi-scalar governance, particularly in relation to the role of the Northern Way, city region initiatives, the new LDF process, and the role of Yorkshire Forward, which leads on the Regional Economic Strategy, and has a relatively strong investment capacity. This said, the various regional strategies in Yorkshire and the Humber were generally felt to be reasonably well aligned at a strategic level, providing a good basis for the RSS. All the main regional strategies take account of the integrated strategy for Yorkshire and the Humber, *Advancing Together*, and as a matter of policy each of the main strategy documents cross-refers to policies in the others. They are less well integrated on their actual contents, which perhaps understandably have different core objectives, plus different time horizons (Counsell *et al.* 2007).

However, there was a feeling that with all these diverse pressures coming into play, there was considerable 'noise' in the system as the various policy communities involved in each strategy responded to various government initiatives, so that integration appeared rather better on paper than it worked out in practice. Despite such concerns, the RSS was seen to be an important core document for the region, so many stakeholders spent many hours helping to produce the documentation and getting involved in the various consultation processes. The strengths of the overall process were seen to centre on the way in which institutional actors were brought together through the RSS system, with several people telling us that the main benefits from the partnership involved individuals making links as much as the policies put on paper. The RSS's main failings were, according to most critics, essentially down to its inability to integrate transport planning in any meaningful way and failure to broker consensus on housebuilding allocations within the region. Some of those involved also felt that the plan's strong economic development and housing allocation orientation overrode all other considerations, which are relatively weakly framed by comparison. It is worth noting that, though there is a Regional Transport Strategy chapter in the RSS, it is weak in giving a coherent spatial overview and in making a link to the rest of the strategy.

Two quotes give a reasonable sense of the range of comments encountered during our interviews:

> At the regional level I think spatial policy is pretty joined-up . . . you do get a sense that there are linkages between topics . . . there's been quite a lot of debate about what areas to include and how they relate to each other . . . There's been a lot of interest in how strategies link up . . . and about how sustainable development fits in . . . I get the sense overall that the joining-up is pretty good both spatially, thinking about how the city regions, subregions and local authorities match with the regional level plan . . . and also at the topic-level thinking about how the different parts of sustainable development relate to the RSS.
>
> (E35, regional economist, 2007)

> There's so much happening all at the same time . . . in parallel . . . and there isn't a clear synergy between one process and another process, and I think if you were to put all of the documents on one table – if you had a table big enough – you might find that things approximate on the broad principles but when you get beneath the skin of what they actually say, are they actually consistent in real terms?
>
> . . . Nor in my view does it fully integrate economic policy with housing policy and transport policy as well as it ought to . . . Connectivity was the buzz word early on in preparing the RSS . . . and

by this they meant transport as a way of connecting different parts of the region . . . and also communications technology . . . it was different things to different people . . . And then it emerged that 'don't get too enthusiastic about levels of infrastructure investment because there isn't any money on the table'. So the connectivity theme tended to dissipate . . . and it didn't shine through as strongly as it ought to.

(E29, local planner, 2006)

To summarise the interview findings around some of the main themes for regional spatial planning, good consultation was felt to have occurred involving strong relationship building, especially among 'regional' scale actors. However, it was not clear that this was leading to greater policy integration, nor to enabling the partners to broker difficult decisions and implement new policy approaches. For some of our respondents the RSS was still largely a compromise document, representing an amalgamation of subregional agreements on priorities rather than a distinctive strategy for the region as a whole. Attention to sustainable development has long been felt to be a strong characteristic of the Yorkshire and Humber approach, with a leading role in the use of sustainability appraisals for regional strategy documents (Haughton and Counsell 2004; Counsell and Haughton 2006a). However, there was a feeling that it was key individuals again that set the tone for this work and that not all institutions had bought into it. In particular there was a strong feeling that sustainability appraisal might be good at throwing up challenging issues, but not at resolving them, and that all the fine sentiments on sustainability in the RSS tended to be undermined by an inability to shift transport investment in favour of public transport, cycling and walking. Yorkshire Forward, the RDA, was seen to be a reasonably progressive force in terms of sustainability thinking. Overall, however, the broader systemic pressures from local authorities keen to prioritise economic development and government initiatives such as the Northern Way seem to have resulted in the Yorkshire and Humber Plan being broadly similar to other regional spatial strategies in its approach to sustainable development. Finally, there are five mentions of polycentricity and one of the ESDP in the final Yorkshire and Humber Plan. Our interviews on this subject can be summarised as an acceptance that there may have been some early influence from European planning thinking, but in truth it does not appear to have been a key driver in shaping spatial thinking at the regional scale (but for the experience in South Yorkshire, where high levels of EU funding helped ensure that European planning thinking appears to have been more prominent in the subregion, see Dabinett and Richardson 2005).

In order to accommodate the city region approach the Yorkshire and Humber Plan adopted seven functional subregions (Leeds City Region, South Yorkshire, York, Humber Estuary, Vales and Tees Links, Coast, and Remoter Rural), which purposefully allow a continuing element of fuzziness with the adoption of a Leeds City Region which has overlapping boundaries with two other functional subregions, York and South Yorkshire. Policy YH1 covers

'Overall approach and key spatial priorities', indicating a clear role for Leeds to 'Manage and spread the benefit of continued growth of the Leeds economy as a European centre of financial and business services' (GOYH 2008: 11). Allied to this, concern is expressed about the overheating of already success-ful areas, not least congestion and deteriorating environmental conditions, which is linked in turn to the need to build on the latent strengths of under-performing areas (GOYH 2008: 12). In the main section on the Leeds City Region, the area is said to have the greatest potential in the region for growth, but despite its success it was underperforming relative to European competi-tors. For the city to contribute more to the success of the region requires:

> Encouraging growth and accommodating high levels of growth in households and jobs in sustainable locations, making best use of brownfield land and infrastructure and minimizing the need to travel is therefore an essential part of the Plan's strategy. Infrastructure improvements will be needed; these will be targeted and coordinated.
>
> (GOYH 2008: 41)

Each of the district councils in the Leeds City Region has to prepare a Local Development Framework, which has to conform with the RSS and identify detailed locations to accommodate the strategic development policies in the RSS. Most controversial of these are perhaps the housing growth targets, which are established first for the whole region, then allocated through the RSS to individual local authority districts and aggregated into administrative subregions – in the case of Leeds this involves 'West Yorkshire' and not the emergent Leeds City Region.

Subregions and city regions: flexible spaces of governance?

Work on the concept and practicalities of a Leeds City Region was already well established among a small group of local authorities before the Northern Way document surfaced, reflecting a series of local concerns about the Leeds growth phenomenon. On the part of Leeds City Council there was a concern about how best to balance job creation with the demand for new housing, leading to a growing acknowledgement that the Leeds travel to work area and housing markets extended far beyond the city's political boundaries and indeed beyond the boundaries of West Yorkshire. Led by a small core of offi-cers in Leeds City Council, working with colleagues elsewhere, research was commissioned to identify the functional geography of the city region, while partnership working with neighbouring authorities gathered pace.

As we noted earlier, central government called on the three RDAs of the north to work on a coordinated strategy called the Northern Way, *Moving Forward: The Northern Way – First Growth Strategy Report* (Northern Way 2004), which identified Leeds as one of eight city regions said to be the main drivers of economic growth in the north. This publication inevitably provided the impetus for the emergent Leeds City Region Partnership to cohere in its membership and aspirations, motivated not least by the need to be involved early on to ensure that each authority was able to maximise any gains to be had and minimise any potential negative impacts. The other side of this was that in raising the political and financial stakes, pressures emerged from those potentially excluded, while the expectations of some of those included were raised rapidly and perhaps unrealistically, given the small capacity of the city region team of around five officers.

Reflecting the emergent work of the Northern Way, the Leeds City Region was also identified in the second Regional Economic Strategy as a major driver of the region's economy (Yorkshire Forward 2006). The RES is important as it guided the investments of Yorkshire Forward, whose investment programmes up until recently have been based on subregional partnerships not city regions. The difference is important to those involved as it affected how they might expect to both influence and bid into Yorkshire Forward's funding systems. The West Yorkshire subregional partnership covers the five metropolitan districts of Leeds, Bradford, Calderdale, Kirklees and Wakefield. By contrast the Leeds City Region stretches into both North Yorkshire and South Yorkshire, covering all or part of ten local planning authorities, plus the North Yorkshire County Council.

The Leeds City Region partners agreed a development programme in 2006 which provided a vision of future growth which would see the creation of an additional 150,000 jobs by 2016 and a growth in GVA of up to £21 billion (Leeds City Region Partnership 2006). It also identified a 'wish list' of investments it wanted government to fund, not least improving transport links, with connectivity identified as a major constraint on achieving the growth targets.

The very flexibility in the city region boundaries used in the first Northern Way documentation created initial consternation among some actors, not least about the proliferation of subregional governance spaces that were emerging during the early 2000s. The main concerns were twofold. First, which level of strategy was going to have precedence when it came to government investment and legal status – the Northern Way meta-region, the Yorkshire and Humber region, the administrative subregions, or the city regions? Second, which areas were definitely within the city region's jurisdiction, and following on from this would areas which lay outside become marginalised in terms of government policy and investment? These concerns were very much evident in the early days of the Leeds City Region (Counsell and Haughton 2007). As discussions progressed over the period 2004–2007 it gradually emerged that the city region would become the preferred spatial unit for subregional strategies, being adopted in both the RSS (Figure 7.2) and by the board of Yorkshire Forward, which agreed in 2006 to shift its investment planning to a city regional basis within four years.

At the time of our interviews these decisions were still being taken, creating an air of uncertainty around the politics and the practicalities of this 'rescaling in motion'. Some of the people we interviewed accepted the arguments for flexibility in defining functional subregions, typically based on a belief that city

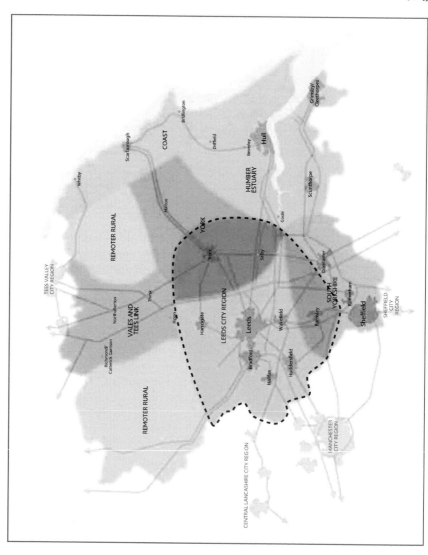

7.2 Yorkshire and the Humber subregions and Leeds City Region

regions better represent the way people live their lives and the economic relationship between a city and its surrounding area. Flexibility in this sense was helpful in 'allowing people to come together in looser coalitions around a specific issue, but without thinking that the solution to this is to change administrative boundaries' (Interview E20, regional body, 2006). Others, though, sought better alignment of boundaries, not least because some 'people don't quite know which structure they're supposed to be integrating with' (Interview E35, regional body, 2007). Aware of the frustrations among some about the potential for multiple boundaries to create confusion, central government civil servants working on Multi-area Agreements were keen to see the emergence of single 'all-purpose' boundaries for city regions from a government perspective. 'What we wouldn't like really is places like Leeds having five or six different subregions, each of which operates separately, when it could actually be one that encompasses most of the issues within that subregion' (Seminar, civil servant, 2007). These responses represent something of the tension that we found among actors at both regional and national scale, involving an abstract desire for the flexibility and fuzziness of new functional spaces, allied to a pragmatic acceptance that at some stage firm boundaries would be required for administrative convenience and clarity.

Soft spaces versus hard spaces: allocating housing growth

One of the reasons for the rapid politicisation of city regional thinking in planning terms was the inevitable tensions among local authorities about how allocations for new housing development were shared among them. This quickly emerged as a contentious issue during the preparation of the *Draft RSS for Yorkshire and Humber* as it tends to do in most English spatial plans given that housing is the biggest consumer of land (see Haughton and Counsell 2004). One of the key issues in the Leeds City Region was whether growth could be allocated directly to the city region or whether, as is normally the case, it would be allocated to individual local authority areas. The logic of using local government boundaries is that the detailed allocation of new sites for housing is determined in Local Development Frameworks which are prepared by local authorities. By contrast there is no formal planning authority covering the city region which might broker a binding agreement between constituent authorities on the distribution of new housing targets between them. Nevertheless, the Leeds City Council view was that its housing allocations in the draft RSS were too high and that some of this growth could be accommodated elsewhere in the city region, reflecting what it argued was the reality of a functional Leeds housing market. For regional planners this created a major headache:

> Yes . . . resolving the distribution of housing in Leeds City Region . . . it's the most difficult part of the region . . . and at the end of the day it wasn't resolved. The document then was put to the vote and the decision was made by the Assembly . . . Leeds voted against it because they didn't like it.
>
> (Interview E22, regional planner, 2006)

By contrast Leeds planners expressed concerns about the mismatch between developing economic policy based on city regions and then basing housing allocations on local authority boundaries (Interview E29, local planner, 2006), a point supported by some other actors: 'So, on the one hand they work with this economic city region, while housing is local . . . The two arguments aren't sustainable really' (Interview E35, regional economist, 2007).

Competing logics appeared to be at work here. The panel of inspectors at the public examination explored the distribution of housing from the perspective of seeking a balance between housing and employment so as not to encourage commuting over long distances, influenced by UK planning's articulation of sustainable development thinking. To achieve this, they focused on the local housing allocations in the RSS and attempted to balance these with the potential for growth in local employment. Given that the city of Leeds is the main driver of employment growth the panel argued that there should be higher levels of housing growth in Leeds than proposed in the RSS and a great deal more than the city council wanted.

> [T]here is perceived to be a disproportionately high number of jobs being created in Leeds in comparison to the amount of housing. Quoted figures vary, but GOYH state some 40,000 jobs are envisaged, but only 23,000 houses over the period 2006–2016. There is already a high number of daily commuters into Leeds and this is likely to grow with the jobs-homes distribution being proposed, with a consequent knock-on effect on sustainability and climate change.
>
> (Offord and Hill 2007: 171)

Leeds not only lost its case for allocating some of its housing growth to other parts of the city region, but also must now face the prospect of a very large increase in housing numbers over and above what was proposed in the draft RSS. In the final version of RSS (GOYH 2008), it is made clear that the district of Leeds must rapidly increase its new housebuilding, from an indicative annual gross build rate of 2,700 in 2004–2008, to 4,740 for 2008–2026. Even at this level, the rate of new build is expected to be less than the rate at which new jobs are created (Figure 7.3). The written commentary makes clear the logic involved in this decision:

> Leeds district already accommodates more jobs than households and job growth is expected to continue to be strong. It is an essential part of the strategy to significantly increase the supply of homes in the district in order to meet housing needs and reduce the need for more and longer distance commuting.
>
> (GOYH 2008: 163)

While soothing words are added about ensuring that adequate infrastructure is put in place to support such growth, some local actors had already expressed their concerns that such fine sentiments might not result in actual provision.

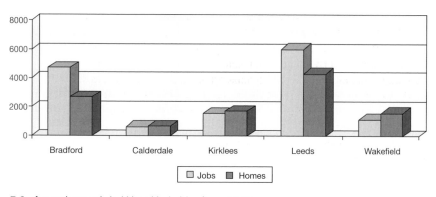

7.3 Annual growth in West Yorkshire from 2008

Source: Government Office for Yorkshire and Humber (2008: Figure 12.2a).

The upshot of all this rather abstract debate is that there will need to be a major change in approach within Leeds in how it addresses future housing needs, after a period of years in which it has managed to encourage substantial growth in new development on brownfield sites, in particular with a boom in city centre apartment building. Even before the housing market slump of 2007–2009, the signs were clear that this market segment was saturated (Chatterton and Hodkinson 2007; Hodkinson and Chatterton 2007). In this context, the RSS decision to require continuing high levels of future house-building within the city council boundaries will put further pressure on green belt, suburban and peripheral communities alike.

Our governance line methodology is helpful in exploring this issue down to the more local level, where we looked at housing and infrastructure issues in the suburban area of Guiseley and Menston. Guiseley is a former mill town in the Leeds City Council area, now experiencing considerable growth in new housing as a result of its proximity to Leeds, allied to a rapid and frequent train service between Leeds and Ilkley. It adjoins the neighbouring town of Menston, a prosperous suburb within the Bradford local government area, also served by the same railway line. Central government policies to encourage higher proportions of new development on brownfield land and the strategic push for higher levels of housing growth have led to substantial development pressures in Guiseley. For local residents in both Guiseley and Menston a major concern with the high levels of recent housing development is that it is causing severe strains on the public transport and road systems, and on social infrastructure in this area. Local planners preparing the Local Development Framework for Leeds were all too aware of this:

> As a result there has been a significant amount of housing growth . . .
> so much so that we have difficulty talking to local people about the
> wider city regional needs for housing growth . . . and the impacts on
> their daily lives . . . not being able to park their cars . . . not being able
> to get on the trains . . . the buses are full . . . there's no supporting

growth in social infrastructure . . . So I do take their point, and we've had some difficult public meetings.

> (Interview E52, local planner, 2007)

The emerging awareness of the problems associated with the new development, much of it on quite small sites, meant that public meetings and consultations on planning-related matters were very well attended. Inevitably local politicians responded to this groundswell of concern, including the Leeds Member of Parliament Paul Truswell (Labour), who has taken the matter up in House of Commons debates:

> Communities in my constituency are in constant conflict with planners and developers about excessive and overbearing housing and office projects. It is hardly surprising, therefore, that community involvement in the planning system is seen as very much on the debit side of developers' balance sheets . . .
>
> Applications for over-intensive developments have been and continue to be made across my constituency. I am referring to places such as Pudsey, Yeadon, Horsforth, Rodley and Farsley. In my Adjournment debate, I cited the experience of the town of Guiseley, where planning permissions over the past six or seven years have given the go-ahead for about 1,200 extra homes – a major increase in the size of the town without any commensurate improvement or increase in the local infrastructure to support it. Clearly, that is not a sustainable approach.
>
> (House of Commons Hansard debates for
> 12 December 2006, www.publications.parliament.uk/pa/
> cm200607/cmhansrd/cm061212/halltext/61212h0002.htm)

Here we see some classic themes played out around the politics of new development, but with the interesting addition of concern that new development was creating problems through lack of infrastructure provision. As the parliamentary debate started to intimate, the main concerns for residents in Guiseley and Menston alike are congestion on local roads and rail services and a lack of capacity in local schools and health facilities.

At a public consultation on future growth plans for the area that we attended, we were told of developers approaching businesses in older industrial buildings (potential brownfield sites) with a view to buying them out so that they could convert the site to new housing. This provides an interesting twist on the RSS's comments about increasing housing numbers to reduce long-distance commuting. An attempt by Leeds City Council to discourage the loss of local employment sites to housing in a recent review of the Leeds Unitary Development Plan (UDP) fell foul of government policies prioritising housing development on brownfield land.

> There are policies in the UDP that make developers jump through hoops to demonstrate their site is not suitable for alternative employment use before allowing residential . . . then going for a mixed use

rather than going for purely residential. We tried to strengthen that policy in the UDP review adopted in 2006 but that was not supported by the Planning Inspectorate. They said the key objective here was to find more land for housing . . . and these are brownfield sites in a sustainable location . . . close to good transport routes . . . and strategically Leeds is the focus of regional growth so it must accommodate more residential development.

(Interview E52, local planner, 2007)

Perhaps the largest recent development has been on the site of a former psychiatric hospital, High Royds, where some buildings are being converted to residential units and some of the land is being used for new build housing. The site is in Leeds, but borders on to Bradford. Planning permission was sought for a mixed-use development in 2003, with plans for conversion of some of the old hospital buildings to 212 homes, offices and a clinic, plus 262 new build homes. A public consultation meeting in 2003 attracted over 300 people, with more turned away at the door (*Bradford Telegraph and Argus*, 13 February 2003). Interestingly, High Royds also attracted critical debate in the House of Commons (18 July 2007), between Bradford MP Philip Davies (Conservative) and Leeds MP Paul Truswell (Labour):

Philip Davies: . . . I do not know whether my local authority is unique in terms of the problems that it has experienced. I suspect not, because the issue of housing developments going up and the infrastructure not being there to support them has been raised in virtually every local authority in the country. There are certainly places in my constituency where houses are built and where every available piece of land is sold off to developers and built on. Yet no extra roads or infrastructure is put in place to support those houses, which exacerbates people's frustration about the number of new houses that are built. The hon. Member for Pudsey [Mr Truswell] will know that well, because there is a new planning application on his side of the constituency boundary near Menston, which borders my part of the constituency. A heap of houses are going up on an already congested road, but there will be no more roads built to support them, which just creates more problems for local residents . . .

Mr. Truswell: I assume that the development that the hon. Gentleman is talking about is High Royds. We have known about it for 10 years or more, so the local authority had a huge amount of time to plan, but it never did. That is the point that Labour Members are trying to make: planning powers are not being used as effectively as they could be to create a framework that anticipates pressure on the infrastructure.

(Hansard Debates, House of Commons, 18 July 2007, column 102WH, www.publications.parliament.uk/pa/cm200607/ cmhansrd/cm070718/halltext/70718h0007.htm)

The importance of the relationship between land use planning and infra-structure provision comes through strongly in such debates, not simply on a site by site basis, but also as a result of the cumulative impacts of successive new developments coming on stream in an area. Certainly the plans to build 450 new homes on green belt land adjacent to Menston were presented locally as problematic because of the cumulative impact when added to the 550 new homes planned at High Royds. Being on the boundary of two local authorities was said to be a confounding issue when it came to identifying the nature of the 'massive infrastructure problems' facing Menston, according to one disgruntled councillor voicing his frustrations to the local press (*Telegraph and Argus*, 8 July 2004, http://archive.thetelegraphandargus.co.uk/2004/7/8/99234.html).

More positively it is worth noting that as a prime site in the green belt, High Royds has been of a sufficient size and significance to allow planners and developers to negotiate a series of mitigation measures, including a green travel plan for the development, which will see local residents provided with a free public transport pass for a year to encourage use of public transport, plus a financial contribution to allow new rolling stock to be bought for the rail service. Land has also been allocated for sports and social facilities for use by all within the town, not just the new residents, plus a new doctors' surgery. For the government, this constitutes best practice (Department for Transport 2005), but for existing residents of Menston and Guiseley, what they see is a major new road intersection being built to allow residents onto the already congested main A65 road which serves the site and not being able to get seats on peak hour trains (Figure 7.4).

7.4 New development and access road, High Royds former psychiatric hospital site in Menston

Returning to the Regional Spatial Strategy, the Guiseley and Menston case begins to reveal some of the remaining tensions in turning broad strategies into deliverable high-quality development. Given the boundary issues involved, it ought to be a classic case of where the City Region scale ought to have been helpful. But for all the recent debate on city regions, the practice has mainly been about economic development and the transport infrastructure needed to support that, and not the wider infrastructure needs of building sustainable local communities. Instead, what we see is how city region ideas were deployed selectively by both Leeds and Bradford local authorities to argue that they should be allocated lower housebuilding targets than the government expected, on the grounds that they were part of a larger Leeds City Region. Rather than provide new spatial horizons for helping resolve difficult decisions, lacking any democratic mandate of its own the emergent city region scale is simply another parallel arena in which old battles can be fought within. City regionalism in this sense is essentially a political tactic not simply at the macro scale, but also at the micro scale.

Delivering on spatial development in the Leeds City Region

Delivery has been described as a defining feature of spatial planning (University College London (UCL) and Deloitte 2007: 36), and indeed central government planning policy guidance makes much play of the expectation that policies in RSSs and LDFs should be deliverable (ODPM 2004b, 2004c). For example, RSSs should be 'focused on delivery mechanisms which make clear what is to be done by whom and by when' (ODPM 2004b: 3), while guidance on LDFs (ODPM 2004c) also identifies the need for a coordinated approach to delivery, in this case emphasising links with Sustainable Community Strategies prepared by Local Strategic Partnerships (LSPs). The very fact that these fine and entirely uncontroversial sentiments are given such a regular airing suggests something of the government's unease about the planning system's ability to shape future development patterns through the process of strategic spatial planning. In essence this reflects that many of the investment decisions necessary to progress from plan to implementation lie with other actors, from the actions of planners at other scales, to private investors, utility companies, and government agencies and departments. More than this there is a gap between the theoretical and rhetorical impetus of written spatial strategies, agreed through various partnership and consultation mechanisms, then getting partners to deliver their part of the agreement, which they have to negotiate through their own separate budgetary and investment processes. In practical terms too delivery of the RSS's spatial policy for the Leeds City Region will partly be achieved through the detailed policies and land allocations decided upon in the various Local Development Frameworks of the constituent local authorities, none of which have yet been completed.

One of the first steps for most policies involving physical development will be securing the commitment of substantial public sector investment in physical and social infrastructure, requiring favourable decisions by bodies that may well not have been very heavily involved in preparing the spatial plans or even in consultations, including national organisations such as the National Health Service and Department for Education. While the Regional Assembly formally prepares the Regional Spatial Strategy, as a small organisation it has little or no capacity for achieving delivery itself. Recognising the need to coordinate the programmes of a wide range of organisations, the draft RSS envisages a delivery plan that will 'bring together the RSS/LDF and the investment programmes of the Sub-Regional Investment Programme [RDA], Sub-Regional Housing Partnership, Local Transport Plan Partnership and the City Region Development Programme' (Yorkshire and Humber Regional Assembly 2005: 76). What we begin to see here is the emergent chasm between the English regions and the devolved administrations in Scotland and Wales, in terms of control over budgets and power to ensure investment in diverse sectors, in broad conformity with the relevant spatial plan.

Our interviewees commented about a range of problems associated with aligning the delivery of spatial policy with investment, in one case even within the same institution. There are problems, for example, of national versus regional priority, something that regional planners are all too well aware of:

> There's been an awful lot of debate about to what extent you can bind those agencies to spend money in certain ways in certain areas . . . The interesting point is . . . that government sets rules about how its agencies spend money . . . and those criteria aren't joined up. So the Environment Agency will tell you it has to spend money in certain ways . . . And the problem then comes when you try to join at the region . . . that the regional arm of that agency will say well we can't do this because we have certain ways we have to do these things nationally. So there is a problem there and it is going to take time to work through . . . big spending departments just go out and do things . . . closing that hospital. They just say that's their business, whatever the spatial effects . . . and they can be huge.
>
> (Interview E21, regional planner, 2006)

Similar frustrations exist at the local level, where local authority planners told us that even within their own organisations conflicts existed between the longer timescales associated with spatial planning compared to financial planning:

> Notwithstanding the benefits of the new system, it still takes a long time . . . perhaps several years to get documents to fruition and other parts of the council might want to work at a different pace . . . may have to because of the way the financial provisions work. They're pulling the plan along when ideally it should be the other way round.
>
> (Interview E17, civil servant, 2005)

When it came to city regions, a clear disjuncture emerged between the decisions on investment priorities taken by city region partners and planners producing the Regional Spatial Strategy:

> Those [city region development programmes] are very much bottom-up . . . and the first cut of them . . . I think even those people within the Northern Way thought that there was a bit of misalignment because it was bottom-up . . . and all very different . . . And some of them were probably wish lists . . . very aspirationally driven . . . They were led through Chief Executive policy units, without perhaps sufficient connection to spatial planning within their own authorities.
>
> (Interview E21, regional planner, 2006)

Although some responsibility for public sector investment has been devolved to the regions, this remains partial in sectoral coverage and a small part of overall government spending at the regional level. So while Yorkshire Forward's Single Pot budget for 2006–2010 amounts to £1.5 billion and £542 million has been assigned to Yorkshire and the Humber through Regional Funding Allocations for 2005/6 and 2007/8 (HM Treasury 2005), the reality remains that the majority of public investment in the region is directly funded by central government departments and agencies. Even with the financial devolution that exists, there are some doubts about whether regional and local strategies exert much influence on Whitehall expenditure (Pearce and Ayres 2006), not least since much of it stems from local bids to regional entities:

> It's interesting looking at the work of the Regional Transport Board . . . we've had indicative regional transport allocations going for the next ten years . . . and the Board has been anxious to ensure that funds are available for schemes coming forward. They've asked local authorities to submit schemes . . . and they've had submissions that amount to four or five times the money available. So there's an issue there . . . it's not worth putting time and effort into working up all those schemes if only one in five can be fired . . . So there is an onus on planning authorities to produce spatial plans that don't depend on infrastructure that isn't likely to be available.
>
> (Interview E17, civil servant, 2005)

Once again it appears that the spending decisions of many central and local government departments are being taken without much regard to the regional spatial strategy deliberations, and to an extent they are actually driving spatial development patterns rather more clearly than the written strategy. The chances of coherent, integrated policy remain as remote as ever, it seems, despite all the months of negotiation and collaborative activity involved in producing the RSS.

Despite the previously remarked upon move to Regional Funding Allocations, a frequent concern we encountered was that the government's spending remained strongly tied to national priorities and PSA targets, rather than to regional priorities. The biggest government spending sectors – health and education – between them invested £13 billion in Yorkshire and the Humber in 2004 (Yorkshire Forward 2006) but these are the sectors that our research reveals to be least well aligned with spatial planning. This said, in Yorkshire and the Humber, the health authorities have been more active in the preparation of the RSS than in many parts of the country, helped by a member of staff being seconded to work with the Regional Assembly. The result of this, incidentally, is a reasonably strong chapter in the final RSS covering health and recreation, which lacks much in the way of spatial detail but does contain clear commitments to ensuring good access to facilities. But more generally the problem remains that the RSS lacks a clear mechanism for mustering resources behind its vision and must necessarily rely on the actions of its various 'stakeholders' in government and beyond. This is a problem which afflicts others too, even the Regional Economic Strategy, which highlights its lack of influence over strategic expenditure on infrastructure, noting the low level of government investment in transport compared to the south-east region – £355 million in 2004 compared to £797 million in the south east (Yorkshire Forward 2006). Government rhetoric might say otherwise, but the financial figures do not lie. The government's national competitiveness agenda clearly leads it towards giving greater priority to supporting growth in the south east rather than regeneration in the north.

Not surprisingly then, the lack of influence over national expenditure on infrastructure was a frequent theme in our interviews. For instance, in Leeds, a long-running saga has been the efforts by local politicians and officers to get approval for government investment in a new super-tram system for the city, which has considerable congestion on its roads and parts of its public transport network. With the project now seemingly abandoned, planners were left wondering how they could plan for major new housing developments, forced on them as they saw it, while central government refused to invest in public transport infrastructure necessary to ensure this did not create gridlock in the city's transport system:

> [Investment in infrastructure] strikes at the heart of it for us because the RSS is looking for the bulk of strategic growth . . . physical growth . . . to be in West Yorkshire . . . the majority of the housing growth to be in Leeds . . . as the driver of the city region . . . and we are beginning to see some problems now in terms of infrastructure capacity. If we are going to plan for that level of growth, and also the 'step-change' that is talked about in RSS, given the demise of the super-tram we have concerns about the capability of the infrastructure to sustain the growth set out in RSS.
>
> (Interview E29, local planner, 2006)

Even central government planners, we found, could see the problems faced at the local level by such impasses, reflecting different aspirations and philosophical drivers of investment between different arms of government:

Planners in some respects are caught between a rock and a hard place . . . In terms of Leeds . . . focusing development in Leeds city centre clearly makes sense in sustainable development terms . . . and in terms of many planning policies . . . but the indication is that [transport] networks for getting people to jobs in the city centre are at capacity . . . and it's very difficult for planners . . . Do they turn round and say because we're not sure about funding of infrastructure we will allocate land elsewhere?

(Interview E17, civil servant, 2005)

Delivery might then be a defining feature of spatial planning, but it is a problematic one, dependent on the vagaries of government departments' spending commitments and the coordination of a range of policy sectors and investment programmes. To put it mildly, our research suggests that despite all the reforms intended to promote greater coordination and to achieve integrated approaches to spatial development, we remain some way yet from achieving a system that delivers this.

Conclusion

English planning has undergone a dramatic and still continuing process of rescaling since the late 1990s. While a coherent 'national' scale of strategic English planning has not yet emerged, regional planning has been substantially enhanced, including a mandate to work at subregional level, while county-level planning has been undermined. Thinking at the city region scale has also started to influence planning (again), but as it is driven very much by an economic agenda its impacts on planning have largely been to unbalance further the system's attempts to provide a 'balanced' interpretation of sustainable development at its heart. Broadly speaking, our work in Yorkshire and the Humber, and specifically in Leeds, suggests that most planning decisions in effect follow decisions made elsewhere (particularly infrastructure investment decisions) at least as much as they follow the guidelines set out in strategic planning documents. We can see that spatial planning is one among many tools for attempting to integrate policy decisions, but despite the initial high hopes of the planning profession taking a lead in providing integrated policy so far its achievements in this respect are limited. Part of the reason for this is that in the English system there is little compulsion on government departments to follow the guidelines set out within strategic planning documents. Others may have to abide by planning policies, but government departments can and in some cases do largely ignore them. There are exceptions, naturally, and one of the achievements of recent work on strategic plan-making has been to draw into the process a greater range of stakeholders than hitherto, some of whom have been better than others at subsequently supporting the adopted spatial strategy. But in truth, even within any given body, different factions too often pull in different directions, not simply at the level of national government, but also within local authorities. As for the much heralded duty to pursue sustainable development in planning, this is being largely sidestepped by those outside planning who wish to promote economic growth as a priority, while planners have used it to pursue a policy of urban compaction which in itself is a useful approach, but when taken to extremes seems to be implicated in a pattern of urban development which is likely to be little more attractive in twenty years' time than the large edge of town public estates of the 1960s or their private estate counterparts in the 1980s and 1990s.

What we begin to see from the Leeds case study is how the 'soft spaces' of planning such as city regions are not yet spaces for strategic spatial decision-making. While there are policies for the Leeds City Region in the RSS they tend to be generalised and well intentioned rather than directive. When it comes to 'hard' decisions such as allocating housing growth, these inevitably focus on the hard spaces of planning – regions and local authority areas. The reasons for this are largely to do with practical considerations concerning legal appeal by parties at some stage in the process. This leaves a question mark against exactly what spatial planning issues if any will be determined at the city region scale under the present planning system in England. Despite its having long been recognised as a key scale for strategic planning and transport policy, the city region appears in government publications principally as a scale for economic policy and governance (DCLG 2006a; HM Treasury *et al.* 2006, 2007). Until it is viewed as a scale for holistic policy-making, however, the city region simply becomes an impediment to spatially informed, coordinated delivery of development. In the meantime, our research in Leeds suggests that city regions are best characterised as spaces that bridge the two formal spaces of planning, the regional and local scales, rather than spaces for taking decisions about the location of development.

There is an interesting contrast between the experience of Leeds and that of other parts of the country, not least the designated growth areas, which we turn to in Chapter 8. For Leeds, the problem is that it is expected to cater for substantial growth without any recognition that it might need a delivery vehicle capable of providing a holistic approach to development, something which neither the formal planning apparatus at local and regional levels, nor the putative city region arrangements are currently able to deliver. The result is that rather than a double devolution dividend, Leeds faces a double whammy, where powers are being devolved asymmetrically across sectors and spatial scales, creating newly empowered regions and city regions that seem incapable of addressing the needs of the area, which finds itself landed with lots of responsibilities, but very little in the way of powers or resources. It is difficult to know whether this is central government unable to think creatively about how to deal with growth outside the charmed 'south east', or Leeds seeking to use the planning system to attract employment growth while resisting housing expansion. Either way, the people of Leeds lose out, with a housing market that is currently dysfunctional, with high prices, new developments filled with vacant properties of a type wanted by only a few and built in places where only a small segment of the market want to live, while finding resistance to new development is widespread elsewhere. For some, high prices may be a good thing of course, as is fending off new development that might adversely affect property prices. For the poor, benign neglect is as much as the planning system appears to be able to offer, given the lack of funding for new affordable housing, made worse by creeping redevelopment of former public sector estates that seems to be whittling away at the stock of affordable rented accommodation. In the meantime the road and public transport systems are congested and with little prospect of improvement ahead. Spatial planning may well have supported the economic growth of Leeds, but it has yet to deliver in terms of a wider vision of inclusivity, sustainable development and integrated policy-making.

8

Congested governance and the London Thames Gateway

The concept of the Thames Gateway has been around since the 1980s, recognising the potential to provide much needed new housing for the south east of England in an area with considerable industrial dereliction and urban deprivation. The Thames Gateway extends 40 miles eastwards from London Docklands, and at its maximum 20 miles north and south of the Thames, with 1.45 million existing residents and 637,000 people (ODPM 2006) working within a diverse area, ranging from the financial hotspot of Canary Wharf to areas of substantial economic decline and social deprivation. Those promoting the Thames Gateway concept have emphasised its role in unlocking the hidden potential of the area and providing a counterbalance to the enormous growth pressures being felt elsewhere in the capital, particularly to the west. Nor has it been the only effort to kickstart development to the east of London. The *longue durée* of economic and social change in the area, overlaid with successive strategies and institutional arrangements for regeneration, provides a unique opportunity to explore the shift from a 'top-down' tightly focused development-orientated form of government typified by the London Docklands Development Corporation (LDDC) in the 1980s, through a more regionally and spatially orientated approach in the 1990s to a more 'bottom-up' partnership-led spatial governance style in the 2000s. Onto this evolving governance and planning approach further exogenous 'shock' can be added, such as the need to accommodate London's successful 2012 Olympic bid.

The principles of a more spatial approach to planning would on paper appear to lend themselves well to dealing with the range and complexity of issues that need to be dealt with in promoting new growth in the Thames Gateway. However, as we will go on to demonstrate, the experiences of planning in the area highlight both the advantages and disadvantages of spatial planning as well as the possible trade-off between coordination and delivery.

The Thames Gateway area is frequently cited in its publicity material as one of the largest and most ambitious regeneration projects in the UK and indeed one of the largest in Europe. The overall objective is to bring about a rebalancing of spatial growth and regeneration in London, with the present targets being that it should accommodate an extra 225,000 new jobs and 160,000 new homes, plus the substantial infrastructure required for the resulting massive increase in residential and working population. The wider context for this concerted housing effort lies in new government targets for building 3 million new homes in England by 2020, which rely in large part upon the success of areas such as the Gateway. More than this, however, the Thames Gateway is held up as a potential exemplar for how to bring about large-scale regeneration rapidly, in a better integrated fashion than hitherto, while delivering development meeting higher environmental standards than in typical new developments. Delivery of regeneration in the Thames Gateway is therefore projected as a national priority, both in its own right and in setting higher aspirations for the standards of new development across the country.

As well as the country's largest regeneration challenge, the Thames Gateway is also arguably its most demanding contemporary governance challenge (Allmendinger and Haughton 2009).[1] As yet it shares its boundaries with no other statutory body. Reflecting its importance to the future growth of London, and with this national growth, there is a Thames Gateway Strategy team within the Department for Communities and Local Government (DCLG),[2] charged with providing leadership, integrating the work of various central government departments, and direct intervention with partners when necessary (National Audit Office 2007: 14). In addition there is a Thames Gateway Strategic Partnership which involves stakeholders from across the area and certain government agencies, which is chaired by the Minister of Housing and Planning.

The Gateway also has within it a range of new sub-areas, few, if any, conterminous with existing political or functional boundaries. The resulting complexity would seem to be an exemplar for testing whether it is possible to achieve coordination and integration of different scales and policy sectors through a spatial approach to planning. But in many ways it is an extreme case, such that the challenges of spatial planning in the Gateway dwarf those of other regions and can rightly be seen as an example of the 'congested state' (Sullivan and Skelcher 2002).

- It covers parts of three different standard government regions (Greater London, South East, East England), involving three sets of regional spatial strategies, regional economic strategies, housing strategies, and more. This also means dealing with three separate Government Offices for the Region, two different regional assemblies, and the Greater London Authority and London mayor.
- The Thames Gateway has three subregional partnerships: Thames Gateway London, Thames Gateway South Essex and Thames Gateway Kent Partnership.
- There is also a disparate network of local delivery partners, with varying governance styles, including two urban development corporations, one urban regeneration company and six other local partnerships.

- On top of these there is the Olympic Delivery Authority, responsible for accelerating development of the Olympic Park area for the 2012 London Olympics.
- A total of 16 local authorities lie wholly or in part within the Gateway, each with its own planning, housing, regeneration, recreation, education and transport plans.
- On top of this there are the essential services to consider: police, health and fire authorities, plus water, gas, electricity, telecommunications, environmental protection, flood management, sewerage, and others, each with their own administrative geographies.

It is useful to address some of the political particularities of London within which a large part of the Thames Gateway project and area sits. As the nation's capital and the focus of much of its economic impetus, political centre of gravity and a key node in many financial, transport and other networks, it occupies a unique position in the national space economy. Recognising this, it has had its own distinctive governance arrangements over the years, albeit being adapted as political ideologies have changed, with four systems of governance introduced since the late 1960s (Travers 2004). The two most recent changes were the abolition of the Greater London Council (GLC) in 1986 by the Conservative government and the creation of a Greater London Authority (GLA) in May 2000. This represented part of the devolutionary agenda of Tony Blair's new Labour government, which included giving considerable strategic powers to a newly created post of elected London mayor. Welcome though the move was to re-establish a greater role for London-wide governance, the resulting arrangements have clear limits. As Goode and Munton (2006) point out, the devolution package on offer reflected the fact that both central government and the 32 London boroughs were unwilling to cede many of the powers they had gained following the 1986 reforms. In consequence, the Greater London Authority has restricted powers to raise funds and a very small staff compared to its GLC predecessor. The mayor oversees various London-wide bodies, including transport, police, fire, and economic development, and sets the budget for the GLA. Crucially, however, the mayor has responsibility for the London Development Agency (LDA), the functional equivalent of RDAs in the English regions, and for the London Plan. The London Plan is the Regional Spatial Strategy for the capital, which unlike its counterparts in other English regions achieves statutory status directly rather than as a document formally published by the government. The elected members of the Greater London Assembly have limited powers, essentially those of scrutiny over the mayor and the GLA, plus the potential to veto the budget and initiate investigations of importance to London (Hall 2006).

For all these reworkings of London's democratic and governance arrangements, there are two widely agreed themes that dominate political discourse about the future of the capital. The first involves a virtual consensus around the success of London in recent years in terms of economic growth, the second concerns the degree to which this economic success has resulted in a more polarised society, where the rich in particular have got richer. Sub-narratives to this are the ways in which all the relevant governance agencies have naturally claimed their centrality in achieving the 'economic success' aspects of the London storyline, while emphasising the extent to which their hands were tied in addressing the social problems of the capital. This is not a new tactic, one which held sway as much in the days of the LDDC as it does nowadays with the GLA.

As both Massey (2007) and Hall (2006) argue, it had become unthinkable for the writers of the new London Plan to do anything other than accept the 'inevitability' of and need for further employment and population growth within London. As a result, in the first draft London Plan released for public consultation in 2002, much emphasis was made of the need for ensuring the growth of London's economy for the national good, with the City and financial services seen as the major engine of this growth. After much criticism about this narrow emphasis the final Plan, released in 2004, addressed such concerns by paying greater attention to creating a more sectorally diverse economy and to the role of London's other centres and suburbs (see Figure 8.1). But as Massey (2007: 87) points out, this did not involve any pulling back from the original emphasis, more a shoring up with greater recognition of the other aspects of London's spatial economy. London's growth is still presented as both an inevitable and a good thing, requiring planning policies that allow this to be taken forward, with two themes dominant, as Hall (2006) sums it up: 'go east' and 'raise densities'. The Thames Gateway and the government's urban renaissance agenda then provide London's planners with their solution to finding a home for the anticipated new growth, handily in both cases meaning local policy can claim to be backing national policy agendas rather than bucking them.

This is not to say, however, that the planning regime in London has been simply market enabling. There is much that is distinctive that has been tested, proposed or introduced in Greater London which has been influential more widely, including the introduction of a Congestion Charge and target policies to increase the proportion of 'affordable housing' in new developments, to as high as 50 per cent. The GLA has also sought to introduce a liveable wage for Londoners, setting an example itself and seeking to work with private employers, and creating strategies for energy, air quality, biodiversity, food and waste, and a walking plan among other activities (Massey 2007).

The London Plan was viewed positively by most of our interviewees, who commented on it as a useful and innovative departure, the most akin to spatial planning of any English regional plan to date. In particular it was seen to have done more than any other regional plan to address a wide range of issues and engage with a wider than usual set of stakeholders. Reservations did exist, inevitably, about whether its growth orientation made sense in terms of the wider English spatial economy and whether it could have done more to address social equity matters. The main criticism though came from a national housebuilders' representative, who objected strongly to the London approach,

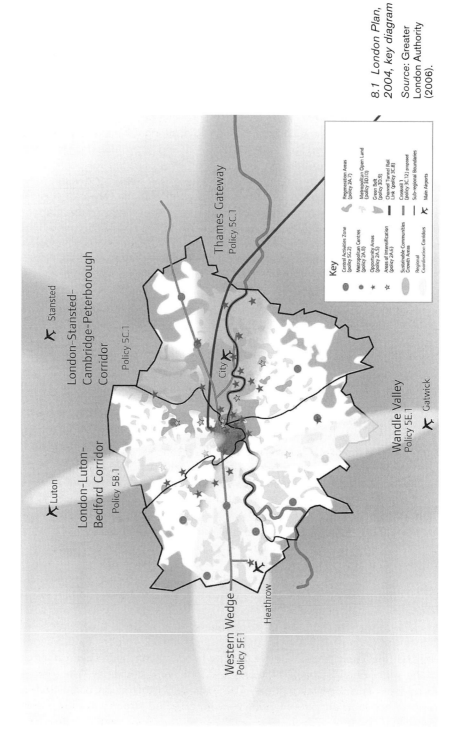

Luton ✈

Stansted ✈

London–Luton–
Bedford Corridor
Policy 5B.1

London–Stansted–
Cambridge–Peterborough
Corridor
Policy 5C.1

Western Wedge
Policy 5F.1

Heathrow

City ✈

Thames Gateway
Policy 5C.1

Wandle Valley
Policy 5E.1

Gatwick ✈

Key

● Central Activities Zone
  (policy 5G.2)

● Metropolitan Centres
  (policy 2A.8)

★ Opportunity Areas
  (policy 2A.5)

☆ Areas of Intensification
  (policy 2A.6)

⬭ Sustainable Communities
  Growth Areas

Regional
Coordination Corridors

Regeneration Areas
(policy 2A.7)

Metropolitan Open Land
(policy 3D.10)

Green Belt
(policy 3D.9)

Channel Tunnel Rail
Link (policy 3C.8)

Crossrail 1
(policy 3C.12) proposed

Sub-regional Boundaries

✈ Main Airports

8.1 *London Plan,
2004, key diagram*

Source: Greater
London Authority
(2006).

because it is far too detailed. Basically Ken [Livingstone, then Mayor] wants to be the planning authority for London . . . so he's basically produced a plan that gives the local authorities very little space in which to manoeuvre . . . So he's effectively trying to run the unitary authorities of London by providing too much detail.

(Interview E1, housebuilder, 2005)

This was a tension also noted by some of our other interviewees, albeit from different perspectives, for instance, the senior Labour GLA assembly member who explained to us that:

There are clearly tensions . . . one of the biggest tensions is the territoriality tension . . . the boroughs will see themselves being sovereign over the individual land use issues and they will expect the spatial strategy to set themes and general direction for their work . . . As a consequence of that, any sane mayor will want to exercise their authority in a more detailed spatial fashion . . . so there is a tension between the aspirations of the London Plan which is sort of general and enabling and the desire to be prescriptive . . . and the desire of the boroughs to maintain their own turf.

(Interview E43, local politician, 2006)

We also asked interviewees whether there was much that was distinctive in the approach taken to the London Plan. Even for the underwhelmed there were some positives, but also some concerns:

[Has the GLA made a difference . . . are they doing something distinctive?] I think that the way they were able to do things like the congestion charge . . . that probably wouldn't have happened without the GLA . . . But then I would say there might be a bit less difference than some people might see . . . For example all regions have RSSs . . . ours is just called the London Plan . . . and Ken's [Livingstone, the London Mayor] CO_2 reduction targets are actually less in the revised London Plan than they are in the existing one . . . and less than the Yorkshire and Humber region will have in theirs . . . We supported having a GLA . . . and I think it's the right thing to have . . . this strategic thinking . . . So I think it definitely does make a difference . . . The difference is perhaps that it is more accountable . . . because there is the elected assembly.

(Interview E41, national environmental NGO, 2006)

Mostly, however, the consensus was that London's devolution had provided the platform from which the mayor was able to push a distinctive agenda through the spatial planning process, displaying political leadership rather than getting too bogged down in observing administrative protocols and procedures. In spite of the limited powers, financial resources and staff then, the new arrangements in London do seem to have gradually built up into an integrated policy agenda, whose aims are necessarily worked out with other local partners, since it is these that will ultimately need to be responsible for introducing changes. In this sense the limited powers of the mayor and GLA means they have had to pay attention to relationship building across the public, private and voluntary sectors in order to broker new understandings of what is possible and desirable for the future direction of London's growth, a new form of governance indeed.

Returning to the Thames Gateway, we can begin to see how important it is not only for national government, but also for the aspirations of the Greater London authorities, providing much of the necessary space for London's future economic and population growth. It has been the focus of considerable national government attention, notably New Labour inherited plans for a Millennium Dome, while announcing its own plans for a Millennium Village on the Greenwich Peninsula in 1997, its first year of office. Subsequently the government announced that the Thames Gateway would be one of its four selected national growth areas in 2003 and set up the governance arrangements for taking this forward rapidly, with the GLA in effect one of many interested parties. In July 2005 the announcement that London had been successful in its bid to host the 2012 Olympics added further urgency, as the main site was located in the east London part of the Thames Gateway. Moreover, the role of the Olympics in making a positive and sustainable impact on the regeneration of a run-down part of the capital had been a key part of the bid. With the need to ensure that the capital's infrastructure was capable of coping with the large numbers of visitors and with the eyes of the world on it for the duration of the Olympics, the stakes were raised considerably. More than this, the prominence of the Thames Gateway more generally means that the quality and timeliness of all aspects of infrastructure provision will be one of the main criteria on which the future success of the area can expect to be judged.

The context of the Thames Gateway

The redevelopment of the area now known as the Thames Gateway goes back many decades, first achieving national prominence through the establishment and work of the London Docklands Development Corporation (LDDC), which was the flagship of the thirteen Urban Development Corporations (UDCs) established by the Conservative governments of the 1980s (Raco 2005). The LDDC was an experiment in combining deregulation of planning controls with massive public investment and subsidy in development and infrastructure. While the record of many UDCs was patchy the impact of the LDDC upon the area was significant. Much to the chagrin of many on the left as well as local people, the LDDC led a physical and economic transformation of the area within its control. However, what some saw as the embodiment of neoliberal governance (e.g. Imrie and Thomas 1999) was not a success for a 'hands-free' approach'. The LDDC very much benefited from financial deregulation in the

City of London and the associated demand for huge amounts of commercial floorspace as well as large amounts of public subsidy and investment.

One of the key experiences of the LDDC concerns the negative consequences of divorcing development from wider planning frameworks. The LDDC was a 'black hole' within both local and strategic planning frameworks (Allmendinger and Thomas 1998). One outcome of this was the lack of coordination of development within its boundaries between bodies and their plans and strategies. The connecting transport infrastructure, for example, is still regarded as inadequate for the scale of development in the area. Other issues included the stark 'boundary effect', the lack of 'trickle-down' benefit to local people and the extent to which local people and stakeholders were excluded (Brownill 1990).

The latter years of the LDDC witnessed a greater attempt at integrating and coordinating the development of the area with other bodies and their plans and strategies and a far more concerted effort to engage with local stakeholders. The experiences of the LDDC and the swing of the pendulum away from the idea of 'development for development's sake' had an important legacy in the form of a much greater subsequent emphasis upon partnership-led development.

The Thames Gateway concept, initially known as the East Thames Corridor, emerged out of the government's planning department during the early 1990s. The idea briefly generated considerable political enthusiasm and a unique subregional edition of Regional Planning Guidance was produced specifically for the Thames Gateway, known as RPG9a. This set out the rationale for a large-scale regeneration initiative of this type and a broad spatial vision for the area: this document remains the core planning document for the Thames Gateway. Despite the fanfare at the time, the Thames Gateway faded from the headlines quite quickly, with progress tending to be patchy and rather slow. With political interest waning, no political leadership and no specific governance body, the Thames Gateway seemed destined to become the Cinderella of the planning system, never quite making it to the ball. Things began to pick up pace in 2003 when it was designated as one of the four national Growth Areas in the Sustainable Communities Action Plan, and new stretching targets set out for the new housing and jobs that would follow. The House of Commons ODPM Housing, Planning, Local Government and the Regions Committee also published a report on the Thames Gateway that year (House of Commons 2003) which argued for the need to integrate future development in the area better with, in particular, water and transport infrastructure. This was not entirely unexpected, with the question of where water would be sourced for the enlarged population a long-standing concern for critics (Haughton *et al.* 1997; Haughton 2003). The government responded positively and in 2005 announced its intention to produce a Strategic Framework for the Thames Gateway by November 2006 which would be linked to the Comprehensive Spending Review in 2007.

In the mean time in March 2005 the government published *Creating Sustainable Communities: Delivering in the Thames Gateway* (ODPM

2005a). With a lengthy introduction by the Prime Minister and the Deputy Prime Minister, this document set out further details of the government's objectives and targets, including information on the funding arrangements being put in place for transport, green space, education and health to reflect the way in which high growth levels were anticipated in parts of the Thames Gateway. It was also announced that the Prime Minister would chair a committee of Cabinet ministers to ensure it achieved high priority, and development in the area would be coordinated between the relevant government ministries. In 2006 the government appointed a so-called Thames Gateway 'Tsar' in an attempt to underline the need for coordination and integration of policy. There has also been a team of central government civil servants overseeing the Gateway for some time.

Partly in response to the changes to the Thames Gateway scheme brought about by the decision to hold the 2012 Olympics in London and partly in response to criticisms of complexity and a lack of delivery (Roger Tym and Partners 2005; Deloitte 2006), the DCLG published a policy framework and interim plan for the area in November 2006 (DCLG 2006b) with accompanying analysis (DCLG 2006c). At this stage projections for new housing were raised from 120,000 to 160,000.

Despite the additional clarity which the interim plan introduced, criticism over the complexity of the project and institutional landscape has continued:

> The department [DCLG] has encouraged the development of several forms of partnership at regional, subregional and local level to help coordinate investment across the Gateway. This has allowed local ownership, accountability and flexibility to adapt to local circumstances. But the complexity of the decision-making and delivery chains makes it difficult for potential investors, developers and Government itself to understand the programme and integrate investment as a whole.
>
> (National Audit Office 2007: 5)

In November 2007, the Committee of Public Accounts (House of Commons 2007) claimed the government still lacked leadership over the project and had yet to provide a clearly costed implementation plan. It was particularly sceptical over claims that the governance systems for the Gateway were constructed effectively, with unclear chains of command said to persist even after the government had respond to the National Audit Office (NAO) report by establishing a cross-government coordination board for officials. To substantiate some of its claims, the report pointed to the fact that the earlier NAO report had found that local partners and government officials did not feel the programme was well integrated across Whitehall departments:

> Major sites are being delayed due to a lack of joined-up infrastructure investment. For instance the building of 9,400 homes at Barking Riverside is reliant on further transport infrastructure that is not

included in the Transport for London or the Department for Transport's spending plans, while development of 30,000 homes in Kent Thameside is reliant on agreement from the Highways Agency, 12 years after they first knew the Channel Tunnel Rail Link would lead to housing growth in the area.

(House of Commons 2007: 8)

This criticism is particularly important since major infrastructure projects have been seen as central to unlocking the potential of the area, both to cope with the demands of new growth and to replace existing decayed infrastructure. Most notably there have been controversial plans for a new road bridge over the Thames, initially backed by the GLA, but turned down after a planning inquiry. The Channel Tunnel rail route also runs through the area with new connecting railway stations built at Stratford and Ebbsfleet, both of which will as a result become major focuses for growth. Plans are at an advanced stage for introducing a new east–west rail link for London, Crossrail, and for extending the Docklands Light Railway to Woolwich. In the midst of the public criticisms noted above, in November 2007 the government announced plans to support the Gateway with public investment of £9 billion, involving the building of eight new hospitals and the building or refurbishment of twenty-seven schools and three new university campuses, while also increasing the jobs target to 225,000 (DCLG 2007).

While all concerned agree that coordinated infrastructure spending is key to the future of the area, it is proving to be one of the most difficult governance challenges, requiring actors and funding arrangements used to their own administrative geographies to think creatively about the wider interests of a meta-region that has no true electoral or administrative base. There has, however, been growing effort by other bodies to provide strategic documents which either directly or indirectly reflect the geographies of the Thames Gateway and its subregions. For instance, there has been a greenspace strategy, Greening the Gateway, released in 2004, the Environment Agency is working on Thames 2100, which extends beyond the Gateway boundaries and, as we shall see later, some innovative efforts in the field of social infrastructure. One thing the area is not short of is strategies.

These Gateway-wide efforts have since 2003 been paralleled by considerable activity at subregional level, with separate strategies now published for specific parts of the Thames Gateway by the new delivery agencies (Figure 8.2). For instance, in 2005 the London Thames Gateway Development Corporation (LTGDC) published its *Engines for Growth: Our Vision for the Lower Lea Valley and London Riverside* (LTGDC 2005) while the Olympic Delivery Authority (ODA) has its own plans and Olympic Park Delivery Programme (ODA 2006). The Thurrock Thames Gateway Development Corporation has been particularly active, publishing a regeneration framework in Autumn 2005, a spatial plan in August 2007, and is now working on four master plans covering smaller parts of its jurisdiction. Such subregional and local plans and strategies exist alongside a host of other plans and

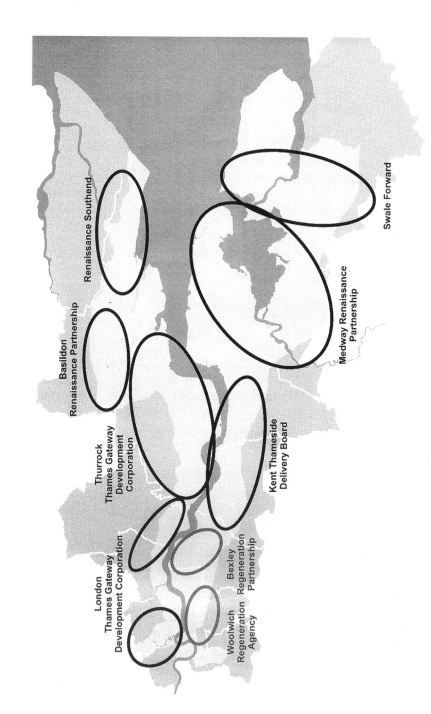

Renaissance Southend

Swale Forward

Medway Renaissance Partnership

Basildon Renaissance Partnership

Thurrock Thames Gateway Development Corporation

Kent Thameside Delivery Board

London Thames Gateway Development Corporation

Bexley Regeneration Partnership

Woolwich Regeneration Agency

8.2 Local delivery structure in the Thames Gateway

strategies from a variety of delivery agencies, not least local authority plans and strategies.

The House of Commons (2007) report noted that there were over 100 bodies involved in the work of the Thames Gateway at various levels of government and in the private and voluntary sector, involving multiple funding streams and multiple lines of reporting. The true figure is much higher. It helps maybe to take the example of the London Thames Gateway Development Corporation, whose website in July 2008 listed its 51 public partners (covering local authorities, government departments and agencies, regional bodies), 26 privates and independents (covering builders, social housing providers, universities, port authority) and nine voluntary and community groups. Multiply all these partnership connections for the many other agencies involved in strategic and delivery work in the Thames Gateway and the mammoth nature of the governance task underway for all those involved, as lead agencies, partners, stakeholders or consultees, becomes apparent. In effect there is a dense web of partnership links, such that charting these as a network diagram for the whole Gateway would be near impossible, a mass of black ink.

Something of the frustrations felt by those involved in the Thames Gateway can be summed up by the views of two of our interviewees:

> I'm firmly of the view that the government needs to take an axe to the whole of this and create a single body for the Gateway . . . which is a UDC in the true sense of the word . . . whose sole objective is delivery of the government's objectives for the Gateway.
>
> (Interview E36, housebuilder, 2006)

> There is no one in overall control . . . Different actors are doing different destructive things . . . It's going to be guerrilla war again . . . Just because it's screwed up . . . there's so many loose ends . . . nobody's coordinating it.
>
> (Interview E46, local partnership agency, 2006)

We examine below the tensions involved between what are in effect two rival claims. One, that coordination and integration (spatial planning) is 'not working', i.e. the situation is too complex and that attempts at coordination are thwarting development delivery. Second, that coordination is not happening. On the face of it both of these cannot be simultaneously the case and yet there is clear evidence that this is the on-the-ground experience of many of those working in the Thames Gateway.

The remainder of this chapter explores the role of spatial planning in delivering regeneration in the Thames Gateway by, first, focusing upon three issues that run through this book; scale, policy integration and major infrastructure provision. Our governance line at the subnational level incorporates the Thames Gateway as a whole, plus its relationship to the Greater London Authority and at the local level, existing and planned initiatives on the Greenwich Peninsular.

Spatial planning in the Thames Gateway

The scale and complexity of delivering, integrating and coordinating development across the Thames Gateway is not in dispute, only whether the challenge is being met. There are several questions we wish to pose. First, can the claim that the Thames Gateway is being planned in a spatial way be justified? Second, is spatial planning as a broadly constituted set of practices for coordinated spatial strategy-making, facilitating or hindering development in the Thames Gateway? Is there a point at which institutional thickness reinforces complexity rather than helps unpick it? Can 'over-planning' be seen as a downside of spatial planning, amounting to what Sullivan and Skelcher (2002) term the 'congested state'? Or is spatial planning the necessary decongestant to what is inevitably a fragmented and diverse landscape of bodies and boundaries?

We now move on to analyse in more depth the recent experiences of regeneration and spatial planning in the Thames Gateway using the three themes raised in Chapters 1 and 2, namely scale, coordination and infrastructure.

Reworking the scales of planning: vertical rescaling and the new planning spaces of the Thames Gateway

> The challenge for governance and delivery in the Gateway is to put in place structures and processes that are 'fit for purpose', given the nature, complexity and scale of the Gateway project. In terms of governance, there needs to be strong leadership and strategic direction from the top and a clear understanding of how to balance top-down coordination with bottom-up initiatives.
>
> (DCLG 2006d: para.13)

This section sets out some of the tensions involved in balancing top-down and bottom-up approaches to strategic and delivery activities in the Thames Gateway, focusing on the national through to local aspects of the governance line (few of our interviewees were moved to comment on the impact of ESDP thinking on their activities in the Thames Gateway, other than as a sop to officialdom in written documentation). In setting about this task we address in empirical terms the theoretical issue raised in Chapter 2, namely the possible conflict between 'formal' scales and strategies created and operated by democratically accountable governmental organisations and the strategic and delivery activities associated with more 'informal' or soft spaces of governance.

National coordination

Reflecting the growing concerns of national government to deliver on (and in) the Thames Gateway, it has been granted some unique governance arrangements, including dedicated Delivery and Strategy units within the main planning department of government, currently DCLG. One of the main aspects of the Thames Gateway Strategy Unit's remit is to ensure that the various departments of government work together productively in pursuit of the Thames Gateway strategy. We spoke to civil servants in these two units and within a wide range of government departments, including those responsible for policy development in relation to Transport, Highways, Environment, Culture, Treasury, Planning, and Industry, and at subregional level those involved in issues such as spatial planning and health planning. Inevitably the main focus of such national actors was on issues of strategic importance, including attempts to ensure that each department's investment planning reflected the government's priorities for rapid growth in the area. The importance of this is that traditionally government departments use trend forecasts to guide investment decisions, while the very unusual and rapid development in the Thames Gateway is of its very nature attempting to buck the local trends, requiring investment greater than, say, population change figures for the previous decade might have suggested. Although the main focus of national actors was at this strategic level, we were also taken by the extent to which this interest extended into the area of promoting delivery, ensuring that their various delivery partners were aware of the national priority attached to the Thames Gateway.

One of the most notable changes in planning at national level since the election of New Labour in 1997 has been the rapid growth in both formal and informal consultation around changes to the planning system, typically involving the major stakeholders in the planning process, the professions, developers and a range of lobby groups. These groups and indeed the general public are now routinely invited to comment on Green Papers, White Papers, draft PPS statements, and a whole variety of other issue papers, including, for instance, the Sustainable Communities plan and more recently proposals to create Eco-Towns. Less immediately apparent is the extent of interdepartmental liaison and lobbying that takes place within central government, a process which runs in parallel to the formal processes of external consultation. Indeed a key finding of our research was the pervasive nature of such consultations between central government civil servants, and the extent to which key government planning policies emerged through negotiations with other national government departments. In some ways, this is not entirely surprising; it is what one would hope was happening behind the scenes to ensure policies were not being developed in separate sectoral silos. But for the most part planning research has been notable in the past for not making direct use of interviews with national planners, and for assuming that planning was something essentially limited to the activities of land use and transport 'planners'. Such assumptions were always problematic, of course, made more so in recent years by the extent to which planners' interaction with other policy actors appears to have both grown and become more formalised.

Perhaps the most high-profile example of this is the way that the Treasury has recently taken to making very public interventions in planning debates, most conspicuously through commissioning the economist Kate Barker to write reports suggesting changes that might be made to ensure the planning system is better able to promote the government's national agenda for building new housing. There is a parallel here with the way in which the Irish government's interest in national strategic spatial planning appears to have been kickstarted by the Irish finance department (see Chapter 3). In the case of England, political changes are an essential part of the evolution in thinking, given that

> one of the things that is different under New Labour is that the Treasury has got more involved in planning . . . and it's more spatial than it was . . . So you can plan on the assumption that the infrastructure might follow the plan . . . which you perhaps couldn't do previously.
>
> (Interview E39, civil servant, 2006)

Part of the rationale behind this growing interest in spatial planning has been the recognition that it could make a difference, for better or worse, to the national growth agenda. The extent of this interest became clearer to us on interviewing two of the main economic departments. One of them, for instance, made it clear that their interest was in both strategy and delivery:

> [Is the sustainable communities work within your remit?] It is . . . the spending implications and delivery of those are very much our concern . . . from a public finance point of view, but also from an economic point of view in terms of wanting to see the macro-economic effects of Barker being implemented and stability being achieved in the housing market . . . for example, we were involved in negotiations with ODPM over what the funding should be for the growth areas [such as] Thames Gateway . . . so we're in discussion with them over delivery . . . they'll come to us for example when they're setting up Urban Development Corporations, to speed up housing delivery.
>
> (Interview E10, civil servant, 2006)

The other economic department stressed that it saw its role as ensuring that economic factors and the needs of business did not get drowned out by those lobbying for social and environmental issues to be prioritised: 'What's effectively happened is that plans and strategies are so much more important now . . . and I think the business world is behind' (Interview E2, civil servant, 2005). Pursuing what they regarded as a 'standard deregulation line', this department scrutinised draft Planning Policy Statements, for instance, to ensure that the interests of the business community would not be unduly compromised.

The other strategic scale is for the whole Thames Gateway and its main subregions. Notwithstanding the views of civil servants, there was broad agreement, as we set out above, that the Thames Gateway was 'over-planned' in the sense that there are too many strategies, plans, partnerships and agencies involved. In stark contrast, the government's perspective is that coordination is already in place, providing a multilevel approach that largely builds on the existing institutional infrastructure while adding new bodies where specific problems or potential existed:

> It's not so complex if you're working in an individual area . . . It's only when you look at the whole picture . . . which none of the deliverers are actually doing. It's only when you look at the whole picture when you start to get worried about the complexity.
>
> (Interview E37, civil servant, 2006)

As we have seen already, there is a strong subregional tier within the Thames Gateway, with its three formal subregions and below these a range of other subregional bodies each seeking to blend strategy and delivery. This scale is what we would call 'sub-subregional', above the level of the individual site and possibly crossing the boundaries of political units such as local authorities. Not only are these rarely aligned with existing political or administrative areas, but also we would go further and argue that it is very much part of the rationale of these emergent new spaces of regeneration and area planning, that they represent a break from existing political entities. The argument for change may be formally couched in terms of somehow better reflecting real world problems or development potential, but frequently it is also about realigning stakeholders so that they can break free of negative, ingrained responses to suggestions for trying to turn around an area. Typically the identification and re-branding of such 'new' areas will involve the commissioning of a consortium of consultancies (architects, landscape architects, planners, ecologists, regeneration and property experts) to prepare a draft strategy, or, at local level, master plan. Responsibility for delivering the master plan is then charged to some kind of formal multisectoral partnership, which will aim to remove blockages to development, stitch together funding sources, coordinate infrastructure investment and deliver the output targets demanded by the various funding bodies.

Curious about these emergent soft spaces (see Chapter 2), we asked some of those involved about their rationales for whether to create new institutional geographies or to empower existing institutional arrangements. Typically the decisions were seen to be apolitical, technical decisions about what works best in different circumstances:

> You've got to realise why the boundary was drawn where it is . . . it's not to fit where the bodies are . . . it's to fit where the complex opportunities are . . . So it's where government intervention is seen to be needed . . . So no . . . the boundaries don't map with anything . . . The closest thing they map to is roads . . . the A2 . . . and the A13 and A127 . . . It's more to do with the geographical nature of the landscape . . . in that those kinds of industries based themselves that side of the roads to be close to the river. So no, you're right, they don't map at all.
>
> (Interview E38, civil servant, 2006)

More than this, however, for some of the officials involved in creating these new administrative geographies there was a sense of dissatisfaction with the existing tools for creating new territorial understandings of what is possible in a particular place, with spatial planning still seen as tied into a system more associated with inhibiting than provoking new thinking:

> What you find in spatial plans . . . spatial plans are pretty static regulatory tools . . . and this is where I go off message . . . They are by definition really . . . they're based around concepts of creating places of equilibrium really rather than creating places of change . . . So they're not particularly visionary . . . what they do do is carry with them this element of political authority and community consultation.
>   . . . You can say what you like in statutory plans . . . and get it through . . . But whether it's market-real or not is desirable but not essential . . . Spatial plans are largely . . . exciting political realism coupled with planners' concept of balance . . . So they look good . . . and you can say 'we don't want lots of growth there because we don't want commuting into London . . . We want self-contained sustainable communities' . . . Whereas the reality of it is . . . you take the opportunity . . . and you turn it into a strategic benefit. Canary Wharf . . . which is now the largest shopping centre in east London . . . It's captured the market . . . That kind of thing . . . you'd never plan it . . . But it's a triumph of non-planning I suppose in that sense.
>   (Interview E39, civil servant, 2006)

What we can begin to see from the comments of this civil servant centrally involved in the Thames Gateway is the extent to which it is creating a new framework which is simultaneously consciously rooted in a rhetoric of spatial planning and a reality of creating structures that simultaneously allow for a degree of 'free expression' outside the formal planning system itself. But the changes are not simply of spatial planning, this is just part of the intellectual and delivery apparatus. Much of the rising sensitivity to spatial issues lies with Labour's interest in social equity issues, such that while civil servants might not explicitly engage with planning when closing down schools or hospitals and rebuilding elsewhere, they will nonetheless be sensitive to the government's social agenda and environmental agenda and make some efforts to place their decisions within that perspective.

Achieving policy integration then is both explicitly through these more informal processes and the emergent patchwork of regeneration and planning strategies and agencies. This process can look very confusing from the outside, but to an extent it appears to have its own internal logic, one that recognises that a perfect institutional landscape does not, indeed cannot exist for a development project as complex, as multi-nodal and as multi-scalar in nature as the Thames Gateway. More than this, there is a degree of path dependency in how institutions develop and a political desire to both 'break free' of entrenched oppositional forces while remaining wedded to the democratic apparatus of formal planning and the desire to consult with the public on the strategies being produced outside this formal process. Faced with this, as one civil servant put it:

> You can't spend all your time reforming the administrative processes . . . You'll spend all your time on that and not getting on with the job in hand. In Thames Gateway the reason it is such a spaghetti of poli- cies is because the Thames is a body of water and bodies of water are always boundaries.
>
> (Seminar, civil servant, 2007)

This Janus-faced ideological turn was evident at the local level too, where we regularly encountered the view that planning could not be expected to deliver exciting new developments, only to facilitate them. The answer, we were told on various occasions, was to provide light touch planning which would be responsive to changes in the market. Using the case of Canary Wharf once again, but this time emphasising its office core, one of our interviewees made the link to more recent efforts to open up parts of London to new forms of development:

> I'm also quite interested in the idea of permitting the unexpected to happen . . . Canary Wharf would be considered the unexpected in that context . . . In the 1980s there was a view that Canary Wharf would become . . . like sheds . . . industry . . . Then these crazy peo- ple came along and put offices there . . . and since then it's been a striking new office district . . .
>
> So there you are . . . you need a framework which is sufficiently loose that it allows unexpected things to happen . . . Stratford City . . . we got very excited a while ago . . . we said here is the master plan . . . this is what's going to happen . . . [however] the market will decide how most of that will happen . . .
>
> City East is arguably a strategy that was dreamt up by Lord Rogers about two years ago . . . But it doesn't feature in the London Plan . . . it's a good example of where people say if we look again at this area perhaps we will find another node for growth which wasn't described in the London Plan, but maybe is valid . . . What does that tell you about the balance between prescription and facilitation? I don't know.
>
> (Interview E43, local politician, 2006)

Opposite Canary Wharf lies the Greenwich Peninsula, which provided the local dimension to our London/Thames Gateway governance line, an area on the south side of the Thames in the London Borough of Greenwich, which for years lay mostly derelict. Its fortunes began to turn around with the decision to build the Millennium Dome there; after the millennium celebrations the Dome lay empty until it reopened in 2007 as an entertainment centre, the O2 Arena (Figure 8.3). The Dome was accompanied by a new tube station on the

8.3 Aerial view of the Greenwich Peninsula
Source: English Partnerships.

Jubilee line, and bus interchange, helping to open up the area not only for visitors but also for new development. Further development impetus came in 1997 when the new Labour government announced a competition to create a Millennium Village on the peninsula, intended to be a national exemplar for sustainable development. By this stage much of the land on the peninsula, a 121-hectare site, had passed from its former owner, British Gas, to the government's development agency, English Partnerships. From 1998 English Partnerships invested massively in site restoration, including decontamination, remediation of land, plus installing considerable new basic infrastructure, costing around £217 million. A masterplan for the Millennium Village was produced in 1997–1998 following a design competition, with development quickly following, such that by 2008 it included around 1,100 new homes, plus a new integrated primary school and health centre, adjacent nature reserve and supermarket, fourteen-screen multiplex cinema and retail ware-house zone, surrounded by a large car park (Figure 8.4). A second masterplan was then commissioned to take forward the next stage of development to cover the rest of the Peninsula, which started in 2008, with the first commercial building opening in 2009.[3] The new masterplan, developed by Terry Farrell Architects, envisages 10,000 new homes being built in a mixed-use development around four new neighbourhood zones, accommodating 20,000 residents.

The development here has much to tell us about the nature of the new spatial planning and its learning processes. We can see, for instance, the interplay between various scales of government: national government in the shape of the work of the DCLG and Thames Gateway strategy and delivery

8.4 Greenwich Millennium Village

teams, plus English Partnerships; the GLA and its development arm, the LDA; the Greenwich Partnership as the local strategic partnership; the development consortia working on specific developments on the Peninsula; and Greenwich metropolitan council. The main delivery agency in formal terms from a Gateway perspective appears to be English Partnerships, which is working alongside the local authority to orchestrate developments on the Peninsula. Apart from the broader context setting work of the London Plan in establishing targets for new housebuilding, the role of the GLA and LDA seems fairly low key, reflecting that the plans are relatively mature, allowing the LDA to focus on other priority areas, notably the Olympic sites. The Peninsula may not be a classic example of 'soft space' governance then, not generating a specific new governance body but instead a development consortium, but it is nonetheless, a classic case of developing a large area in ways that challenge planning orthodoxy, attempting to create new senses of place for the Peninsula as a whole and its new 'neighbourhoods'.

In terms of multi-scalar governance, some of those involved in the development did note that the different strategies created some scope for confusion, as planners in Greenwich explained to us:

> There's a little bit of overlap or duplication with those [London Plan documents] . . . but our starting point is always . . . that the UDP [local unitary development plan] is the number one document because it's the most up-to-date and relevant. Whereas in 18 months' time the London Plan will have been reviewed and so that will be more up-to-date and will have more status.
>
> (Interview E50, local planner, 2007)

The Millennium Village itself is a strange mixture of building design that seeks to promote sustainability, both in the residential and retail buildings, plus an eco-reserve and plenty of cycle path provision. But looking at the bigger picture, it also incorporates substantial car parking for the retail and leisure facilities, attracting considerable car-borne traffic and undermining much of the 'eco' credentials of the area. More than this, however, the giganticism of the commercial facilities undermines the potential for smaller local retailers to establish themselves. It is then a very English vision of what a mixed-use development might look like, rather than the mainland European model of a more fine-grained urban texture of multiple shops encouraging pedestrian and cycle movement and with this, it is claimed, a certain type of civility. This said, the first stage of the Millennium Village is seen by local planners as having attracted only limited opposition within the community, though in practice local groups did lead a vociferous campaign against aspects of the development, as one campaigner explained to us:

> John Prescott wanted this eco-village there . . . which was all well and good . . . but it was an absolute classic of not being able to look at the bigger picture . . . [English Partnership sold land for a large supermarket and car park next to the eco-village] which meant clearly that no small local shops would be able to flourish in the eco-village . . . If you're really thinking about building a community . . . and not just a little housing estate you have to think about living . . . working . . . reducing the need to travel . . . local ownership . . . and having money rotating in the local area . . . So allowing this monster [supermarket] next to this eco-village was a classic mismatch . . . that was a complete failure of spatial planning . . . of sustainable thinking . . .
>
> [Were there any successes . . . they built a school . . .?]
>
> Yes . . . and a health centre . . . and the housing itself is relatively energy efficient . . . low water use . . . low energy . . . Car parking standards weren't particularly amazing . . .
>
> [Did local people get involved in any of those decisions?]
>
> Yes . . . we did . . . we got some nominal changes to the car parking . . . and I think we shamed them on that retail into making it as green as possible . . . although it was a bit tokenistic . . . a wind turbine . . . although all it actually did was light the store sign at night . . . to attract more cars off the Blackwell Tunnel approach!
>
> (Interview E41, national environmental NGO, 2006)

One of the interesting issues that emerged from our interviews was the way in which the proposals for the Peninsula, and the Millennium Village in particular, appeared to have triggered a rethinking of standard development practices. For instance, the higher eco-standards expected of buildings in the Millennium Village were said by local planners to have influenced them to raise expectations elsewhere in the Borough.

Coordination and spatial planning

In Chapter 2 we discussed a range of influences that have led to the move in the role of the state from one of 'steering' to one more akin to 'rowing'. This shift from government to governance involves a diverse and fragmented range of institutions and bodies, operating at a variety of different spatial scales. Local government generally, and planning in particular, have been charged with coordinating and integrating the plans and strategies of these bodies. Such processes have been instituted both formally and more informally. At a formal level local Sustainable Community Strategies have been introduced as the 'plan of plans'. Working through Local Strategic Partnerships and led by local authorities, Sustainable Community Strategies are charged with coordinating the plans and budgets of a wide range of bodies towards common goals. At a more informal level the concept of spatial planning has been advanced as a parallel way of thinking about the processes and products of planning in an integrated way, with Local Development Frameworks providing guidance on the spatial aspects of development. The point here is that the broadening out of the tentacles of spatial planning has its counterpart in how other statutory and non-statutory agencies are being required to engage more widely in their governance and stakeholder systems. This process is central to creating the interlocking, multi-scalar processes that Jessop (2003) refers to as metagovernance in the shadow of hierarchy (see Chapter 2).

The experiences of delivering 'joined-up governance' on the ground highlight some of the difficulties involved, particularly in a complex arena such as the Thames Gateway. On the positive side, more government departments are now taking the Thames Gateway seriously, recognising it as a central government priority and not simply a local issue to be sidelined, with health and transport perhaps the main positive contributors through the spatial planning process. Other departments have engaged with the Thames Gateway too, but not necessarily in a particularly strategic or spatial way, essentially operating through 'old-fashioned' departmental bidding systems or through providing ad hoc support.

Government departments then appear to be working together on the Thames Gateway in a way that is increasingly spatially informed and if not integrated at least showing signs of greater coordination. There appears to be a gradually awakening awareness that national government is committed to some form of planning and public consultation over changes to the system. This makes it much more difficult to expect national government to override its own regulatory apparatus than in the 1980s. For economic development and regeneration in particular, planning was seen as an important aspect of their work, whether it was impeding or helping achieve their goals. This recognition of the potential value of working through (rather than against or in ignorance of) the planning system was emerging faster in some sectors than in others, with Health the most notable convert and Education easily the most reluctant to engage. This perhaps explains the recommendations in the RTPI and central government-funded study on effectiveness in spatial planning that various departments, including education, should disseminate internally advice on the need to give appropriate attention to spatial planning in capital and infra-structure work (UCL and Deloitte 2007).

In effect the broad spatial outline set out in RPG9a in 1995 still provides the main guidance for future development in the Thames Gateway, while more recent strategies have started to fill out the detail for particular sectors and for particular sub-areas. Driving forward the new processes has been a com-bination of government targets on housing, jobs, residential density, and proportions of new development on brownfield sites, bidding for departmental funding under the Treasury's Comprehensive Spending Review round, plus a series of ad hoc announcements of new investments. For instance, the new investment in three university campuses does not appear to have any basis in an integrated analysis of projected demand, phasing over time, spatial pattern or in relation to existing provision. All that will have to come later as strategies are developed around the pre-given targets (in this case new university campuses) and the release of government funding. Central government civil servants working on the Thames Gateway were quite open with us about how targets could be simply made up and put out for consultation, which would then lead to refinement of the proposed figures. Housing targets for the Thames Gateway, for instance, were announced in the Sustainable Communities Action Plan in 2003 and refined in the interregional planning statement on the Thames Gateway in 2004:

> We came up with 120,000 homes . . . and split them between these different locations . . . based on plan . . . What happened is that . . . we thought 90,000 was what was in the RPG figures . . . and they said what can you jack that up to in terms of density directive . . . new transport infrastructure . . . brownfield land . . . and we thought 120,000 . . . or originally up to 216,000 . . . That wasn't an absolute limit . . . So we said 120,000 . . . but the statutory planning author-ities were always uncomfortable with this . . . us coming along and telling them where to put their houses . . . And they did an estimate of growth in the zones of change which came to 128,000.
>
> (Interview E39, civil servant, 2006)

Subsequently there emerged an interesting pattern of revised targets for housing and jobs in the Thames Gateway being announced by ministers as they issued press releases on new government investment plans, always moving upwards naturally. The regularity of these changes makes it difficult to trace what the official targets were at any given moment in time.

Is this 'perfect' spatial planning? Certainly not. But is it a viable way forward given the political exigencies of the times? Quite possibly. As we have remarked elsewhere, with planners often co-opted into the strategic and deliv-ery bodies of other sectors, planning is increasingly diffuse and difficult to pin down as a sector, leading us to conclude that there is no 'sectoral' privileging at work in the Thames Gateway (Allmendinger and Haughton 2009). So where planners were perhaps demonised and marginalised during the earlier experiments in, for instance, London Docklands, the current governance arrangements for the Thames Gateway see planning not as a necessary formality or a standalone statutory enforcement mechanism. Rather, we found planning a pervasive professional influence in many different bodies, but certainly not a lead or dominant influence.

(Allmendinger and Haughton 2009: 627)

At more local scales spatial planning and sectoral policy integration was not always easy to discern. Vertical integration has proved to be difficult because different parts of the Thames Gateway – while functionally related – are aligned with different Regional Spatial Strategies, Regional Economic Strategies and Regional Housing Strategies. The upshot of this has been that the RSSs themselves have 'stood back' to some degree on the question of strategic planning in the Gateway. While an interregional planning statement was produced by the three regional planning bodies, it contains nothing of great substance that we can discern, other than reasserting the principles set out in RPG9a and pulling together housebuilding targets from various documents (ODPM 2004a). This statement builds upon the earlier 2003 coordinating statement (ODPM 2003a), which if anything had more substance, perhaps benefiting from not being seen as part of the formal planning system which might then be used in future planning appeals. In short, as far as the Thames Gateway is concerned regional and cross-regional plans and planning statements seem to be limited to broad statements of vision, principle and intent, which are difficult to either dispute or pin down, plus housing targets which are to all intents and purposes set by central government.

Regional plans, including the London Plan, walked a tightrope between criticisms of being bland and of being over-prescriptive, in effect overriding local planning authorities. So while they note the Thames Gateway's importance, they add little new in terms of strategic vision or detail. Filling out the spatial detail was largely left to non-statutory subregional development frameworks which were produced over the next few years, although strangely the Thames Gateway subregions were not coterminous with the subregions used in, for instance, the London Plan. Following on from the London Plan work soon began on developing the East London Development Framework, covering districts north and south of the Thames. This reasserts the London Plan statement that the area would be the main development focus for London's future growth. While the consultation draft was rather weak on social infrastructure issues and delivery issues in general, by the time of the final document considerable further work was evident, which resulted in stronger statements on both hard (e.g. economic and transport) and soft (or social) forms of infrastructure. The Framework goes down to the next spatial level of disaggregation by providing detailed annexes setting out challenges, priorities and timelines for development in the main growth or opportunity areas, one of which is the Greenwich Peninsula.

For those in other sectors, this twin-track strategic planning process was not always easy to understand, with the East London subregion running alongside but separate to the Thames Gateway London subregion. Despite this, most agencies were more bemused than anything by this institutional congestion.

More pertinently perhaps, it was at the subregional level that some progress started to be made in interfacing with the work of those in other sectors. The health sector was particularly interesting in this respect, with good working relationships established early on with planning and regeneration agencies for the Thames Gateway, leading to the publication in 2003 of a joint report by the (then) three London Strategic Health Authorities, *London Thames Gateway Health Services Assessment 2003–2016* (London Thames Gateway Partnership Board 2003). Known as the 'Blue Book' (now sadly unobtainable), this represented a considerable step forward for the UK health sector in how it addressed future investment plans in a more spatially informed way. Followed by a useful guide to social infrastructure investment (NHS Healthy Urban Development Unit 2006b), this generated considerable praise as an exemplar for others to follow during our interviews. One of the key breakthroughs was moving away from official census-based trend population projections to working with the government's aspirational population targets for the Thames Gateway. In effect this created the potential for new investment to be phased to be in line with planned population increases rather than always lagging behind and leaving the new population centres under-provided for.

This work on health was in many ways a pioneering activity for spatial planning within the UK, providing an example of how successful cross-sectoral and multi-scalar coordination might work, as other actors respond to the government's plans for the area. Having been criticised for when investments have failed to be integrated across sectors, naturally in our interviews national civil servants were keen to stress that this success story was no accident:

> The strategic framework that we're publishing feeds into the other departments as well so they're starting aligning their plans . . . We work with the Department of Health for example . . . they've aligned their spending to Thames Gateway and they're giving extra spending to the growth areas now . . . But we also work with the PCTs and strategic health authorities . . . so that they know what's going on in the area . . . and they can respond to where the need is going to be . . . so again it does tailor . . . although there are quite a few different layers.
>
> (Interview E37, civil servant, 2006)

Perhaps inspired by the work on health infrastructure planning, further work was then undertaken on the wider sphere of social infrastructure planning in the Thames Gateway. This work ought to be better known as it is quite simply ahead of anything being undertaken anywhere else in the UK that we are aware of. The Thames Gateway Social Infrastructure Study was funded by the LDA and ODPM, managed by the NHS Healthy Urban Development Unit, with the work undertaken by consultants and published in 2006 (NHS Healthy Urban Development Unit 2006a). It set out the case for better planning of social infrastructure and the barriers to achieving this, and then provided a 'Toolkit to guide decision-making at the local level', including analysis of how best to map and forecast future social infrastructure needs.[4]

As ever there is the 'theory' of such strategic-level work and the practice, as we discovered during some of our interviews. While the progress made in the health sector was generally acknowledged and praised, there were some caveats. Commenting on the national picture of integrated policy working, for instance, one planning official noted that though there was often lip service paid to the idea:

> it is not always two-way. If you take health . . . they are very keen to have an influence on the pattern of development and to ensure there are policies in RSSs that assist them . . . but I am not sure it works the other way round . . . What's driving the siting of hospitals is economics not sustainable development.
>
> (Interview E50, local planner, 2006)

This sentiment was echoed in the London Thames Gateway area where we were told that

> The health authority's a big beast . . . which is slow to change direction . . . For example they're still disinvesting in town centre sites that they've got . . . yet their strategy is to invest in the town centre sites with multiple use to link the new clinics to social services . . . and other services . . . And town centres are the right sites for that multiuse . . . yet the property arm keeps disposing of town centre sites because they are the most valuable to dispose of . . . so they haven't achieved institutional consistency between their policy and their purchasing strategy.
>
> (Interview E46, local partnership agency, 2006)

For all the doubts raised about such issues, and the ability of health authorities to plan over long-term time horizons, the sector remains an example of successful coordination. However, it is the exception rather than the rule. And ironically this much praised exemplar of strategic long-term thinking appears to have fallen victim already to short-termist measures, with a decision taken to close the dedicated Thames Gateway health sector coordination unit in early 2007 as part of a national chain of cutbacks in the face of possible NHS overspending.

At the local level too there are some signs that there is a growing momentum behind work for delivering social infrastructure in a more coordinated way, facilitated by the emphasis on social infrastructure in the East London subregional development framework. So in the case of Greenwich Council, we were told by planners there that:

> Our strategic development section are producing a social infra-structure framework at the moment . . . delivering everything across the board . . . In addition we've produced an SPD [Supplementary Planning Document] on planning applications . . . so there's overlap between those two . . . to make sure we're getting what we should do out of development.
>
> (Interview E50, local planner, 2007)

After years in the wilderness then, social issues are gradually re-emerging as an important consideration for planners to take account of. This may seem a strangely upbeat assessment of an obviously still faltering conversion to non-British readers, but it must be seen in the context of the backlash against 'social engineering' brought about by the Conservative governments in the 1980s, and the narrowing of the scope of planning to a regulatory land use role in this period (Haughton and Allmendinger 2007).

Spatial planning and investing in major infrastructure

> Unlocking the delivery of infrastructure is the key to unlocking whichever part of the region that you are in.
>
> (Interview E36, housebuilder, 2006)

One of the main challenges for the Thames Gateway, perhaps inevitably, is finding money to develop the area to the high standards that the government aspires to. The political agenda has changed dramatically since the last great experiment in major new urban expansions. The New Towns and Growth Areas of the post-war period were largely funded by the state, which ran many of the major utilities itself, and subcontracted much of the rest of the building to private companies. Now the utilities are mostly privately owned and need to raise funds either internally or on the market, and must operate under the ever vigilant eyes of their shareholders and their respective regulators, with regulators particularly keen to prevent companies from over-spending on capital investment ('gold-plating') in a bid to be able to raise the prices they charge customers. The problem with this is that (despite what the regulators might say) it is a system which ingrains short-term cost savings over long-term, society-wide benefits such as moving towards renewable energy, unless there is a clear government directive to the contrary.

Government departments also need to align their spending to address local needs, working through highly varied systems for devolving and spending funds at local levels. Recognising some of the problems faced by large centralised bureaucracies meeting local needs and priorities the government has recently introduced indicative regional budgets for some aspects of gov-ernment investment spending, mainly for economic development, transport and housing. It has also placed more emphasis on longer term investment planning to provide greater stability to the system than, say, yearly budgets. At the time of our interviews in 2006 negotiations were in place between the Treasury and individual government departments on their spending needs for the next three years as part of the Comprehensive Spending Review. Responding to criticisms of slow progress in the Thames Gateway, the government had previously announced a dedicated funding package of £373 million over three years to assist in site assembly, land remediation, affordable housing and providing local infrastructure (DCLG 2006c). This was intended to be supplementary to mainstream spending by government departments in the area, not to replace it. An interesting issue here is that for much of its earlier lifetime the Thames Gateway as a corporate entity did not carry sufficient institutional weight or capacity to bid for the usual regeneration funding programmes – indeed, it was the wrong scale to fit in with most government initiatives of the 1990s.

With problematic sites or in areas of 'market failure' development might need to be kickstarted through some form of government subsidy; for instance, many brownfield sites with a legacy of industrial contamination will not be commercially viable without some form of subsidy to allow remediation and to install basic infrastructure. In such circumstances delicate negotiations are required as government officials seek to ensure they are not spending taxpayers' money unnecessarily and in the process boosting developers' profits. Planning also provides a mechanism to encourage developers to contribute directly or indirectly to wider infrastructure provision in the shape of planning gain or planning obligations. These are legal agreements under Section 106 of the Town and Country Planning Act 1990. Typically such agreements might include social or affordable housing or contributions such as land for a new school or clinic, or highway improvements to facilitate the larger traffic movements that a new development might bring. In recent years these have become standard practice as a device, and the range of activities funded has broadened and become more imaginative. Mitigation agreements can also be negotiated if development is on a particularly sensitive site, requiring a developer to mitigate for any on-site environmental loss of quality by protecting or remediating another site in the area, so that overall there is in theory a net environmental gain.

It is in this context then that efforts to promote development in the Thames Gateway need to be seen, with each site having different characteristics and levels of financial viability. Here we focus on the need to establish area-wide infrastructure rather than site-specific measures. For smaller developments housebuilders will be primarily concerned with ensuring that 'hard infrastructure' is in place, such as roads, energy, water and sewerage connection; however, with larger developments it is also necessary to deliver social or 'soft infrastructure' in the shape of policing and other emergency services, plus facilities for leisure, education, healthcare, and nursery and elderly care facilities. Indeed the quality of these facilities is typically to the fore in the advertising materials for large new developments.

One of the main concerns of many of those we interviewed was overcoming the obstacles to the timely provision of infrastructure – both soft and hard. Given the considerable attention devoted to this issue in strategic documents at various scales, the feeling from interviewees in the Thames Gateway was that agreement over what infrastructure would be required, and when, was less of a problem than deciding who should pay. Related to this was a wider concern that spatial planning appeared to be orientated towards coordination rather than delivery, leaving the partners to deal with ensuring that funding was identified from various sources, packaged, and put into effect.

Two related issues emerged. First, timescales for the redevelopment of the Thames Gateway are much longer than most financial planning periods and land use plans and strategies, while different types of organisation will typically invest to different timescales. This is where planning ought to be able to provide a sense of vision and continuity, both more generally and specifically in the Thames Gateway. Even so, we were told, in the Thames Gateway effective delivery of development is:

> going to take generations to achieve ... and that longevity is something that's rarely seen in government programmes when the minister's focus is always on the next election ... The type of challenges here are not going to be resolved within a four-year cycle ... some of these individual sites are taking fifteen years to develop ... so they are massively complex and massively long term and in our mind ... it's going to take twenty or thirty years ... Thames Gateway isn't going to be seen as a finished thing until at least 2030 if not beyond.
>
> (Interview E37, civil servant, 2006)

The timing issue is more than simply the length of time to completion. Several of those involved in seeking to develop in the Thames Gateway explained to us that they suffered because Treasury rules were not sufficiently flexible to allow either central government departments or local delivery agencies to structure their investments over the longer term. A longer term investment horizon, for instance, might allow public bodies to buy prime sites for schools early on when land was cheaper, or to buy and develop land to release in stages onto the market as land values rose. Instead the Treasury tends to pressurise public authorities to release 'disposable' land onto the market as soon as possible, motivated by a concern that in the past development sites had been sterilised by 'land hoarding'. This approach though is counter-productive in the case of large development sites, where releasing land in stages as prices rise would allow the public sector to recoup more of the money it had put into the early stages of a regeneration project.

The second issue concerns capacity and skills. Planning has not been centrally involved in 'delivery' since the early 1980s. For most of this period governments have dealt with this apparent failure not by re-empowering planning to widen its horizons, but by continued reference to the apparent failures of planning and the need to put in place alternative delivery mechanisms to deal with this, such as UDCs, Enterprise Zones and various other area-based initiatives. Based on the twin rhetorics of 'market failure' in the land market, and 'planning failure', the approach was to keep planning to a tight land use remit and to limit the ambitions of strategic planning on the grounds that ultimately the market would decide and that long-term plans would frequently be undermined by changing market conditions and societal preferences. One result of this shift is that there is now little capacity within planning bodies concerning development finance and infrastructure costs and delivery.

As planners seek to re-engage with these aspects of delivery for large development projects such as the Thames Gateway they are finding quite how complex parallel changes in governance have made their task. For instance, the English water companies are now largely privately owned, they vary hugely in their size and ownership, they are subject to regular intense media scrutiny of their behaviour, and are responsible to at least three sets of UK public regulators, and subject to EU legislation. As well as providing water supply, the water companies provide drains and sewerage capacity, though local authorities have responsibility for parts of the system too, cleaning gullies and monitoring drinking-water quality. So getting water companies to invest in major new infrastructure capacity involves a negotiation between the aspirations of planners, developers, local authority departments, company shareholders, numerous lobbying 'stakeholders' and various regulators. This exercise in negotiating complexity then has to be matched by similar efforts with the various other utility companies, for energy and telecommunications, privatised bus and rail companies, plus the various quasi-state agencies responsible for waste, flood control, land decontamination and transport infrastructure.

It is worth emphasising here that the Thames Gateway is not an infrastructure-less desert, a popular misperception, according to one of our interviewees. Indeed, de-industrialisation has left some under-utilisation of infrastructure capacity, though the bigger problem is outdated poor-quality services, not least school buildings. This said, there will be new communities developed in parts of the Thames Gateway, notably Barking Reach, Ebbsfleet, and the area around the Channel Tunnel Rail Link. It is these which present some of the most severe problems, ones where Section 106 agreements are never likely to be sufficient to make up for the infrastructure gap:

> land value in theory is high here . . . The market's stronger here . . . but often the costs are so enormous . . . Barking Reach . . . you've got transport costs . . . decontamination costs on a massive scale . . . how do you turn this area into an attractive residential area . . . which more than swamps Section 106 . . . What we're finding in Barking Reach is that someone is going to have to fund the transport infra-structure because the Section 106 . . . will only go so far.
>
> (Interview E39, civil servant, 2006)

So in attempting to put together a development, there is a need to negotiate the balance between the mainstream funding programmes of government, themselves subject to intense bidding pressure through the Comprehensive Spending Review, competing for area-based regeneration funding, negotiations over developer contributions, and of course developers need internally to argue the case for their investment.

> Using Greenwich Peninsular as an example, there is a requirement for one if not two school sites . . . The way that in old-fashioned terms was negotiated was . . . 'All right, developer you provide the site for free and we the council will trust to luck that we can get the funding for the school based on the number of people who are going to be living around there . . . in due course.' Completely unsustainable, because . . . you need the school . . . before the people are there. . . .
>   This was slightly exceptional . . . but the primary school and health centre that was built at Greenwich Millennium Village, English Partnerships actually funded . . . not only the site [but] the building as well. Simply to demonstrate the point that unless you get social facilities . . . the school . . . the health centre . . . there almost before the first resident moves in, the first resident is going to send little Johnny down the road three miles in a car . . . and your whole drive to cut down CO_2 emissions is shot before you start. . . .
>   There is still a debate about the great mismatch between service providers delivering social infrastructure . . . because however well the developer and the local authority plan it, if the primary care trust won't play ball you're stuffed. So there is a bit of an issue . . . which I take to be part of spatial planning.
>   (Interview E40, national regeneration body, 2006)

Rather than shrink from such complexity, the challenge has been for all involved to get on with absorbing it into their processes, such that working in partnership, packaging funding and working out deals is now the norm, for planners, developers and others:

> Locally . . . in these days of LSPs . . . perhaps it's second nature . . . working with the health authority . . . water suppliers . . . power suppliers.
>   (Interview E39, civil servant, 2006)

> So most developers who are any good . . . are very adept at pulling people together and working through compromises and trying to get these things to happen.
>   (Interview E40, national regeneration body, 2006)

And as if all these difficulties were not enough, then there is the racial politics of development in east London, which provides the often unspoken backdrop to negotiations over what type of development should take place, where, and for whom. Planners, regeneration professionals and local politicians tread carefully to avoid inflaming local concerns about incomers gaining preferential treatment over existing residents and businesses, a difficult issue given that everyone may agree change is necessary, but not what type of change. In east London a related issue has been the rise of the far right British National Party (BNP) with a racial agenda which feeds on allegations of white indigenous working-class populations suffering because of 'bias' towards ethnic minority groups. Here the planners can play a major role in attempting to work with communities and also attempting to defuse some of the tensions, setting out negotiation frameworks which give people the opportunity to have a say on how best to balance and distribute benefits, while recognising that not every one will gain to the same extent:

> We are sensitive to the views of local communities on development . . . On housing . . . there have been issues about the ways that social housing is allocated . . . in fact it's broader than that . . . It's about who's coming to live in any of the housing . . . and this has fuelled the growth of BNP in the area . . . Barking/Dagenham has now got twelve BNP councillors . . . That was fuelled by . . . housing allocations . . . and why new houses were being built in Barking and Dagenham . . . So whatever land use it is, there are sensitivities about its impact on existing communities . . . and we're sensitive to the way things are perceived as well as the way things are done.
>
> (Interview E44, local development body, 2006)

Conclusion

What the London and Thames Gateway case study reveals is that, despite the many claims of right-wing think-tanks, UK planning systems are actually potentially very flexible, capable of adapting to local circumstances and requirements, including negotiating settlements to suit the needs of a particular development or area. The system was originally designed to facilitate this which has meant that major legislative reform has not been required to change the direction of planning: changed national priorities and policies can be adapted into its loose framework. One of the consequences of this is the enduring ability of local planners and planning agencies to adapt to pressure, a point made well by a previous study of different local planning 'styles' (Brindley *et al.* 1996).

For large-scale development programmes such as the Thames Gateway, we need to recognise that both coordination and delivery take place simultaneously at multiple scales. Analytically, focusing on just one scale for policy and its subsequent implementation no longer makes sense, if it ever did. Instead what this chapter suggests is the need to look at how coordination takes place across the scales and sectors of development-related activity, looking for evidence of both barriers to delivery and innovative ways of unblocking blockages. It was in this vein that we first began to realise the importance of seeing how hard and soft spaces of planning worked off each other in moving towards implementation, and more than this that there might usefully be multiple soft spaces in evidence, quite possibly at different scales, in this case the transregional, subregional and sub-subregional. Had we looked for planning delivery through the lens of the formal planning apparatus, we would have missed its essence – that successful planning takes place outside as well as 'inside' the planning apparatus.

In the Thames Gateway both subregional strategy-making and sub-subregional delivery fit between statutory scales of spatial and regulatory planning. New scales for strategy-making have emerged which run alongside the formal scales of statutory planning, the regional and local, as government experiments with new forms of strategic and delivery bodies. The insertion of these new scales of strategy-making in effect promote a rethinking of the geographies of development, which might be construed variously as either supplementing or sidelining the role of local government. In effect these new spaces create the opportunities for pro-development actors to coalesce while destabilising oppositional tendencies, whether these be within the local government apparatus itself or the 'stakeholder' bodies that have adapted to lobbying at the scale of local authority boundaries.

This reworking of the geographies of development is very much one of 'scalar flux' at the local level, which appears to be motivated primarily by those seeking to create new possibilities for thinking about place-making and future development. In effect we are witnessing a degree of separation between the new scales of regeneration and the formal scales of planning and democratic representation. But it seems to us that there is an alternative reading of this, which is that the soft spaces of regeneration are actually an important part of the glue that holds together the realities of the development process, which requires the legitimacy, due process and certainties associated with the formal planning process, plus the dynamism and willingness to experiment that comes when actors are brought together into new ensembles and invited to think and work creatively. There is a reworking then of the politics of development through this rescaling process. This could create tensions between the two systems, as it did in the past, for instance, with the UDCs in the 1980s. But what we appear to be witnessing here is that the emergent new spaces are intimately interwoven with multiple other regeneration geographies, including formal local and regional planning scales (Allmendinger and Haughton 2009). We do not want to invest too much optimism in these soft spaces of governance as a 'solution' to development problems, and certainly we do not see them as some form of universal panacea for addressing development blockages. So a degree of caution is necessary here – soft space forms of governance may well address certain shortcomings, while bringing problems of their own, not least accountability issues, while possibly displacing problems elsewhere. In the wrong hands, or used insensitively, they may well become part of the problem for future planners to address.

This chapter has also pointed to an emergent fuzziness in the professional boundaries of what it is to be a planner. While large amounts of planning remain focused on land use planning as a regulatory function, the boundaries of the profession are increasingly open as planners necessarily learn how to work with others, who bring new expertise, resources, priorities and insights. We would not want to underplay the continued dominance of experts, professions and professionals in policy development and decision-making (Allmendinger 2006), but looking beyond this, we can see how spatial planning is being reconstituted so that it can and must operate within new associational networks, in the process gradually becoming more deeply embedded in governance systems at all levels.

At a theoretical level, these findings point to the need to develop a more relational understanding of the remaking of spatial planning in its broadest sense, as an institutional practice within broader governance systems and as a set of evolving professional practices and discourses, where planning knowledge is continuously challenged and remade through its encounters with others. At a practical level, our findings point to the benefits of rethinking planning in terms of the hard and soft spaces of development, something which practitioners themselves are quite possibly already aware of:

> Fuzziness is probably a good thing . . . We have legal processes and structures . . . the statutory planning system . . . but it's good that within that statutory system . . . those constraints . . . you have enough room for manoeuvrability to come up with plans that cover functional areas . . . that are actually fuzzy . . . that are flexible . . . that are actually responsive to the real geography of place.
>
> (Seminar, civil servant, 2007)

9

New planning spaces and the new spatial plannings

Revisiting our aims

One of the purposes of this research was to explore the widely held view that devolution would encourage policy experimentation and an element of diversity. Letting 'a thousand flowers bloom' in the post-devolution sun, it was hoped, would breed innovations and developments which could be learnt from and applied elsewhere. Returning to this broad context, this final chapter sets out to respond to the two large questions that underpin our investigation. Has spatial planning delivered, particularly in its aspiration to contribute to a more integrated approach to development? Has devolution delivered, in particular in terms of opening up planning to greater experimentation? Our interest was essentially with the remaking of planning as a professional practice, the rethinking of the scales and scope of planning, and the value of the governance line methodology that we introduced in Chapter 1.

When we began our research in 2005, the time was ripe for a study of the new systems of planning which were emerging post-devolution. National spatial strategies had recently been produced, with the Regional Development Strategy for Northern Ireland (2001), the National Spatial Strategy in Ireland (2002), the National Planning Framework in Scotland (2004) and the Wales Spatial Plan (2004), plus the London Plan (2004) and the introduction of Regional Spatial Strategies as statutory documents in England in 2004. It was against this background that we set out to explore how planning practices were evolving across the UK and Ireland in an era of devolution, interested both in how the plans came about and how they then operated within the multi-scalar governance arrangements of contemporary planning.

Reworking spatial planning

Chapters 1 and 2 set out in some detail the context for the reworking of spatial planning practices to embrace a wider perspective than the largely regulatory role for planning of the 1980s and early 1990s. The argument introduced there emphasised the role of structural factors in shaping the emergence of new planning concepts and practices, while acknowledging the role of influential agencies in government, professional bodies and beyond in shaping how these gained purchase in particular national and subnational contexts. Influenced in part by European thinking and in part by the reality of growing governance complexity and fragmentation, a wider role for strategic spatial strategies was envisaged by those in government and elsewhere pushing forward what might be broadly termed a 'spatial planning' agenda. From the mid-1990s a new generation of spatial plans was encouraged which it was hoped would help planning to break out of its fairly narrow confines to become better integrated with other policy domains, more strategic and more spatially informed. Linked to the integrated definition of sustainable development which was then emerging, spatial planning was recast as more than a regulatory apparatus, aspiring towards a more general role in policy integration.

Our methodological approach involved interviewing a wide range of potential stakeholders in spatial planning. This was inspired by the belief that if planning was to be truly a tool for policy integration, we might begin to see 'spatial planners' reaching out into new policy arenas and influencing parallel sectoral strategies where a spatial development perspective would help. Similarly, we expected to see spatial plans in turn influenced by more thoroughgoing engagement with the new, wider constituency of actors drawn into the spatial planning policy community. This type of mutually reinforcing cross-sectoral working would appear to be essential if spatial planning is ever to reach its full potential. Broadening our range of interviewees to the wider group of policy-makers and activists with a potential interest in spatial strategies meant that we were able to look at planning within its wider meta-governance context. Reflecting on this approach we would now argue that to understand spatial planning researchers always need to look beyond the formal system. In effect by looking at planning from the outside in, we were able to analyse planning as a practice that is closely woven in with, and shaped by, broader changes to territorial management that work selectively and recursively across a range of policy domains.

At a theoretical level we addressed these concerns through what we have described as the 'politics of scope' (Allmendinger and Haughton 2007), that is looking at the reworking of the fuzzy boundaries of planning as strategy-making and planning delivery. Situating this alongside our work on the rescaling of planning leads us to the conclusion that the search for new scalar fixes in planning is always paralleled by changing governance arrangements related to the *scope* of planning, as its reference communities are reworked and new arrangements instituted for connecting selected actors across scales and sectors. The reworking of scale and scope in planning is in effect part of a search for a new territorial management fix, always bound up in socio-political struggles over establishing strategic directions and priorities.

Rethinking planning

At a theoretical level this book has drawn on both state theory and recent work on post-structural and relational geographies to rethink how best to undertake research on spatial planning. Informed particularly by the debates in geography and elsewhere on rescaling and the state (Jessop 2000; Jones 2001; Goodwin *et al.* 2005), plus the challenges to this approach raised by work on relational geographies (Amin 2002; Massey 2005), the intention has been to engage planning research more closely with state theory. More than this, however, we wanted to challenge the preoccupation of many state theorists with subnational economic development by looking at how such work might benefit from considering how governance worked in the more tightly regulated policy domain of planning (see also Haughton and Counsell 2004). While we had hoped to find more evidence of planning providing a forum for challenging neoliberalism's privileging of economic growth and subordination of social and environmental objectives to this, in practice we found economic growth was very much in the ascendant in all the post-devolutionary planning systems covered here. So while new governments in Scotland, Wales and Northern Ireland made much of their commitment to environmental and social objectives, all explicitly asserted economic growth as their primary objective. Despite widespread adoption of a 'balanced' approach to sustainable development within planning and beyond, there was little evidence that this disrupted the political priority accorded to economic growth. Instead we found a series of ways of rationalising public commitments to both balancing economic, environmental and social objectives and to privileging economic growth. In effect each administration provided its own reworking of neoliberalist formulations, using the consultation apparatus of planning and its stakeholders to find ways of rationalising the wider project of a market-led approach to economic growth, where the worst excesses of unbalanced growth might be (rhetorically at least) mitigated through various actions negotiated through the planning system and other related sectoral strategies. Rather than challenging neoliberalism then, spatial planning appears to be implicated in helping to rationalise it by providing a set of principles and practices for mitigating, obfuscating or palliating some of the externalities associated with promoting high economic growth above other aspects of societal well-being.

One of this book's main theoretical contributions has been a critical interrogation of 'soft spaces' and 'fuzzy boundaries' as a way of understanding how much of the real work of planning is operating not so much outside the formal apparatus of planning as on the interface between planning and other parts of the development process (Allmendinger and Haughton 2007). The argument we have developed here is that some of the strategic and delivery work of planning is now operating at various in-between scales, often involving arm's-length institutional arrangements which do not so much isolate planning as create new institutional formats and constellations of actors which can operate without the rigidities of the statutory regulatory framework of planning, yet whose links to planning provide a central part of their legitimacy. There is considerable scope here for further conceptual and empirical work to test these ideas, but already it provides some useful conceptual and empirical insights into the complexity of how state spatialities are being remade in the context of planning and regeneration.

Devolution and policy experimentation

Looking at devolution in terms of governance lines helped to highlight the ways in which the different parts of the planning system knitted together across both new and existing planning spaces, where experimentation was unleashed not simply at the scale of the new territorial administrations. In terms of our interest in whether devolution led to a new period of policy experimentation for planning, in summary it is fair to say that there is some diversity of experience emerging, but perhaps not as much as we had expected (see Tables 9.1 and 9.2). This said we did uncover plenty of examples of innovation, not least in the strategy-making process and in the undoubted growing tendency to create new planning spaces, often initially at least introduced using the tactic of fuzzy boundaries to create what we have termed soft spaces. But perhaps the most important 'new' planning space of all has been the development of national spatial plans subsequent to devolved political powers, notably in Wales, Scotland and Northern Ireland, which often struggle to be contained within easy categorisations.

The reasons why we found less experimentation in turning strategies into implemented policies than we had expected appear to be fourfold. First, devolution prompted a British Isles-level policy community for spatial planning, with considerable sharing of experience taking place (see Chapter 5; see also Keating 2005; Harris and Hooper 2006). Second, devolution appears to have encouraged greater participation in the opportunities to exchange experiences at a European level, through various projects funded by Community Initiatives such as INTERREG. Third, the devolution settlement was neither open-ended nor without restraints. While planning was a devolved function in the UK (primary legislative in Scotland and secondary legislative in Wales) there were constraints upon autonomy. For instance, there was a deliberate attempt to ensure coordination through the signing of concordats between the devolved bodies and Westminster that agreed processes and common goals. Also, some important sectors such as energy were not devolved, limiting some of the scope for autonomy. The final reason we found for limits upon experimentation was the significance of EU environmental regulation. Estimates vary on the extent, but it seems clear that mechanisms such as Strategic Environmental Assessment and Environmental Impact Assessment dictated the scope of spatial planning to a considerable degree, with the UK's adoption of 'sustainability appraisal' an overt attempt to reweight these technical mechanisms in favour of economic growth and social justice. The result is that experimentation is taking place, but this is at least as much evident at a system level as it is within individual territorial administrations.

Table 9.1 Governance innovations in planning post-devolution

	Fuzzy boundaries	*Soft spaces of governance*	*New planning spaces (post-devolution)*	*Double devolution in planning*
England	City regions in Northern Way, also some use at micro level	Subregions and city regions and meta regions (e.g. Northern Way, Thames Gateway)	Regions, subregions, city regions	Largely illusionary, strong central control still, regional planning made statutory
Wales	New subregions	Partnerships for new subregions	Wales Spatial Plan and subregions	Strong central control
Scotland	Not used	West Edinburgh (Planning Framework)	New formal city regions	Some improvement to city regional arrangements
Ireland	Not widely used	CASP	National Spatial Strategy and regional planning guidelines introduced. Also city regions (Cork and Dublin) and cross-border strategies	As the regional tier remains weak there is limited evidence of a further cascade of powers to local authorities
Northern Ireland	Not used	Belfast Metropolitan Plan and new cross-border region and subregions, (e.g. North West)	Regional Development Strategy, Belfast Metropolitan Plan and new cross-border region and subregions	Stronger national framework, plans afoot to empower local authorities in planning

Table 9.1 provides a brief summary of some of these trends, which usefully highlights the uneven adoption of, for instance, fuzzy boundaries as part of the new spatial planning. In both this and Table 9.2 (p. 247) the judgements made are ours and are of course subjective to an extent, based on our collective assessment of the many different viewpoints we heard during the course of a two-and-a-half-year study in which we talked to over 140 people and read many plans, draft plans and background submissions. We readily accept that these are only summaries of some broad trends, masking some important

differences over time and at different scales and locations within each plan-ning system. In addition, it is very difficult to compare England with its many regions with, say, Wales and Scotland, as the different entities vary so widely in scale and complexity. Despite the misgivings we and others may have, the fact that people will dispute and argue over our conclusions is probably a positive thing in opening up debate on comparative planning. From our per-spective the justification is that we have tried to bring together and summarise our findings here, based on a shared research methodology explicitly con-structed to capture the dynamics of spatial planning in each of the territories we covered.

What Table 9.1 highlights is that all parts of the UK and Ireland have invented new planning spaces as part of their effort to rework their planning hierarchies. Scotland stands out as the territory which has been least likely to imagine these new subnational planning formations in terms of fuzzy bound-aries or soft spaces of governance. By contrast, in both England and Wales there has been considerable experimentation; indeed in Wales it has been very much a central feature of the new spatial planning there that it has sought to imagine and introduce new planning spaces that disrupt the 'traditional' spaces of regulatory planning.

We turn to look at some of these emergent practices in the next sections.

Overview of key findings

As part of this overview we draw attention not only to particular innovative approaches which appear to be emerging in particular areas, but also to the changing institutional landscape within which spatial strategies are produced. For example, new policy communities are emerging around the development of national spatial strategies as the different administrations learn from each other about alternative ways of taking forward their spatial planning work. We start by looking at devolution overall, then policy integration, followed by a discussion on rescaling and the changing nature of planning, concluding with a section on implementation.

Devolution and the rescaling of planning

Devolution *has* bolstered spatial planning in the devolved territories. While the government offices in the territories always had a strong presence, the recent work on the preparation of national plans and other documentation has high-lighted the work of planners in the devolved administrations. There is also evidence of transnational policy communities having emerged among planning stakeholders at national levels within Northern Ireland, Ireland, Scotland and Wales, where recent experiences and ideas about best practice are regularly shared (for a similar finding with regard to transport planning, see Mackinnon *et al.* 2008). This has, to some extent, limited the degree to which devolution has led to policy divergence as actors share information within these new communities: the Northern Ireland plan was much lauded in the planning profession, for example, and provided something of a starting point for other administrations. Devolution does matter: however, the distinctiveness in spatial planning that we are seeing is both at the system level in terms of divergence from past practices, as well as divergence between the various new and existing administrations.

The contested nature of the rescaling of subnational planning provided a recurrent theme throughout the case study chapters. In addition to a trend towards diversity and fragmentation in the scalar fixes of planning, the continuing significance and dominance of the nation state provided another consistent theme. In two previously highly centralised states (Ireland and the UK) this is perhaps not surprising. To paraphrase one of our Irish interviewees, even decentralisation is centralised. Or to put it another way, decentralisation has been accompanied by a complex set of formal and informal measures for ensuring that the scope for discretion is tempered by the realities of ensuring some level of conformity in pursuit of overriding national interests.

In terms of rescaling and changes in the relative authority of various territorial entities in the UK and Ireland we see two broad trends emerging in relation to planning, which parallel wider tendencies in governance practice. First, there is mixed evidence of strategic and selective 'hollowing out' at the nation state in the UK and Ireland, with little or no transfer of powers to the EU level, and in many ways a strengthening of many of the instruments and powers of national governments, through targets, new legislation and in the case of Ireland, the new national spatial strategy. Fitting better with the hollowing-out thesis is the selective transfer of planning powers to some of the newly devolved territories, notably London, Scotland, Wales, and to a lesser extent Northern Ireland and the regions of England and Ireland. Second, and following on from the above, there has been an equally strategic and selective 'filling in' and reimagining of subnational state spaces in both Ireland and the UK. Seeing the project of devolution as an active and continuously evolving process, we can begin to see how the new institutional forms of the state are actively being constructed and contested. Far from being a simple process of 'filling in', these new state spaces are actively struggled over (Brenner 2004: 76), evident in planning particularly through the creation of new institutional geographies via the multiple (hard and soft) planning spaces that are being experimented with. Devolution then created the opportunity for re-territorialisation and institution building, but did not and indeed could not dictate the outcomes of these processes. Rather, the new arrangements were always going to be contingent on historically and place-specific processes of political contestation (Goodwin *et al.* 2006). This multifaceted process is very much evident in the increased complexity of spatial planning across the UK and Ireland, where devolution has brought about very different settlements and in turn unleashed the potential for different types of planning to begin to emerge at subnational level.

The nations of Northern Ireland, Scotland and Wales have all gained considerable increased autonomy since the late 1990s, while decentralisation and the formation of new regional structures has also occurred in Ireland as part of moves towards spreading growth more equally on a territorial basis. This devolutionary process has been paralleled to an extent in the English regions, although the English devolution process was stalled with the public rejection of elected regional assemblies in 2004. Below this level there is also a growing interest in new approaches to subregional and metropolitan-scale planning. While post-devolution institution building has played out differently across the British Isles, one consistent theme in post-devolution planning has been a greater emphasis upon the building blocks of subregions and city regions.

The filling-in process for planning is essentially twofold. At times it is driven by national governments. The emphasis on city regions in regional spatial strategies in England and the city region authorities created by the 2006 Planning Act in Scotland both had variable degrees of local support but were driven from the respective centres. In other contexts, however, the institutional filling in is more ad hoc and 'informal' (or at least non-statutory) as with the spatial planning arrangements in Cork or the Thames Gateway, though again it is fair to say that national, regional and local forces tend to combine in producing each particular settlement, such that it is rarely the case that a new accommodation is purely 'top-down' or 'bottom-up' in origin. The emergent soft spaces of recent times seem to have become more important, formalised and encouraged through a range of mechanisms such as Multi-area Agreements in England, and the encouragement of 'functional planning' based around travel to work and housing market areas. However, there is also evidence that such forms of rescaling have distinct advantages for planning authorities. In the Thames Gateway, for example, functional planning is not only a way of mapping planning institutions onto the realities of sites and developments but also a way of undertaking planning outside of the lengthy and sometimes confrontational nature of statutory processes. In Cork too an informal approach through collaboration between the city and county councils has had clear benefits, establishing a widely accepted framework for development which has subsequently been incorporated into statutory plans at all scales from national to local.

There is therefore a fine balance between government condoning and even encouraging non-statutory approaches while simultaneously needing to endorse open and democratic planning. This is particularly so given the mantra in the UK since 1997 of the need to focus on ends and not means in a Third Way adoption of a 'what works' philosophy: in some areas the formal, statutory system of planning has been deemed to be not 'working', and planning authorities, with sometimes tacit and sometimes more explicit encouragement, have 'voted with their feet' and created or otherwise opted to work with 'shadow' planning processes. Some 'progressive' planning authorities appear to be deciding on what needs to be done and then selecting and manipulating the tools to achieve their aims, with a careful eye on the need for some approval from central government representatives. Others are perhaps more focused on producing documents that meet their statutory obligations, seeking to innovate within the confines of the statutory processes or struggling to produce a plan at all. There is no saying that one approach is better than the other – and we would want to caution against naive optimism on the potential of non-statutory processes for achieving rapid policy documents. As we saw in the case of North East Wales-West Cheshire, the very nature of these soft space arrangements may speed up the process of agreement, but at the expense of gaining widespread acceptance.

In some areas the rescaling of planning needs to account for even greater diversity of planning approaches than previously recognised or even known, as statutory and non-statutory systems combine to create multilayered, multi-faceted plannings. This is not a universal trend. In other areas the processes of rescaling have been more formalised in nature. In Scotland, for example, legislative change and statutory processes have led much of the restructuring of planning. This has sometimes led to the creation of new or bolstered organisations with responsibility for plans with hard boundaries. In other places the malleable nature of the UK and Irish planning systems has been used to create policy mechanisms and institutional infrastructure on a short- or medium-term basis aimed at the delivery of particular plans or strategies, as in our Thames Gateway example. This temporal dimension adds a further dynamic to the rescaling of planning and highlights the extent to which rescaling is a process rather than an outcome.

The 'layering' and overlapping of formal and informal scales of planning has some significant implications in terms of democratic deficits and the sheer complexity and opacity which results from institutional proliferation. The creation of institutions to deliver regeneration and spatial planning, in the Thames Gateway, for example, can be seen as a way of cutting through a cluttered governance landscape. However, there is a clear paradox here in that they create further clutter and add to the obfuscation for non-specialists. The experience of Leeds too highlights both the complexity and adaptability of the dynamics of scalar change. The emergence of the Northern Way plan and its city region focus, with its unclear 'other' status outside the planning system, created considerable uncertainty for the local authorities and other bodies involved. The ability of planners and others to 'muddle through' and reach agreement on issues such as housing allocations and infrastructure provision provides a way forward in the short term. However, without any clear legal status such arrangements have tested the ability of greater scalar complexity to accommodate growth. This was the case too with the Cork Area Strategic Plan. The consensus around a good paper plan covering Cork and its hinterland was paralleled by the widespread feeling that the plan's innovative vision for a spatial reordering of the metropolitan region was being undermined by incremental and short-term decisions, particularly a failure to enforce growth controls in overheated areas.

Devolution then is creating a more varied set of institutional accommodations for spatial planning across the UK and Ireland. It is perhaps helpful to think of these variations in a similar way to the classifications for the emergent UK territories put forward by Cooke and Clifton (2005) for economic governance post-devolution. In Northern Ireland, the spatial planning process is one of 'fragmented centralisation', with a strong prescriptive element in the form of housing targets, allied to a weak roll-out of planning responsibilities as yet to the local level. Wales has developed a 'state-centric and evolutionary' approach to spatial planning at the national level, where the emphasis to date has been on corporate policy integration and giving substance to new sub-national 'area' identities. The approach is one of high-level visioning with no prescriptive dimension. Instead the statutory system runs parallel and indeed largely separate to this more 'visionary' corporate process. In Scotland, the approach remains largely formal and hierarchical, involving a state-centred model for delivery, allied to some experimentation with new institutional arrangements at the subnational level. At national scale, the National Planning Framework is high level, lacking the prescriptive elements of English regional plans and the Northern Ireland strategy. In London, the London Plan is unique among the regions for being a statutory plan produced and approved by the mayor and Greater London Assembly. The approach is 'local state-centric with a strong inclusiveness agenda' in which policy integration is also a strong feature. Nonetheless, the London approach is very heavily shaped by external conditions, including government housing targets and an economic growth agenda allied to the fortunes of central London and its financial services sector. Elsewhere, the English regions are best characterised as 'planning through borrowed powers', borrowed from local authorities who constitute the regional planning bodies, and from central government which formally approves the plans and sets a series of constraining targets. The result is conformist plans, largely lacking individuality and only limited experimentation, something in turn reflected in local plans. Ireland is unique in its combination of 'high-level vision backed by spatially informed investment', provided by the National Spatial Strategy and the National Development Plan. Regional planning guidelines and local plans complete the Irish system, providing a clear hierarchical statutory framework.

Planning's role in policy integration

A distinctive feature of the new spatial planning is the aspiration to create a more considered cross-sectoral, spatialised understanding of the likely needs and impacts of future development, though in practice this has proved difficult to achieve. This is perhaps understandable, given that different sectors work within different regulatory constraints and the long-standing issues of poor interdepartmental policy coordination in government.

An interesting issue to emerge from our work was the ways in which planning as an object of governance was being considered in areas of government away from its normal institutional home. Thus, in the UK Treasury several teams were concerned with different aspects of planning and as we saw in Chapters 7 and 8 contributing actively to debates on the future shape of planning. The Department of Trade and Industry (now the Department for Business, Innovation and Skills) likewise had a small dedicated team working on planning issues, seeking to ensure improved linkages between the department's work and the planning system. In Ireland there is a high-level ministerial committee overseeing planning and infrastructure, an approach also adopted in Wales. In Wales the preparation of the national plan was undertaken by a separate team rather than as part of the planning department in national government, with strong ministerial leadership. Sub-area work in Wales too is led by ministers. At one level these might be seen as examples of integration in action or of planning being taken more seriously elsewhere in government. This was partly true but they also represented struggles over institutional power, including defining the parameters of the planning system and its evolving modus operandi. We can see it as a clash of paradigms too, with planners attached to an integrated definition of sustainable development while departments such as the Treasury have a decidedly neoliberal market orientation, influencing how they sought to challenge planning's ways of doing things during a period of considerable reform to the system. Whether this planning work outside the mainstream planning institutions continues and extends will be an interesting issue to monitor, not least in terms of whether it leads to a more integrated approach to policy or simply exercises a disciplinary effect on planning to bring it fully behind the dominant ethos of financial departments. It is far from clear whether the two-way exchange of views is taking place on an equal basis.

This said, clear efforts are being made to join up government policy better in both Dublin and Whitehall, partly driven by the greater involvement in shaping planning policy by central departments such as the Irish Department of Finance and the UK Treasury. In addition to influencing policy, both governments are seeking to improve the alignment of their investment with regional priorities, and in the case of Ireland with the National Spatial Strategy. The Irish approach is the more sophisticated, involving a process of aligning government investment with territorial development, guided by a clear national spatial strategy. The Welsh Assembly Government too has a clear written commitment to align its spending behind the Wales Spatial Plan, but in truth the limited amount of financial devolution to Wales plus the limited amount of spatial detail in the Wales Spatial Plan renders this a fairly empty gesture at the present time. In England, Regional Funding Allocations represent a limited but encouraging step in the right direction towards devolving responsibility to regional actors to determine their own priorities, though this has been an unsophisticated process, lacking meaningful engagement with spatial thinking, more an unfiltered wish list from local authority chief executive departments rather than a multi-agency process of debate over regional priorities.

This is perhaps a slightly harsh assessment of progress in the UK, since we also found some evidence of movement towards more effective integration between policy actors at subnational levels, particularly in relation to economic development, transport infrastructure and environmental protection. Most encouragingly, we saw a widening of the planning policy community; for instance, work on water infrastructure in Scotland was contentious, but progress was being made through constructive engagement. In the Thames Gateway, plans for substantial and rapid population growth were being addressed by greater collaborative work between planners and the health authorities, seeking to respond to plans for growth rather than simply react after development was in place. It should be stressed, however, that such exemplars were exceptional. For the most part, we are seeing improved dialogue between planners and other policy sectors, but only limited evidence of impacts on each others' fundamental policies.

In theory, and in practice, interdepartmental coordination appeared to have a better chance of making progress in the younger and less entrenched administrations in the devolved administrations, where size of place is helpful in coordinating agendas, more so than in the larger and more diffuse administrations in England. We found evidence that this was occurring in Scotland and Wales in particular. In Ireland too we found that interdepartmental committees of ministers and senior civil servants were helping drive through a more integrated approach to policy-making than hitherto, particularly through linking investment decisions to the National Spatial Strategy. This is suggestive of the need for greater investment autonomy to parallel devolved responsibilities for strategy-making in the devolved territories of the UK.

The technical apparatus of spatial planning is interesting here. Some of the new national spatial strategy documents are clearly positioned as statements of corporate intent on behalf of the new administrations, where the expectation is that the contents of the plans will inform whole-of-government approaches. In this sense, spatial planning is indeed becoming more than a regulatory planning system. However, this is best seen not as a shift from one system to another, but rather as the creation of a new parallel system with varying levels of attachment to regulatory planning systems, from arm's-length in Wales, to separated through departmental barriers in Northern Ireland, to hierarchically ordered in Ireland, and of course in England national spatial planning is still a pipe-dream. But the technical apparatus of spatial planning involves more than the written strategies, it also encompasses any formalised statutory elements, such as targets for brownfield site redevelopment and new housing allocations. Running alongside these are ex ante appraisal systems such as sustainability appraisal (Counsell and Haughton 2006b) and policy integration tools, the latter in many ways emblematic of the new devolved planning systems in Wales, Scotland and Northern Ireland, and ex post monitoring systems of varying levels of sophistication.

New planning spaces: the reworking of the scale and scope of planning

One outcome of scalar complexity and the growing significance of partnership and networked governance is the (re-)emergence of 'soft spaces' and 'fuzzy boundaries'. Subregional planning arrangements have added a further dimension through the reworking of formal administrative boundaries and processes into more fluid and ephemeral joint arrangements. The issue here is that while the main statutory basis for spatial planning is at the new national, regional and local scales, there is a strong focus too on spatial strategy work at non-statutory scales, what we term the 'soft spaces' of planning. While a new meta-regional scale has emerged, exemplified by work on the Northern Way, most of these new spaces focus on subregional, city region or local delivery scales. Despite being largely non-statutory, these new policy spaces appear to have exerted a strong influence on emerging statutory plans at national, regional and local scales. Our interview results suggest that 'soft spaces' are valued as a mechanism for encouraging more creative thinking, unconstrained by regulation and national guidance, and providing greater opportunities for a range of non-planning actors to engage more productively with planning processes.

Because of their non-statutory nature and concerns about public accountability, these new planning spaces bring with them significant challenges, particularly for governance and alignment with other policy spaces. Arrangements for city region governance range from professionally staffed and permanently established joint committees of local authorities to ad hoc arrangements for the preparation of particular plans and strategies. Where there has been a tradition of working together, such as in Glasgow and the Clyde Valley, spatial plans appear stronger and better aligned with delivery. Indeed, in Scotland city regions are set to become formal spaces of planning as a result of new planning legislation.

Fuzzy boundaries have also become an issue, most notably perhaps with the Northern Way (Chapter 7) and the Wales Spatial Plan (Chapter 6), both of which define sub-areas without definite boundaries. The fuzziness of these boundaries has caused concerns to peripheral local authorities and those on the boundaries between different subregions, over issues such as are they in or out when it comes to public investment, and participation in policy-making processes. Perhaps the epitome of fuzzy boundaries is to be found in the Wales Spatial Plan (WSP), leading to work in establishing six new subnational territorial areas, not least as it is clear in this instance that these were deliberately created to provoke new territorial thinking in the expectation that this would encourage greater innovation in developing new policies, not least by demanding new territorial alliances not wedded to previous practices and ways of thinking.

Soft space and fuzzy boundary issues are also apparent in a rise in attempts at cross-border planning. Here new spaces for planning are being created to deal with cross-border questions. In North West Ireland, Thames Gateway and Cheshire and North East Wales we see interesting examples of plans being developed along lines which are said to reflect certain spatial realities better than existing administrative boundaries. In some cases such efforts were performed through local authority planning teams, lessening the criticisms of governance clutter. Alternatively the generation of additional strategies to those developed in statutory arenas in the latter case could be said to be adding to a cluttering of the policy landscape. There are also issues arising here when statutory processes encounter the useful work done in these other, more informal arenas, for instance, about transparency and the translation of work done outside the statutory system into statutory plans, as in the case of North East Wales.

Fuzzy boundaries and soft spaces appear to have a number of practical advantages for those involved. In the Thames Gateway they are being used to facilitate and coordinate scales of development which cross administrative boundaries, such that fuzziness was almost a necessity for implementation. In other areas too, fuzziness and soft spaces were used as a way of overcoming administrative boundaries that were unhelpful in relation to planning for housing and employment.

Nevertheless, the case studies also highlighted the downsides of such approaches. In Wales there were mixed feelings about the use of fuzzy boundaries, where the WSP was felt to have 'imposed' fuzzy boundaries. Local authorities initially preferred clarity and complained that, in some cases, they did not know which area and policy regime applied. However, parts of the private sector were more welcoming, claiming that they reflected the way people live and work, though housebuilders longed for greater certainty rather than ambiguity. Likewise the introduction of the Northern Way plan in Leeds and the focus on city regions and fuzzy boundaries created uncertainty over which geographical scale was to have precedence when it came to government investment, while local planners used the emergent city region space as a means of contesting housing allocations to meet RSS targets. In short the rescaling of planning through soft spaces was not unproblematic, becoming embroiled in political battles over practical aspects of implementation, even when agreement had been reached on broad visions and principles.

The interesting irony here is that fuzzy boundaries and soft spaces seem to be preferred by their proponents as ways of breaking out from the rigidities of statutory planning's fixed procedures and processes, which are seen as time-consuming and costly. Yet it would seem that soft space arrangements may only displace the points at which dissent arises, putting the onus for those involved not so much to bypass the system as to work carefully alongside it. Soft space approaches can be a useful part of the strategic planning repertoire in terms of facilitating development and creating competitive advantage, in part, through minimising regulations or short-circuiting and partnering developments through formal processes. The danger though is that they might be used to mainly sidestep wider responsibilities, not least those relating to the social justice and environmental aspects of sustainable development.

It must also be stressed that fuzzy boundaries and soft space arrangements are almost invariably condoned and even encouraged by central government, not least through preferential access to government funding. But more fundamentally they also reflect the discretionary and flexible nature of UK and Irish planning discussed in Chapter 2. The combination of flexible plan areas and processes, multiple scales of plan combined with statutory plan areas and processes creates a maelstrom of strategy that can diminish rather than enhance implementation and understanding. Arguably there may well be an optimal level of coordination and fuzziness beyond which the complexity and uncertainty of arrangements mitigate against implementation.

Taken together, one of the most distinctive messages from our work is the importance of non-statutory 'soft spaces' and 'fuzzy boundaries' within the development process. Our argument is not that these new spaces of planning compete with existing formal scales of planning, but rather that they are being introduced by government departments and others as part of a very specific political project to destabilise and counteract those oppositional interests which are effectively organised at existing scales of planning. As such they are introduced as 'flexible' and aligned to the 'real' geographies of problems and opportunities while doing some hard political work in ensuring that post-devolution agendas are taken forward.

Fuzzy planning: new policy communities and the porosity of planning

Despite the different contexts for spatial planning provided by devolution, it is apparent that there is a strong sense of networking and mutual learning among planning administrations. Lead officers in the UK administrations and Ireland meet regularly to discuss issues of common interest. Planning in the British Isles also forms part of a wider European spatial planning community where officers participate in joint inter-regional projects and in research projects through the European Spatial Planning Observation Network (ESPON).

While these new 'supra-national' policy communities can help share good practice, previous studies suggest that established policy communities tend to be conservative and, consciously or otherwise, tend to preclude radical policy options from emerging, a reason perhaps for the similarity of technical approaches that we found in spatial plans in the British Isles. Differences in the way spatial planning is delivered appear to result from different institutional arrangements and different political and geographical contexts, rather than from different professional approaches or planning cultures. As one Irish civil servant told us:

> The group of people doing this type of work is quite small . . . and that does make people share their approaches. But I think the spatial contexts in the territories are very different . . . so it would be difficult to find a one size fits all.
>
> (Interview IR2, civil servant, 2005)

We found some intriguing differences across the devolved administrations of the UK, not so much in policy content as in how planning worked in the different territories. The very act of devolution, allied to the smaller size of the policy communities in Scotland and Wales in particular means that they appear to have been well placed to create more cohesive policy communities which are working towards better integrated policy at a corporate level.

Spatial planning is presented by its supporters in government and beyond as fundamentally different in scope to land use planning by providing the broad context for the development of a territory, rather than playing a role in framing development management (Planning Officers Society 2005; DCLG 2007). In this way spatial planning activity is encouraged rhetorically to focus more on planning's place-making agenda and less on its role in regulating and managing conflicts over land use (Rydin 2004). In summary the evidence suggests that the wider remit of spatial planning is leading to planners reinventing themselves not as experts in other policy domains, but rather as part of a network of actors who between them bring different forms of expert knowledge. What planners bring to these wider networks is an expectation that not only planning but other forms of strategic thinking adopt a more explicitly 'spatial' dimension. Planners then are reworking their professional boundaries not by extending their own 'internal' expertise, for instance, into social justice or biodiversity, but by linking into the networks within which these various bodies of expertise exist. Within these wider associational networks, the value that spatial planners seem to bring is their ability to think over the long term about future development, an awareness of the need to anticipate likely impacts that will result from development beyond land use itself, their statutory role in regulating future land use, and a willingness to engage in consultative processes with a wide range of stakeholders as a means of bringing shared ownership and legitimacy to decisions that will necessarily always create winners and losers, and with this disagreement.

Implementation: delivering integrated spatial policies

We found considerable evidence of better strategy-making processes, but that few of the claimed local delivery successes appear to stand up to detailed critical scrutiny. This is not to underestimate the importance of what has been achieved. Policy-makers have become much better at working with each other to ensure that their strategies support rather than contradict each other, and there is some evidence of better integration of aspects of infrastructure development with spatial planning, particularly for transport, economic development and environmental protection (Counsell *et al.* 2006). Less well integrated are social issues, though again, examples of progress do exist, for instance, work around health agendas in the Thames Gateway and Glasgow-Clyde Valley (see Chapters 5 and 8).

Overall, however, our research leads us to conclude that there has been considerable success in creating better strategy documents, but rather less success in implementing them, a perennial issue for spatial planners (Newman 2008). Coordinating the delivery of development and especially infrastructure proved a vexed issue in all administrations, requiring cooperation *horizontally* with delivery agents in different sectors and *vertically* with national governments, which fund much of the infrastructure, and local delivery agencies. Coordination proved problematic for a variety of reasons: the non-alignment of policy and investment geographies used by different public sector institutions; reliance on investment by bodies which are not directly party to a spatial plan and work in different regulatory environments; the different timescales which many of these bodies work to – planning is essentially long term, and investment programmes are often short term, linked to public spending rounds and the short-term political nature of much decision-making over projects such as transport infrastructure.

There are interesting theoretical challenges here in thinking through at what scale(s) policy integration might be most likely to be effective, and what happens when powerful actors at different scales have to combine to make things happen. In England, where powers are so diffuse across actors and scales, it is difficult to see how powerful cross-sectoral, multi-scalar alliances can take shape. Despite some progress on local area agreements and the like, local authorities still struggle to exert authority, having been systematically stripped of powers and funding over many years. This is in contrast to the historical experience of powerful local authorities mobilising growth through planning, Birmingham in the 1980s, Manchester in the 1990s. In this context, we can begin to see how in the new, smaller national territories their very size and new-found political status helps to foster agendas around a national and subnational set of plans and priorities that are easier to promulgate.

It is a moot point whether the profusion of new strategies is helping promote policy integration, an issue clearly evident in the Thames Gateway, our London case study and itself a relatively new policy space involving three different regional planning authorities and sixteen local authorities. Here a host of emerging formal plans and strategies together with a proliferation of new policy and delivery agencies has created a complex network of planning and regeneration spaces. The nature of large sites combined with the necessity of huge infrastructure costs required the coordination of a wide variety of public and private partners. The push for delivery in such a nationally significant growth area often required such plans to be negotiated around rather than through existing planning structures and plans, raising the question of whether action followed policy or policy followed action.

Devolved governments were often elected with a promise to be consultative (Keating 2005). We found that, if anything, this had gone 'too far' with increasing calls to get things done coming from many stakeholders; business communities in particular. This in itself caused problems. Being new institutions, there was limited history and capacity to undertake and commission research that would help take decisions (Keating 2005), and little cultural capital to draw on when it came to using such work to take decisions and make policy (Mackinnon *et al.* 2008). National plans were often seen as lacking in statements of clear priorities as a result of these institutional difficulties, coupled with planning's failure to elevate itself to a metagovernance role capable of providing a framework within which such investments might be considered. Procedures to judge competing investments were seen as lacking as a result and the resultant portfolios of projects, in NPF2 in Scotland and the Leeds City Region, for example, frequently had little coherent justification behind them.

In England and at the UK scale, institutional issues become even more complex. A seemingly never-ending series of changes to the planning system and its practices have swamped subnational government, as planners have struggled to keep up with changes within their own narrow regulatory domain, let alone keep abreast of the parallel changes being introduced in the regulatory environments of their many stakeholders. Ironically, while much of the restructuring of planning has aimed to allow local solutions to flourish, it often had the perverse effect of binding local government into an ever more dependent relationship with the centre, sometimes through its regional offices. The language of devolution was not matched by the reality, however honest the intentions.

Planning has always been supposed to be about providing at least a broad context for the provision of distributive infrastructure, such as energy, transport, information communication technologies, water and waste networks. Indeed for many non-planners when they think of what planning might be about they frequently resort to a discussion of infrastructure questions, particularly with regard to transport. In the past, however, spatial planning has under-performed in the task of coordinating and providing for infrastructure provision (Webster 2003). In general terms we found that these issues continued to be problematic for spatial planning.

Winners and losers in the new spatial planning

As we noted in the earlier chapters, policy integration and by definition spatial planning is not a politically neutral process. Rather it is a reordering of priorities and with this comes a reworking of the way in which the benefits of future development are distributed. In effect there is a reshuffling of the winners and losers associated with any spatial plan. At a systemic level too, the adoption of particular types of spatial planning also reorders the way in which positive benefits and negative externalities are distributed across society. Take improved policy integration as an example. We have spoken about two competing paradigms operating in policy circles when it comes to future development, the market-led neoliberal agenda of mainstream economic government departments, and the 'balanced' or integrated approach to sustainable development preferred by planners. Where the integration of policy is led by the funding departments of government, then inevitably a particular vision of what is to be integrated and how, and what is to be prioritised within this, will shine through. So we found plenty of examples of policy rhetoric in favour of integrated approaches to 'sustainable development', which in all cases of large investment seemed to boil down to 'if enough jobs are created, then this outweighs all other considerations'. For instance, in Wales the decision around the Bluestone development highlighted the dominance of economic development. Similarly, the economic development function in Northern Ireland also dominated decision-making. In both cases the implementation of the national/regional spatial plan proved difficult because under pressure not all central agencies and politicians were willing to 'buy-in' to either spatial planning as a concept or the need to underpin sectoral decisions with a spatial strategy.

One outcome is the difficulty in ascribing clear 'winners' and 'losers' under spatial planning and scalar complexity. One winner that emerges from the case study chapters is the central state. While some analyses of rescaling processes highlight both the 'hollowing out' of the nation state and its 'filling in' with new state spaces the actual distribution of power within largely unitary states has not changed significantly. Nor has spatial planning emerged as a strong force for influencing the emergence of major national policy initiatives. Initiatives such as the proposed English Eco-Towns, development connected to the successful 2012 Olympics bid and future major infrastructure projects including nuclear energy have and will lie outside of the formal and informal spatial planning processes. Other major developments such as the third runway at Heathrow may well go ahead despite, not because of, a planning system that has brought together a coalition of interests opposed to it. In England the role of the Treasury in directing planning policy in recent years has been clear. Both Barker reviews of land use planning and the subnational review of economic development originated within and were controlled by the Treasury with close involvement of the CBI (Confederation of British Industry) and others. In some respects the dominance of economic interests overriding others is nothing new (see Healey *et al.* 1988). Nevertheless, it is worth highlighting that spatial planning does not necessarily presuppose more balanced and devolved governance arrangements; nor does it or has it diminished traditional powerful interests.

Table 9.2 provides a useful overview of some of the issues covered here, attempting a broadbrush assessment of the direction of travel that spatial planning has undertaken since 1997 in each of the main territories covered in this book, using some of the key themes identified in earlier chapters. Policy integration is a theme in all of the administrations, more strongly followed through in some than others. Northern Ireland is a unique case in the extent to which policy integration in practice appears to have gone in the wrong direction, at least in terms of planning, with the fragmentation of planning powers between departments and the politicisation of control over departments all playing a part in a system which is competent technically as a regulatory function, but verges on dysfunctional in terms of the wider remit of spatial planning. By contrast, Northern Ireland's progress on improving public participation in planning, in difficult circumstances, has been exceptional. Balanced territorial development is a theme found in all spatial plans, with ESDP concepts particularly evident in Scotland, Wales, Northern Ireland and Ireland. In addition, there has been some evidence of efforts to decentralise the civil service in Wales and Ireland, enjoying a mixed reception from the public, plus some efforts to better align central government investment with regional priorities, though not necessarily those arrived at via the spatial planning system. With the possible exception of Ireland, with its links between national investment planning and spatial planning, there is still only limited progress in moving much beyond good intentions towards an integration of spatial public investment and spatial planning in pursuit of a more balanced form of territorial development. In similar vein, we find limited evidence to date of spatial planning managing to make a clear influence at the implementation level. Likewise, for all the work on sustainability strategies, we would argue that none of the new spatial planning systems has achieved any success in subverting or reworking the balance of political emphasis between economic, social and environmental objectives.

Table 9.2 Direction of travel for some of spatial planning's key features

Spatial planning aims – direction of travel since 1997	Policy integration	Public participation	Emphasis on balanced regional development	Changes to environment, economy and social balance	ESDP influence	Moving from plan to delivery
England	+	++	+	0	0	+
Wales	++	++	+	0	0	0
Scotland	+	+	0	0	+	+
Ireland	+++ at national level + subnationally	+	+++	0	++	++
Northern Ireland	Fragmentation at national level	+++ at national level + subnationally	++	0	++	0

– Deterioration
0 much as before
+ some positive improvement evident
++ strong evidence of improvement
+++ very strong evidence of improvement

The next spatial planning

It is common practice in spatial plans to start with a brief fictional vision of what an area will look and feel like to live in many years hence thanks to the plan. Here we adopt this conceit to end this book by envisioning what a future 'post-national' spatial planning might look like.

> There is no spatial planning department anywhere in the UK or Ireland, all of them abolished by 2029 thanks to the widespread adoption of strategic spatial thinking in all parts of government, the private sector and civil society. The first sign of radical change came with Prime Minister Green and Taoiseach O'Green's 2009 joint statement on governmental transformation for the governments of Britain and Ireland, supported by the leaders of the devolved territories of Northern Ireland, Wales, Scotland, England, London and Cornwall. This statement committed all the elected parliaments and assemblies covered by the agreement to ensuring that all government taxation and spending plans would in future be judged against their ability to support the proposed British Isles Future Territorial Integration Strategy (BIFTIS).
>
> BIFTIS was eventually agreed in 2015, providing a high-level vision document for improving connectivity across the British Isles and with the European mainland. It set out agreed priorities for infrastructure investment, including joint responses to the international climate change agenda agreed at Glossop in 2015. The new approach led to a massive investment in public transport infrastructure, renewable energy systems, and 22 new towns, which now all have long waiting lists of residents and businesses wishing to move in. BIFTIS has no statutory function, a role which lies instead with the territorial development strategies of the various elected parliaments and assemblies, including the new English Assembly. The power of BIFTIS became evident in 2018 when the UK's rogue Department of Transport was required to convert its M666 motorway proposal into a new mainline train service, on the grounds that it went against the BIFTIS strategy. The department was subsequently abolished and replaced with the new Department of Connectivity.

In short we are agreeing with Wildavsky's view that if planning is everything then maybe it's nothing (Wildavsky 1973). In other words perhaps the end of planning as a function will come when everybody thinks and acts spatially. And with that, we say farewell. But we do not think this is a farewell to spatial planning, yet. This book feels like a summary of progress in the early years rather than an epitaph. Spatial planning is a product of its time, and this book necessarily reflects on spatial planning as it is today – the only thing we can predict with any certainty is that spatial planning's fortunes will fluctuate hugely over the next few decades, providing rich material for future academic books and articles.

Appendix

Method matters

The empirical material used in this book is largely based on two sets of interviews, the first conducted at the national scale mostly during 2005, and the second in the case study areas during 2006 and 2007. In total we conducted interviews or roundtable sessions with 147 people, six of them at both stages of the research. The national interviews were conducted with civil servants in a range of government departments in Whitehall, in the devolved administrations and in Dublin, together with representatives of national lobby groups and planning organisations. The second round of interviews focused on policy-makers and stakeholders from the public, private, voluntary and academic sectors in the six case study areas. In Ireland, Northern Ireland and Wales in particular we used academic interviewees as expert commentators, not least of course as we were concerned that we knew less about contextual issues here.

Most of the interviews took the form of taped semi-structured interviews with one or two people, but we also included two roundtable events in Wales and Cork, plus a final summary seminar event to which we invited key figures from across the areas we had studied, which was also taped so that it could be used as evidence. The roundtable events were something we would be careful about in the future. Both were organised with good intentions, but in practice we felt that they were potentially forums in which dissident voices might be either muted or amplified for differing reasons, depending on the composition of the groups. This said, both events did generate a lot of open discussion and debate among attendees about their different perspectives and interpretations of the subjects under discussion, so we have no hesitation in using material from them here.

Interviews were mostly taped and transcribed, although a few in the early stages were summarised from notes. Most people were actually happy for their views to be directly attributed to them personally. However, some were not, so in the event rather than have an uneven approach we have chosen to anonymise all the quotes we use. To protect individuals, some voices are made more stringently anonymous than others. This slightly unusual approach reflects that some of our interviewees were saying things distinctive to their role, some of whom wanted total anonymity while others were relaxed about their views being attributable to them. Indeed several told us their views would really make most sense if they could be attributed. This created a few dilemmas for us. We hope we have fully respected the wishes of those we interviewed, and where we had doubts, in just a few cases, we have provided interviewees with drafts of the text in which we have used their quotes in our analysis. When using quotes directly in the text, we generally choose them for their distinctive voice and ability to express things in ways that usefully capture either a particular widely held view, or a dissident view. Most quotes represent a viewpoint shared with others or that can be triangulated in some other way. Where this is not the case and we are trying to capture a more unique or idiosyncratic opinion, we try to make that clear in how we contextualise the quote.

Documentary analysis in every case includes draft and the final approved strategies at the main national, regional and local levels. In addition, we examined consultation exercise reports and summaries, and individual organisational responses where these had been put online. We use these sources to provide evidence of the diversity of views that the plans generated at the consultations stage and to help triangulate some of the interview material. We also engaged in some Internet searches for further information around specific controversies, particularly local planning issues, a process which generated Hansard debates, media coverage, press releases, and even blogs. We sifted through these carefully, selecting sources that seemed authoritative in some way, whether this be the authority of an entity that had a clear interest in a subject and where opinion appeared to be backed up with some kind of analysis or consultation with a peer group. This was more difficult than it sounds. In the event we ignored blog materials as a direct source, but we did find them useful sometimes in signposting us to other sources that we were more comfortable in dealing with. The line was blurry however and this selectivity may well mean we sometimes overplay the authority of some sources and underplay more underground or anarchist voices, and it is for this reason that we are quite explicit here about our approach. It is not ideal for some purposes, but for our purposes it was felt appropriate.

At the onset of the research, a network of academic experts was established, one for each of the five territories – England, Ireland, Northern Ireland, Scotland and Wales. We interviewed four of these experts as part of the research and the fifth attended the end of project event referred to earlier.

Interviews

England – national

E1   Housebuilder: 2005
E2   Civil servant 1: 2005

E3   Civil servant 2: 2005
E4   National planning body 1: 2005
E5   Civil servant 3: 2005
E6   National planning body 2: 2005
E7   Government agency: 2005
E8   National environmental NGO 1: 2005
E9   National transport NGO: 2005
E10 Civil servant 4: 2005
E11 National planning body 3: 2005
E12 Civil servant 5: 2005
E13 Civil servant 6: 2005
E14 London planner: 2005
E15 National environmental NGO 2: 2005
E16 Civil servant 7: 2005

England – Leeds City Region

E17 Civil servant 1: 2005
E18 Civil servant 2: 2005
E19 Civil servant 3: 2005
E20 Regional body 1: 2006
E21 Regional planner 1: 2006
E22 Regional planner 2: 2006
E23 Regional body 2: 2006
E24 Regional body 3: 2006
E25 Regional environmental body: 2006
E26 Local stakeholder: 2006
E27 Local planner 1: 2006
E28 Local planner 2: 2006
E29 Local planner 3: 2006
E30 Local planner 4: 2006
E31 Local regeneration body: 2006
E32 Regional health authority: 2006
E33 Investment planner 1: 2006
E34 Investment planner 2: 2006
E35 Regional economist: 2006
E52 Local planner 5: 2007
E53 Local education officer: 2007

England – London: Thames Gateway

E36 Housebuilder 1: 2006
E37 Civil servant 1: 2006
E38 Civil servant 2: 2006
E39 Civil servant 3: 2006
E40 National regeneration body: 2006

E41   National environmental NGO: 2006
E42   Civil servant 4: 2006
E43   Local politician: 2006
E44   Local development body 1: 2006
E45   Local development body 2: 2006
E46   Local partnership agency: 2006
E47   Housebuilder 2: 2006
E48   National planning body (second interview): 2006
E49   Local health authority: 2006
E50   Local planner: 2006
E51   Local environmental NGO: 2006

Ireland – national

IR1   Academic: 2005
IR2   Civil servant 1: 2005
IR3   Civil servant 2: 2005
IR4   Civil servant 3: 2005
IR5   Enterprise body: 2005

Ireland – Cork

IR7   Local government officer 1: 2006
IR8   Local planner 1: 2006
IR9   Local planner 2: 2006
IR10   Local government officer 2: 2006
IR11   Local transport planner: 2006
IR12   Local planner 3: 2006
IR13   Local regeneration officer: 2006
IR14   Local government officer 3: 2006
IR15   Academic 1: 2006
IR16   Academic 2: 2006
IR17   Academic 3: 2006
IR18   Regional planner: 2006
IR19   Planning consultant: 2006
IR20   Local community NGO: 2006
IR21   Local environmental NGO 1*: 2006
IR22   Local environmental NGO 2*: 2006
IR23   Local environmental NGO 3*: 2006
IR24   Local environmental NGO 4*: 2006
IR25   Local environmental NGO 5*: 2006
IR26   Local environmental NGO 6*: 2006
IR27   Local environmental NGO 7*: 2006
IR28   Local environmental NGO 8*: 2006

* Attended roundtable discussion

Northern Ireland – national

NI1   Civil servant: 2005
NI2   Former civil servant 1: 2005
NI3   Academic 1: 2005
NI4   Academic 2: 2005
NI5   Academic 3: 2005
NI6   Former civil servant 2: 2005

Northern Ireland – Derry/Londonderry

NI7   Local regeneration body: 2006
NI8   Academic 1 (second interview): 2006
NI9   Academic 2: 2006
NI10 Cross-border group: 2006
NI11 Local planner (Ireland): 2006
NI12 Business stakeholder and former civil servant: 2006
NI13 Civil servant (second interview): 2006
NI14 Civil servant (Ireland – second interview): 2006
NI15 Cross-border body: 2006
NI16 Local planner: 2006
NI17 Environmental NGO: 2006

Scotland – national

S1   Civil servant 1: 2005
S2   National planning body: 2005
S3   Civil servant 2: 2005
S4   Civil servant 3: 2005
S5   Regional planner: 2005
S6   Civil servant 4: 2005
S7   Academic: 2005
S8   Civil servant 5: 2005
S9   Economic development body: 2005

Scotland – central belt

S10 Civil servant 1 (second interview): 2006
S11 Civil servant 2: 2006
S12 National planning body (second interview): 2006
S13 Local planner 1: 2006
S14 Commercial stakeholder 1: 2006
S15 Commercial stakeholder 2: 2006
S16 Local planner 2: 2006
S17 Infrastructure provider: 2006
S18 Housebuilder: 2006

S19 Regional transport body: 2006
S20 Economic development body: 2006
S21 Local planner 3: 2006
S22 Environmental NGO: 2006
S23 Regional planner: 2006

Wales – national

W1 Civil servant 1*: 2005
W2 Civil servant 2*: 2005
W3 Civil servant 3*: 2005
W4 Civil servant 4*: 2005
W5 Civil servant 5*: 2005
W6 Civil servant 6*: 2005
W7 Civil servant 7*: 2005
W8 National planning body: 2005
W9 Housebuilder: 2005

* Attended roundtable discussion

Wales – Bluestone

W10 Local planner: 2006
W11 Local government officer: 2006
W12 Environmental body: 2006
W13 Academic 1: 2006
W14 Academic 2: 2006
W15 Civil servant 1: 2006
W16 Civil servant 2: 2006

Wales – North East

W17 Regional planner (England): 2007
W18 Civil servant 1: 2007
W19 Civil servant 2: 2007

End of project seminar

Seminar 2007: Academic
Seminar 2007: Civil servant 1
Seminar 2007: Civil servant 2
Seminar 2007: Civil servant 3
Seminar 2007: National planning body 1
Seminar 2007: National planning body 2
Seminar 2007: National planning body 3

Notes

1 The new spatial planning: territorial management and devolution

1   Although the EU level is part of our governance line approach, we did not interview European policy-makers specifically; instead we chose to explore European policy influences through our interviews at other scales. A contextual section on European planning follows in this chapter.

2   The rail system in Northern Ireland is separately managed and regulated.

2 Rethinking planning: state restructuring, devolution and spatial strategies

1   See www.communities.gov.uk/news/planningandbuilding/731018

2   A clear exception to this is Scotland, which has a civil law-based approach and a discretionary planning system.

3   This is not to say that continental European planning systems are not spatial. The separation of plan and permission in the UK approaches can mean that spatial planning is achieved both at strategic and detailed (project) levels.

4   There is a clear similarity here with the Eco-Towns initiative currently underway in England.

5   These two paragraphs draw heavily on Haughton *et al.* (2008).

3 Irish spatial planning and the Cork experience

1   NUTS (Nomenclature of Units of Territorial Statistics) is a method used by the European Union to describe regions at different scales. NUTS II regions typically have a population of 800,000 to 3 million and NUTS III regions 150,000 to 800,000.

2   Objective 1 funding is targeted at the most deprived regions in the European Union. To qualify, a region's average Gross Domestic Product (GDP) needs to fall below 75 per cent of the EU average.

4 Spatial planning in Northern Ireland and the emergent North West region of Ireland

1 Unionists tend to use the term Belfast Agreement, while nationalists prefer the term Good Friday Agreement. We use the terms interchangeably here. We discuss the politics of language in Northern Ireland later.

2 An excellent overview of these issues from a spatial governance perspective is provided by Ellis and Neill (2006), while Anderson and O'Dowd (1999a) provide a similarly excellent overview of the contested politics of the region's borders and its broader processes of de- and reterritorialisation over the past 200 years. We draw heavily on both in this section.

3 In general we use the current most widely used term, so we tend to refer to Northern Ireland or the north interchangeably. Similarly, we use either the Republic (of Ireland) or the south. Derry is mainly used here as this is now more widely recognised internationally, being used by the Northern Ireland Tourist Board, for instance.

4 The sources of statistics, unless separately identified, are the Central Statistics Office of Ireland (www.cso.i.e) and the Northern Ireland Statistics and Research Agency (www.nisra.gov.uk).

5 One of the difficulties in comparing socio-economic trends north and south of the border is that statistical data are collected on a different basis and for different time periods, so they are not directly comparable.

5 Spatial planning in a devolved Scotland

1 Though the content is different, this chapter does bear some similarities to an article by Geoff Vigar (forthcoming) on Scottish planning recently accepted for publication in *European Planning Studies*.

2 The Scottish National Party became the party of government in May 2007. It downgraded the cities emphasis in favour of a more balanced geographic approach to economic development. This is reflected in differences between the National Planning Framework One and its successor draft (cf. Scottish Executive 2004a; Scottish Government 2008).

3 Keating (2005) notes that this was a general feature of the Scottish government in its early years.

6 The Wales Spatial Plan and improving policy integration

1 The first strategic plan for Wales appears to have been *A Better Wales*, published on betterwales.com, which is now a commercial website, so we cannot provide a useful reference for it.

2 The terms *Area* and *subregion* are both used, but more recently Area has become the preferred term in official documents.

3 The Celtic League campaigns for the social, political and cultural rights of what it describes as the Celtic nations: Brittany, Cornwall, Ireland, Scotland and Wales.

4 Indeed one or two parts of the press release appeared to us to be misleading or inaccurate, explaining some of the edits evident in this quote.

8 Congested governance and the London Thames Gateway

1   We have written elsewhere about the governance challenges of the Thames Gateway and inevitably there is some element of overlap between that analysis and the current chapter, though we have aimed to write this chapter as a largely separate piece.

2   The government planning ministry at the start of this work was the Office of Deputy Prime Minister (ODPM), changing to the Department of Communities and Local Government in 2006.

3   See 'Greenwich Peninsula in the business of creating a "new view of London" ', available at www.greenwichpeninsula.co.uk/Newsarticle.aspx?urlkey=ln&newsid= 21047 (accessed 4 July 2009).

4   See www.healthyurbandevelopment.nhs.uk/pages/int_social_infra/integrating_ social_infrastructure.html, from which the documents can be downloaded. The same website also reveals the unit's work on using section 106 agreements to help pay for new healthcare facilities in growth areas.

References

Adams, N. (2008) Convergence and policy transfer: An examination of the extent to which approaches to spatial planning have converged within the context of an enlarged EU. *International Planning Studies*, 13(1): 31–49.

Albrechts, L., Healey, P. and Kunzmann, R. (2003) Strategic spatial planning and regional governance in Europe. *Journal of American Planning Association*, 69(2): 113–129.

Allen, J. and Cochrane, A. (2007) Beyond the territorial fix: Regional assemblages, politics and power. *Regional Studies*, 41(9): 1161–1175.

Allen, J., Massey, D. and Cochrane, A. (1998) *Rethinking the Region*. London: Routledge.

Allmendinger, P. (2001a) The head and the heart: National identity and urban planning in a devolved Scotland. *International Planning Studies*, 6(1): 33–54.

Allmendinger, P. (2001b) The future of planning under a Scottish Parliament. *Town Planning Review*, 72(2): 121–148.

Allmendinger, P. (2003) Integrated planning in a devolved Scotland. *Planning Practice and Research*, 18(1): 19–36.

Allmendinger, P. (2006) Zoning by stealth? The diminution of discretionary planning. *International Planning Studies*, 11(2): 137–143.

Allmendinger, P. and Haughton, G. (2007) The fluid scales and scope of UK spatial planning. *Environment and Planning A*, 39(6): 1478–1496.

Allmendinger, P. and Haughton, G. (2009) Soft spaces, fuzzy boundaries and metagovernance: The new spatial planning in the Thames Gateway. *Environment and Planning A*, 41: 617–633.

Allmendinger, P. and Thomas, H. (1998) *Urban Planning and the British New Right*. London: Routledge.

Allmendinger, P. and Tiesdell, S. (2004) Making sense of sustainable communities. *Town and Country Planning*, 73(11): 313–316.

Allmendinger, P., Morphet, J. and Tewdwr-Jones, M. (2005) Devolution and the modernisation of local government: Prospects for spatial planning. *European Planning Studies*, 13(3): 349–370.

Amin, A. (2002) Spatialities of globalisation. *Environment and Planning A*, 34(3): 385–399.

Amin, A. (2004) Regions unbound: Towards a new politics of space. *Geografiska Annaler*, 86B: 33–44.

Anderson, J. and O'Dowd, L. (1999a) Borders, border regions and territoriality: Contradictory meanings, changing significance. *Regional Studies*, 33(7): 593–604.

Anderson, J. and O'Dowd, L. (1999b) Contested borders: Globalisation and ethno-national conflict in Ireland. *Regional Studies*, 33(7): 681–696.

Atkins, W.S. (2001) *Cork Area Strategic Plan*. Cork: Cork County Council and Cork City Council.

Ayres, S. and Stafford, I. (2008) *A Whitehall Response to Regional Funding Allocations*. Project paper, School for Policy Studies, University of Bristol, www.bristol.ac.uk/sps/regionalism/downloads/rfasumm.doc (accessed 9 August 2008).

Baden, T. (2008) Planning to what purpose? *Town and Country Planning*, 77(9): 369–371.

Bailey, N. and Turok, I. (2001) Central Scotland as a polycentric urban region: Useful planning concept or chimera. *Urban Studies*, 38(4): 697–715.

Barker, K. (2004) *Review of Housing Supply: Final Report*. London: The Stationery Office.

Barker, K. (2006) *Barker Review of Land Use Planning: Final Report – Recommendations*. London: The Stationery Office.

Bartley, B. and Kitchen, R. (eds) (2007) *Understanding Contemporary Ireland*. London: Pluto.

Beecham Review (2006) *Beyond Boundaries: Citizen-centred Local Services for Wales*. Cardiff: Welsh Assembly Government.

Bolton, N. and Leach, S. (2002) Strategic planning in local government: A study of organisational impact and effectiveness. *Local Government Studies*, 28(4): 1–21.

Booth, P. (2003) *Planning by Consent: The Origins and Nature of British Development Control*. London: Routledge.

Border Region Authority (2004) *Regional Planning Guidelines for the Border Region*. Cavan: Border Region Authority.

Bowcott, O. (2007) Ireland pledges to pour millions into reviving north. *Guardian*, 24 January, www.guardian.co.uk/international/story/0,,1997125,00.html (accessed 25 June 2009).

Boyle, M. (2000) Euro-regionalism and struggles over scales of governance: The politics of Ireland's regionalisation approach to Structural Fund allocations 2000–2006. *Political Geography*, 19(6): 737–769.

Bramley, G. and Kirk, K. (2005) Does planning make a difference to urban form? Recent evidence from Central Scotland. *Environment and Planning A*, 37(2): 355–378.

Breheny, M. (1997) Urban compaction: Feasible and acceptable? *Cities*, 14: 209–217.

Brenner, N. (2000) The urban question as a scale question: Reflections on Henri Lefebvre, urban theory and the politics of scale. *International Journal of Urban and Regional Research*, 24: 361–378.

Brenner, N. (2004) *New State Spaces*. Oxford: Oxford University Press.

Brindley, T., Rydin, Y. and Stoker, G. (1989) *Remaking Planning: The Politics of Urban Change*. London: Unwin Hyman.

Brindley, T., Rydin, Y. and Stoker, G. (1996) *Remaking Planning: The Politics of Urban Change*, 2nd edn. London: Routledge.

Brownill, S. (1990) *Developing London Docklands: Another Great Planning Disaster?* London: Paul Chapman.

Cabinet Office (1999) *Modernising Government*. London: The Stationery Office.

CAG Consultants (2003) *How Efficiently has the National Assembly for Wales Promoted Sustainable Development? Report to the Welsh Assembly Government*. London: CAG.

Celtic League (2008) Plan for hybrid English-Welsh region causes concern. This is assumed to be a press release from the Celtic League, www.agencebretagne presse.com/fetch.php?id=10697 and www.nowpublic.com/world/plan-hybrid-english-welsh-region-causes-concerns

Central Statistical Office (CSO) (2007) *Census Volume 1: Population Classified by Area*. Dublin: CSO.

Chatterton, P. and Hodkinson, S. (2007) Leeds: Skyscraper city. *Regional Review*, 17(1): 30–32.

Colin Buchanan and Partners with Colin Stutt Consulting (2003) *North West Economic Corridor Study: A Prospectus for Change by the Private Sector*. Derry: North West Chambers of Commerce Initiative.

Collinge, C. (1999) Self-organisation of society by scale. *Environment and Planning D: Society and Space*, 17(5): 557–574.

Commission of European Communities (CEC) (1999) *European Spatial Development Perspective: Towards Balanced and Sustainable Development of the Territory of the EU*. Luxembourg: CEC.

Confederation of British Industry (CBI) (2005) *Planning Reform: Delivering for Business?* London: CBI.

Cooke, P. and Clifton, N. (2005) Visionary, precautionary and constrained varieties of devolution in the economic governance of the devolved UK territories. *Regional Studies*, 39(4): 437–451.

Cooke, P. and Morgan, K. (1998) *The Associational Economy: Firms, Regions and Innovation*. Oxford: Oxford University Press.

Cork City Council (2005) *North Docks Local Area Plan*. Cork: Cork City Council.

Cork County Development Board (CCDB) (2005) *Action Plan*. Cork: CCDB.

Counsell, D. and Haughton, G. (2003) Regional planning tensions: Planning for economic growth and sustainable development in two contrasting English regions. *Environment and Planning C*, 21: 225–239.

Counsell, D. and Haughton, G. (2006a) Advancing together in Yorkshire and Humber? In M. Tewdwr-Jones and P. Allmendinger (eds) *Territory, Identity and Space*. London: Routledge.

Counsell, D. and Haughton, G. (2006b) Sustainable development in regional planning: The search for new tools and renewed legitimacy. *Geoforum*, 37: 921–931.

Counsell, D. and Haughton, G. (2007) Spatial planning for the city region. *Town and Country Planning*, 76(8): 248–251.

Counsell, D., Allmendinger, P., Haughton, G. and Vigar, G. (2006) Integrated Spatial Planning: Is it living up to expectations? *Town and Country Planning*, 43(9): 243–245.

Counsell, D., Hart, T., Jonas, A.E.G. and Kettle, J. (2007) Fragmented regionalism? Delivering integrated regional strategies in Yorkshire and the Humber. *Regional Studies*, 41(3): 391–401.

Cullingworth, B. and Nadin, V. (2006) *Town and Country Planning in the UK*, 14th edn. London: Routledge.

Dabinett, G. and Richardson, T. (2005) The Europeanization of spatial strategy: Shaping regions and spatial justice through governmental ideas. *International Planning Studies*, 10(3–4): 201–218.

Deloitte (2006) *The Thames Gateway Programme: Stage 1 of a Comprehensive Economic Statement for the Thames Gateway. Final Report, February 2006*. London: Deloitte MCS Ltd.

Department for Environment, Food and Rural Affairs (DEFRA) (2005) *Securing the Future: UK Government Sustainable Development Strategy*. London: The Stationery Office.

Department for Transport (DfT) (2005) *Making Residential Travel Plans Work: Guidelines for New Development.* London: DfT, www.dft.gov.uk/pgr/sustainable/travelplans/rpt/ (accessed 25 June 2009).

Department of Communities and Local Government (DCLG) (2006a) *Strong and Prosperous Communities: The Local Government White Paper.* London: The Stationery Office.

Department of Communities and Local Government (DCLG) (2006b) *Thames Gateway Interim Plan Policy Framework,* www.communities.gov.uk/pub/562/TheThamesGatewayInterimPlanPolicyFramework_id1504562.pdf

Department of Communities and Local Government (DCLG) (2006c) *Thames Gateway Evidence Review,* www.communities.gov.uk/pub/632/ThamesGateway EvidenceReviewOxfordBrookesUniversity_id1504632.pdf

Department of Communities and Local Government (DCLG) (2006d) *Thames Gateway Evidence Review: Summary,* www.communities.gov.uk/pub/601/Thames GatewayEvidenceReviewOxfordBrookesUniversitySummary_id1504601. pdf

Department of Communities and Local Government (DCLG) (2007) *Planning for a Sustainable Future: White Paper.* London: The Stationery Office.

Department of Environment, Heritage and Local Government (DoEHLG) (2002) *National Spatial Strategy.* Dublin: DoEHLG.

Department of Regional Development (DRD) (2001) *Regional Development Strategy for Northern Ireland 2025.* Belfast: Northern Ireland Executive.

Department of Regional Development (DRD) (2006a) *PPS14: Sustainable Development in the Countryside.* Belfast: DRD.

Department of Regional Development (DRD) (2006b) *Report of the Panel on the Review of Housing Growth Indicators.* Belfast: DRD.

Department of Regional Development (DRD) (2008) *Shaping our Future: Adjustments to the Regional Development Strategy (RDS) – 2025.* Belfast: DRD.

Department of the Taoiseach (1996) *Delivering Better Government: Second Report to Government of the Coordinating Group of Secretaries.* Dublin: Department of the Taoiseach.

Department of Transport (2005) *Statement of Strategy 2005–2007.* Dublin: Department of Transport.

Docherty, I. and McKiernan, P. (2008) Scenario planning for the Edinburgh city region. *Environment and Planning C: Government and Policy,* 26(5): 982–997.

Docherty, I., Shaw, J. and Gray, D. (2007) Scottish transport policy: A critical overview. *Public Money and Management,* 27(2): 141–148.

Donegal County Council (2006a) *County Donegal Draft Development Plan 2005.* Lifford: Donegal County Council.

Donegal County Council (2006b) *County Development Plan 2006–2012.* Lifford: Donegal City Council.

Drudy, P.J. and Punch, M. (2000) Economic restructuring, urban change and regeneration: The case of Dublin. *Journal of the Statistical and Social Inquiry Society of Ireland,* 29: 155–212.

DTZ (2008) *People, Places, Futures: The Wales Spatial Plan 2008 Report on Consultation.* Cardiff: DTZ.

Dublin Institute of Technology (2008) *Twice the Size: Imagineering the Future of Irish Gateways.* Dublin: Urban Forum.

Eddington, R. (2006) *The Eddington Transport Study.* London: The Stationery Office.

Ellis, G. and Neill, W.J.W. (2006) Spatial governance in Northern/North of Ireland. In M. Tewdwr-Jones and P. Allmendinger (eds) *Territory, Identity and Space.* London: Routledge.

Ellis, G., Motherway, B., Neill, W.J.V. and Hand, U. (2004) *Towards a Green Isle? Local Sustainable Development on the Island of Ireland.* Armagh: Centre for Cross Border Studies.

European Commission (1999) *European Spatial Development Perspective: Towards Balance and Sustainable Development of the Territory of the European Union.* Luxembourg: Office for Official Publications of the European Communities.

Evans, A. (1991) 'Rabbit hutches on postage stamps': Planning, development and political economy. *Urban Studies*, 28(6): 853–870.

Faludi, A. (2000) The performance of spatial planning. *Planning Practice and Research*, 15(4): 299–318.

Faludi, A. (2002) Positioning European spatial planning. *European Planning Studies*, 7: 897–909.

Faludi, A. (2004) The European spatial development perspective and North-west Europe: Application and future. *European Planning Studies*, 12(3): 391–408.

Gallent, N. and Tewdwr-Jones, M. (2007) *Decent Homes for All: Planning's Evolving Role in Housing Provision.* London: Routledge.

Gallent, N., Shucksmith, M. and Tewdwr-Jones, M. (2003) *Housing in the European Countryside: Rural Pressure and Policy in Western Europe.* London: Routledge.

Glasson, J. and Marshall, T. (2007) *Regional Planning: Concepts, Theory and Practice in the UK.* London: Routledge.

Goode, D. and Munton, R. (2006) The Greater London Authority and sustainable development. In M. Tewdwr-Jones and P. Allmendinger (eds) *Territory, Identity and Space: Spatial Governance in a Fragmented Nation.* London: Routledge.

Goodstadt, V. (2007) Strategic planning in the Glasgow metropolitan region. In H. Dimitriou and R. Thomson (eds) *Strategic and Regional Planning.* London: Spon.

Goodwin, M., Jones, M. and Jones, R. (2005) Devolution, constitutional change and economic development: Explaining and understanding the new institutional geographies of the British State. *Regional Studies*, 39(4): 421–436.

Goodwin, M., Jones, M. and Jones, R. (2006) Devolution and economic governance in the UK: Rescaling territories and organizations. *European Planning Studies*, 14(7): 979–995.

Gore, T. and Fothergill, S. (2007) Cities and their hinterlands: How much do governance structures really matter? *People, Place and Policy*, 1(2): 55–68.

Government Office for Yorkshire and Humber (GOYH) (2008) *The Yorkshire and Humber Plan: Regional Spatial Strategy to 2026.* London: The Stationery Office.

Greater London Authority (GLA) (2006) *The London Plan: Sub-regional Development Framework, East London.* London: GLA.

Gunder, M. (2006) Sustainability: Planning's saving grace or road to perdition? *Journal of Planning Education and Research*, 26: 208–221.

G.V.A. Grimley (2004) *West Cheshire-North East Wales Sub-regional Study.* London: G.V.A. Grimley.

Hall, P. (1999) The future planning of city regions. In F. Gaffinkin and M. Morrissey (eds) *City Visions: Imaging Place, Enfranchising People.* London: Pluto.

Hall, P. (2006) London: A millennium-long battle, a millennial truce? In M. Tewdwr-Jones and P. Allmendinger (eds) *Territory, Identity and Space.* London: Routledge.

Hardy, B., Turrell, A. and Wistow, G. (1992) *Innovations in Community Care Management.* Aldershot: Avebury.

Harris, N. (2006) Increasing and spreading prosperity: Regional development and spatial planning and the enduring 'prosperity gap' in Wales. In N. Adams, J. Alden and N. Harris (eds) *Regional Development and Spatial Planning in an Enlarged European Union.* London: Ashgate.

Harris, N. and Hooper, A. (2006) Redefining the space that is Wales. In M. Tewdwr-Jones and P. Allmendinger (eds) *Territory, Identity and Space*. London: Routledge.

Harvey, B., Kelly, A., McGearty, S. and Murray, S. (2005) *The Emerald Curtain: The Social Impact of the Irish Border*. Carrickmacross: Triskele Community Training and Development.

Haughton, G. (1996) Magistracy, city fathers, and partners: Evolving approaches to economic regeneration in Leeds. In G. Haughton and C. Williams (eds) *Corporate City? Partnership, Participation and Partition in Urban Development in Leeds*. Aldershot: Avebury.

Haughton, G. (2003) City-lite – Planning for the Thames Gateway. *Town and Country Planning*, 72(3): 95–97.

Haughton, G. and Allmendinger, P. (2007) Soft spaces in planning. *Town and Country Planning*, 76(9): 306–308.

Haughton, G. and Allmendinger, P. (2008) Soft spaces in local economic development. *Local Economy*, 23(2): 138–148.

Haughton, G. and Counsell, C. (2004) *Regions, Spatial Strategies and Sustainable Development*. London: Routledge.

Haughton, G. and Counsell, D. (2007) Integrating the planning environment: Theory and practice of putting 'urban' in a regional context. In M.S. Geyer and H.W. Richardson (eds) *The International Handbook of Urban Policy*. Cheltenham: Edward Elgar.

Haughton, G. and While, A. (1999) From corporate city to citizen's city? Urban leadership after local entrepreneurialism in the UK. *Urban Affairs Review*, 35(1): 3–23.

Haughton, G., Rowe, I. and Hunter, C. (1997) Thames Gateway and the re-emergence of regional strategic planning: The implications for water resource management. *Town Planning Review*, 68(4): 407–422.

Haughton, G., Lloyd, P. and Meegan, R. (1999) The rediscovery of community economic development in Britain: The European dimension to grassroots involvement in local regeneration. In G. Haughton (ed.) *Community Economic Development*. London: The Stationery Office.

Haughton, G., Counsell, D. and Vigar, G. (2008) Sustainable development in post-devolution UK and Ireland. *Regional Studies*, 42(9): 1223–1236.

Heald, D. and McLeod, A. (2005) Embeddedness of UK devolution finance within the public expenditure system. *Regional Studies*, 39(4): 495–518.

Healey, P. (2004a) The treatment of space and place in the new strategic planning in Europe. *International Journal of Urban and Regional Research*, 28(1): 537–542.

Healey, P. (2004b) Towards a 'social democratic' policy agenda for cities. In C. Johnstone and M. Whitehead (eds) *New Horizons in Urban Policy*. Aldershot: Ashgate.

Healey, P. (2006) Territory, integration and spatial planning. In M. Tewdwr-Jones and P. Allmendinger (eds) *Territory, Identity and Space*. London: Routledge.

Healey, P. (2007) *Urban Complexity and Spatial Strategies: Towards a Relational Planning for Our Times*. London: Routledge.

Healey, P., McNamara, P., Elson, M. and Doak, A. (1988) *Land Use Planning and the Mediation of Urban Change*. Cambridge: Cambridge University Press.

Hetherington, P. (2004) Labour housing plans rejected. *Guardian*, 20 November.

HM Treasury (2004) *2004 Spending Review: Stability, Security and Opportunity for All – Investing for Britain's Long-term Future*. London: The Stationery Office.

HM Treasury (2005) *Regional Funding Allocations*. London: The Stationery Office.

HM Treasury (2006) *2006 Pre-Budget Report Investing in Britain's Potential: Building our Long-term Future*. London: The Stationery Office.

HM Treasury (2007) *Subnational Economic Development and Regeneration Review*. London: The Stationery Office.

Hodkinson, S. and Chatterton, P. (2007) Leeds: An affordable, viable, sustainable, democratic city? *Regional Review*, 17(2): 24–26.

House of Commons (2003) *ODPM Housing, Planning, Local Government and the Regions Committee. Planning for Sustainable Housing and Communities: Sustainable Communities in the South East. Eighth Report of Session*. London: The Stationery Office.

House of Commons (2007) *The Thames Gateway: Laying the Foundations*. Committee of Public Accounts: 62nd report of session 2006–2007, 15 November. London: The Stationery Office.

ILEX (2005) *Derry–Londonderry Regeneration Plan*. Derry: ILEX, the Urban Regeneration Company for Derry–Londonderry.

Imrie, R. and Thomas, H. (1999) *British Urban Policy and the Urban Development Corporations*. London: Sage.

International Centre for Local and Regional Development (2006) *Spatial Strategies on the Island of Ireland: A Framework for Collaborative Action*. Newry: Inter-Trade Ireland.

Irish Central Border Area Network (ICBAN) and the North West Region Cross Border Group (NWRCBG) (2006) *The North West: Roads to Opportunity. Implementing a Vision*. Enniskillen: ICBAN and NWRCBG.

Irish Government (2007) *National Development Plan 2007–2013. Transforming Ireland: A Better Quality of Life for All*. Dublin: The Stationery Office.

James, G. (2004) *Sustaining Spin: An Assessment of the Mainstreaming of Sustainable Development by the Welsh Assembly Government and Local Authorities in Wales*. Cardiff: Friends of the Earth.

Jessop, B. (1990) *State Theory*. Cambridge: Polity.

Jessop, B. (1997) A neo-Gramscian approach to the regulation of urban regimes. In M. Lauria (ed.) *Reconstructing Urban Regime Theory: Regulating Urban Politics in a Global Economy*. London: Sage.

Jessop, B. (2000) The crisis of the national spatio-temporal fix and the ecological dominance of globalising. *International Journal of Urban and Regional Research*, 24(2): 323–360.

Jessop, B. (2002) Liberalism, neoliberalism and urban governance: A state-theoretic perspective. In N. Brenner and N. Theodore (eds) *Spaces of Neoliberalism: Urban Restructuring in North America and Western Europe*. Oxford: Blackwell.

Jessop, B. (2003) Governance and metagovernance: Reflexivity, requisite variety and requisite irony. In H. Bang (ed.) *Governance as Social and Political Communication*. Manchester: Manchester University Press.

Jessop, B. (2008) Avoiding traps, rescaling states, governing Europe. In R. Keil and R. Mahon (eds) *Leviathan Undone? Towards a Political Economy of Scale*. Vancouver: University of British Columbia.

Jessop, B., Brenner, N. and Jones, M. (2008) Theorising sociospatial relations. *Environment and Planning D: Society and Space*, 26(3): 389–401.

Jones, M. (2001) The rise of the regional state in economic governance: Partnerships for prosperity or new scale of state power? *Environment and Planning A*, 33: 1185–1211.

Jones, M., Goodwin, M. and Jones, R. (2005) State modernization, devolution and economic governance: An introduction and guide to debate. *Regional Studies*, 39(4): 397–404.

Keating, M. (2005) Policy convergence and divergence in Scotland under devolution. *Regional Studies*, 39(4): 453–464.

Kelly, R., Sirr, L. and Ratcliffe, J. (2004) Futures thinking to achieve sustainable development at local level in Ireland. *Foresight*, 6(2): 80–90.

Knox, C. and Carmichael, P. (2005) Devolution – the Northern Ireland way: An exercise in creative ambiguity. *Environment and Planning C: Government and Policy*, 23: 63–83.

Leach, S., Stewart, J. and Walsh, K. (1994) *The Changing Organisation and Management of Local Government*. London: Macmillan.

Leeds City Region Partnership (2006) *Eleven Partners One Vision: Leeds City Region Development Programme*. Leeds: Leeds City Council.

Ling, T. (2002) Delivering joined-up government in the UK: Dimensions, issues and problems. *Public Administration*, 80(4): 615–642.

Lloyd, G. and Peel, D. (2005) Tracing a spatial turn in planning practice in Scotland. *Planning Practice and Research*, 20(3): 313–325.

London Thames Gateway Development Corporation (LTGDC) (2005) *Engines for Growth: Our Vision for the Lower Lea Valley and London Riverside*. London: LTGDC.

Lovering, J. (1999) Theory led by policy: The inadequacies of 'the new regionalism' (illustrated from the case of Wales). *International Journal of Urban and Regional Research*, 23: 379–395.

Lowndes, V. (2003) Between rhetoric and reality: Does the 2001 White Paper reverse the centralising trend in Britain? *Local Government Studies*, 28(3): 135–147.

Lowndes, V. (2005) Something old, something new, something borrowed: How institutions change (and stay the same) in local government. *Policy Studies*, 26(3–4): 291–309.

Lynas, N. (2004) The concrete isle. *Guardian*, 4 December, www.guardian.co.uk/weekend/story/0,.1364782,00.html (accessed 25 February 2007).

McCall, C. (2003) Shifting thresholds, contested meanings: Governance, cross-border cooperation and the Ulster Unionist identity. *European Studies*, 19: 81–103.

McDonald, F. and Nix, J. (2005) *Chaos at the Crossroads*. Kinsale, County Cork: Gandon.

McEldowney, M., Sterrett, K., Gaffikin, F. and Morrissey, M. (2002) Shaping our future: Public voices. In Y. Rydin and A. Thornley (eds) *Planning in the UK: Agendas for the New Millennium*. Aldershot: Ashgate.

MacKinnon, D., Shaw, J. and Docherty, I. (2008) *Diverging Mobilities? Devolution, Transport and Policy Innovation*. Oxford: Elsevier Science.

MacLeod, G. (2001) New regionalism reconsidered: Globalisation and the remaking of political economic space. *International Journal of Urban and Regional Research*, 25: 804–829.

Marsh, D. and Rhodes, R.A.W. (1992) *Policy Networks in British Government*. Oxford: Oxford University Press.

Marshall, T. (2002) The re-timing of regional planning. *Town Planning Review*, 73(2): 171–196.

Marshall, T. (2008) Regions, economies and planning in England after the Subnational Review. *Local Economy*, 23(2): 99–106.

Massey, D. (2005) *For Space*. London: Sage.

Massey, D. (2007) *World City*. Cambridge: Polity.

Matthews, F. and Alden, J. (2006) Balanced regional development and the National

Spatial Strategy: Addressing the challenges of economic growth and spatial change in Ireland. In A. Adams, J. Alden and N. Harris (eds) *Regional Development and Spatial Planning in an Enlarged European Union.* Aldershot: Ashgate.

Mawson, J. and Hall, S. (2000) Joining it up locally? Area regeneration and holistic government in England. *Regional Studies*, 34: 67–74.

Maxey, L., Pickerill, J. and Wimbush, P. (2006) New planning opportunities for low impact settlements. *Permaculture Magazine*, 50: 32.

Midmore, P. and Thomas, D. (2006) Regional self reliance and economic development: The Pembrokeshire case. *Local Economy*, 21(4): 391–408.

Milne, R. (2005) Bluestone holiday village plan sees off challenge in the Lords. *Planning Portal*, www.planningportal.gov.uk/england/professionals/en/1115313442594.html (accessed 25 June 2009).

Morgan, K. (2006) *The Challenge of Polycentric Planning: Cardiff as a Capital City Region?* Papers in Planning 185. Cardiff: Cardiff School of City and Regional Planning, Cardiff University.

Morgan, K. (2007) The polycentric state: New spaces of empowerment and engagement. *Regional Studies*, 41(9): 1237–1251.

Morris, N. (2008) Cities in North Doomed says Tory think-tank. *The Independent*, 13 August.

Mulgan, G. and Bury, F. (eds) (2006) *Double Devolution: The Renewal of Local Government.* London: Smith Institute.

Mullally, G. (2004) Shakespeare, the Structural Funds and sustainable development: Reflections on the Irish experience. *Innovation*, 17(1): 25–41.

Murray, D. (1998) *A Register of Cross-border Links in Ireland.* Limerick: Centre for Peace and Development Studies, University of Limerick.

Murray, M. (2004) Strategic spatial planning on the island of Ireland: Towards a new territorial logic? *Innovation*, 17(3): 227–242.

Murtagh, B. and Kelly, B. (2006) Sub regional planning in a cross-border city region: The case of North West Ireland. In J. Yarwood (ed.) *The Dublin–Belfast Development Corridor: Ireland's Mega City Region?* Aldershot: Ashgate.

Nadin, V. (2002) Transnational spatial development and planning: Experiences from the Spatial Vision for North West Europe. In C. Bengs (ed.) *Facing EPSON: Nordregio Report 2002:1*, Stockholm, www.nordregio.se/Files/r0201ch2.pdf (accessed 11 April 2009).

Nadin, V. (2007) The emergence of the spatial planning approach in England. *Planning Practice and Research*, 22(1): 43–62.

National Audit Office (2007) *The Thames Gateway: Laying the Foundations.* London: HMSO.

National Trust (2004) *A Sense of Place: Planning for the Future of Northern Ireland.* Ballynahinch: National Trust.

Neill, W.J.V. and Gordon, M. (2001) Shaping our future? The Regional Strategic Framework for Northern Ireland. *Planning Theory and Practice*, 2(1): 31–52.

Newman, P. (2008) Strategic spatial planning: Collective action and moments of opportunity. *European Planning Studies*, 16(10): 1371–1383.

Newman, P. and Thornley, A. (1996) *Urban Planning in Europe: International Competition, National Systems and Planning Projects.* London: Routledge.

NHS Healthy Urban Development Unit (2006a) *London Thames Gateway Social Infrastructure Framework.* London: NHS, www.healthyurbandevelopment.nhs.uk/pages/int_social_infra/integrating_social_infrastructure.html (accessed 4 July 2009).

NHS Healthy Urban Development Unit (2006b) *The Case for Social Infrastructure*

Planning, www.healthyurbandevelopment.nhs.uk/pages/int_social_infra/integrating_ social_infrastructure.html and www.healthyurbandevelopment.nhs.uk/documents/ int_social_infrastructure/The_Case_For_Social_Infrastructure_02_06_06.pdf (accessed 4 July 2009).

Northern Ireland Executive (NIE) (2008a) *Building a Better Future: Programme for Government 2008–2011*. Belfast: NIE.

Northern Ireland Executive (NIE) (2008b) *Investment Strategy for Northern Ireland: 2008–2018*. Belfast: NIE.

Northern Way (2004) *Moving Forward: The Northern Way – First Growth Strategy Report*. Newcastle-upon-Tyne: Northern Way Growth Strategy Team.

Office for National Statistics (2008) *Labour Market Statistics, May 2008*, www. statistics.gov.uk/StatBase/Product.asp?vlnk=15084 (accessed 4 July 2009).

Office of the Deputy Prime Minister (ODPM) (2003a) *Creating Sustainable Communities, Making it Happen: Thames Gateway and the Growth Areas*. London: ODPM.

Office of the Deputy Prime Minister (ODPM) (2003b) *Government Response to ODPM Select Committee Report on Planning for Sustainable Communities: Sustainable Communities in the South East*, www.communities.gov.uk/archived/ publications/thamesgateway/planningsustainable (accessed 4 July 2009).

Office of the Deputy Prime Minister (ODPM) (2003c) *The Communities Plan – Sustainable Communities: Building for the Future*. London: The Stationery Office.

Office of the Deputy Prime Minister (ODPM) (2004a) *Growth and Regeneration in the Gateway. Interregional Planning Statement by the Thames Gateway Regional Planning Bodies*. London: ODPM.

Office of the Deputy Prime Minister (ODPM) (2004b) *PPS11: Regional Spatial Strategies*. London: The Stationery Office.

Office of the Deputy Prime Minister (ODPM) (2004c) *PPS12: Local Development Frameworks*. London: The Stationery Office.

Office of the Deputy Prime Minister (ODPM) (2005a) *Creating Sustainable Communities: Delivering in Thames Gateway*, www.communities.gov.uk/archived/ publications/thamesgateway/creatingsustainablecommunities3 (accessed 4 July 2009).

Office of the Deputy Prime Minister (ODPM) (2005b) *PPS1: Delivering Sustainable Development*. London: The Stationery Office.

Office of the Deputy Prime Minister (ODPM) (2006) *The State of the Gateway: A Baseline for Future Evaluation*. London: ODPM, www.communities.gov.uk/ publications/thamesgateway/state (accessed 4 July 2009).

Offord, C. and Hill, G. (2007) *The Yorkshire and Humber Plan EiP: Report of the Panel Volume 1 – Report*. Leeds: GOYH.

Olympic Delivery Authority (ODA) (2006) *The Olympic Park Delivery Programme*, www.alastinglegacy.co.uk/content/legacy/oda/

Paasi, A. (1999) Boundaries as social practice and discourse: The Finnish–Russian border. *Regional Studies*, 33(7): 669–680.

Paasi, A. (2001) Europe as a social process and discourse: Considerations of place, boundaries and identity. *European Urban and Regional Studies*, 8(1): 7–28.

Paris, C. (2005) From barricades to back gardens: Cross-border urban expansion from the City of Derry into Co. Donegal. In M. Scott and N. Moore (eds) *Renewing Urban Communities: Environment, Citizenship and Sustainability in Ireland*. Aldershot: Ashgate.

Paris, C. (2006) Housing markets and cross-border integration. In J. Yarwood (ed.) *The*

Dublin–Belfast Development Corridor: Ireland's Mega City Region? Aldershot: Ashgate.

Paris, C. and Robson, T. (2001) *Housing in the Border Counties: Contrasting Images, Continuity and Change*. Belfast: Northern Ireland Housing Executive.

Pearce, G. and Ayres, S. (2006) New patterns of governance in the English region: Assessing their implications for spatial planning. *Environment and Planning C: Governance and Policy*, 24: 909–927.

Peel, D. and Lloyd, G. (2007) Small country, big plans – bigger changes? *Town and Country Planning*, 76(5): 157–159.

Pennington, M. (2000) *Planning and the Political Market*. London: Athlone.

Performance and Innovation Unit (PIU) (2000) *Wiring It Up: Whitehall's Management of Cross-cutting Policies and Services*. London: The Stationery Office.

Perkmann, M. (1999) Building governance institutions across European borders. *Regional Studies*, 33(7): 657–667.

Philpotts, G. and Causer, B. (eds) (2006) *Regional Trends*. Basingstoke: Palgrave Macmillan.

Pike, A. (2007) Editorial: Whither regional studies? *Regional Studies*, 41(9): 1143–1148.

Planning Officers Society (2005) *Spatial Planning: Shaking off the Shackles*, www.planningofficers.org.uk/file/be071d09dc18ad642b4a52ad4ee05853/meeting-notes-260405.html (accessed 4 July 2009).

Powell, K. (2001) Devolution, planning guidance and the role of the planning system in Wales. *International Planning Studies*, 6(2): 215–222.

Purves, G. (2006) Quality and connectivity: The continuing traditions of spatial planning in Scotland. In N. Adams, J. Alden and N. Harris (eds) *Regional Development and Spatial Planning in an Enlarged European Union*. Aldershot: Ashgate.

Raco, M. (2005) A step change or a step back? The Thames Gateway and the re-birth of the Urban Development Corporations. *Local Economy*, 20: 141–153.

Rhodes, R.A.W. (2000) New Labour's civil service: Summing up the joining-up. *Political Quarterly*, 71: 151–166.

Rodríguez-Pose, A. and Bwire, A. (2004) The economic (in)efficiency of devolution. *Environment and Planning A*, 36(11): 1907–1928.

Rodríguez-Pose, A. and Gill, N. (2004) Is there a global link between regional disparities and devolution? *Environment and Planning A*, 36(12): 2097–2117.

Rodríguez-Pose, A. and Gill, N. (2005) On the 'economic dividend' of devolution. *Regional Studies*, 39(4): 405–420.

Roger Tym and Partners (2005) *The Cost and Funding of Growth in the South East*. London: Roger Tym and Partners.

Royal Commission on Environmental Pollution (2002) *Twenty-third Report: Environmental Planning*. London: The Stationery Office.

Royal Society for the Protection of Birds (RSPB) (2005) *RSPB Representation: West Cheshire and North East Wales Spatial Strategy*, new.wales.gov.uk/dpsp/wsp/1335611/RSPB.pdf?lang=en (accessed 25 June 2009).

Royal Town Planning Institute (RTPI) (2001) *A New Vision for Planning*. London: RTPI.

Rydin, Y. (2004) So what does PPS1 tell us about spatial planning? The ambitious goal of spatial planning – as envisaged in PPS1 – needs to be implemented in more ways than through the statutory planning system. *Town and Country Planning*, 73(4): 118–119.

Scotland on Sunday (2006) Labour faces police probe into council 'corruption'. *Scotland on Sunday*, 28 May.

Scott, J.W. (1999) European and North American contexts for cross-border regionalism. *Regional Studies*, 33(7): 605–617.

Scott, M. (2006) Strategic spatial planning and contested ruralities: Insights from the Republic of Ireland. *European Planning Studies*, 14(6): 811–829.

Scott, M., Moore, N., Redmond, D. and Gkartzios, M. (2006) Housing growth, land delivery and sustainable urban management. In J. Yarwood (ed.) *The Dublin–Belfast Development Corridor: Ireland's Mega City Region?* Aldershot: Ashgate.

Scottish Executive (2001) *Review of Strategic Planning.* Edinburgh: Scottish Executive.

Scottish Executive (2002) *Review of Scotland's Cities.* Edinburgh: Scottish Executive.

Scottish Executive (2004a) *National Planning Framework.* Edinburgh: Scottish Executive.

Scottish Executive (2004b) *Making Development Plans Deliver.* Edinburgh: Scottish Executive.

Scottish Executive (2005) *White Paper: Modernising the Planning System.* Edinburgh: Scottish Executive.

Scottish Executive (2007) *Edinburgh and Glasgow City Profiles*, www.scotland.gov. uk/Topics/Statistics/15648/EdinburghCityExcel (accessed 16 January 2007).

Scottish Executive Policy Unit (2000) *Making a Difference: Effective Implementation of Cross-cutting Policy.* Edinburgh: Scottish Executive.

Scottish Government (2007) *Scottish Economic Statistics*, www.scotland.gov.uk/ Publications/2007/07/18083820/11 (accessed 10 October 2008).

Scottish Government (2009) *National Planning Framework for Scotland 2.* Edinburgh: Scottish Government.

Shaw, D. and Sykes, O. (2001) *Delivering the European Spatial Development Perspective.* Liverpool: University of Liverpool.

Shaw, D. and Sykes, O. (2004) European spatial development policy and evolving forms of territorial mobilisation in the UK. *Planning Practice and Research*, 20(2): 183–200.

Shepley, C. and Hurley, M. (2007) *North West Regional Spatial Strategy: Examination in Public – Report of the Panel.* Manchester: Government Office for the North West.

Siggins, L. (2008) Higgins challenges DIT study on spatial strategy. *Irish Times*, 25 September.

Sinn Féin (2007) *North West Charter*, www.sinnfein.ie/pdf/nwcharter.pdf

South West Regional Authority (SWRA) (2004) *Regional Planning Guidelines.* Ballincollig: SWRA.

Stewart, M., Hambleton, R., Purdue, D. and Razzaque, K. (2000) *Community Leadership in Area Regeneration.* York: Joseph Rowntree Foundation.

Stoker, G. (2004) *Transforming Local Governance.* Basingstoke: Palgrave.

Storper, M. (1997) *The Regional World: Territorial Development in a Global Economy.* New York: Guilford.

Sullivan, H. and Skelcher, C. (2002) *Working across Boundaries: Collaboration in Public Services.* Basingstoke: Palgrave Macmillan.

Town and Country Planning Association (TCPA) (2008) *TCPA Response to Wales Spatial Plan Update Consultation*, April. London: TCPA.

Travers, T. (2004) *The Politics of London: Governing an Ungovernable City.* Basingstoke: Palgrave Macmillan.

Turok, I. and Bailey, N. (2004) The theory of polynuclear urban regions and its application to central Scotland. *European Planning Studies*, 12(3): 371–389.

University College London (UCL) and Deloitte (2007) *Shaping and Delivering Tomorrow's Places: Effective Practice in Spatial Planning.* London: Royal Town Planning Institute.

Urban Task Force (1999) *Towards an Urban Renaissance.* London: The Stationery Office.

Valler, D. and Betteley, D. (2001) The politics of 'integrated' local policy in England. *Urban Studies*, 38(13): 2393–2413.

Vigar, G. (forthcoming) Towards an integrated spatial planning. *European Planning Studies*.

Vigar, G., Healey, P., Hull, A. and Davoudi, S. (2000) *Planning, Governance and Spatial Strategy in Britain: An Institutionalist Analysis*. London: Macmillan.

Walsh, J. and Murray, M. (2006) Critical reflections on the National Spatial Strategy and the Regional Development Strategy for Northern Ireland. In J. Yarwood (ed.) *The Dublin–Belfast Development Corridor: Ireland's Mega City Region?* Aldershot: Ashgate.

Wannop, U. (1995) *The Regional Imperative: Regional Planning and Governance in Britain, Europe, and the United States*. London: Jessica Kingsley.

Webster, C.J. (ed.) (2003) *Public–Private Partnerships in Urban Infrastructure and Service Delivery*. Bangkok: UN Economic and Social Commission for Asia and the Pacific, UN Building, Rajdamnern Nok Avenue, Bangkok 10200, Thailand.

Welsh Assembly Government (WAG) (2000) *Learning to Live Differently: The Sustainable Development Scheme of the National Assembly for Wales*. Cardiff: WAG.

Welsh Assembly Government (WAG) (2003) *Wales: A Better Country*. Cardiff: WAG.

Welsh Assembly Government (WAG) (2004a) *Delivering Better Plans for Wales*. Cardiff: WAG.

Welsh Assembly Government (WAG) (2004b) *Making the Connections: Delivering Better Services in Wales*. Cardiff: WAG.

Welsh Assembly Government (WAG) (2004c) *Starting to Live Differently: The Sustainable Development Scheme of the National Assembly for Wales*. Cardiff: WAG.

Welsh Assembly Government (WAG) (2004d) *The Sustainable Development Action Plan 2004–2007*. Cardiff: WAG.

Welsh Assembly Government (WAG) (2004e) *People, Places, Futures: The Wales Spatial Plan*. Cardiff: WAG.

Welsh Assembly Government (WAG) (2006) Minister launches £110m Bluestone project. Press release 20 November 2006, Cardiff: WAG, http://new.wales.gov.uk/news/archivepress/enterprisepress/einpress2006/1090762/?lang=en (accessed 25 June 2009).

Welsh Assembly Government (WAG) (2008) *People, Places, Futures: The Wales Spatial Plan – 2008 Consultation Update*. Cardiff: WAG.

Wildavsky, A. (1973) If planning is everything, maybe it's nothing. *Policy Sciences*, 4(2): 127–153.

Yarwood, J. (ed.) (2006) *The Dublin–Belfast Development Corridor: Ireland's Mega City Region?* Aldershot: Ashgate.

Yorkshire and Humber Regional Assembly (YHA) (2005) *The Yorkshire and Humber Plan: Draft for Public Consultation*. Wakefield: YHA.

Yorkshire Forward (2006) *The Regional Economic Strategy for Yorkshire and Humber 2006–2015*. Leeds: Yorkshire Forward.

Zonneveld, W. (2003) The new European transnational spatial visions. Paper presented at the AESOP-ACSP Conference, Leuven, Belgium, 8–12 July.

Index